SOCIO-ECONOMIC AND CULTURAL DIMENSIONS OF ENTREPRENEURSHIP IN NORTH-EAST INDIA

About the Author

Dr. M. Kennedy Singh, presently working as a Faculty in *Centre for Rural Studies, NIAR, Lal Bahadur Shastri National Academy of Administration, Mussoorie*. He also explored his academic career as an Associate Editor in "The Academy", a monthly newsletter published by Lal Bahadur Shastri National Academy of Administration, Mussoorie. He has interest in Rural Development, Microfinance & Microenterprise Generation in Development Intervention, Human Resource & Institutional Development – focused on study of depressed land Caste in India, National Land Record Management programmes, Action Research and Documentation, etc. He has also worked as a Consultant Faculty in *National Institute for Micro, Small and Medium Enterprises (NIMSME), Yousufguda, Hyderabad, Government of India*.

Dr. M. Kennedy Singh had done M.A., M. Phil, and Ph. D. from University of Hyderabad, Hyderabad. He was qualified for UGC – NET. He has contributed articles in different national and international journals of repute, also contributed articles in edited books. He had attended many national workshops and conferences organized by different national institutes in the country.

SOCIO-ECONOMIC AND CULTURAL DIMENSIONS OF ENTREPRENEURSHIP IN NORTH-EAST INDIA

M. Kennedy Singh

CONCEPT PUBLISHING COMPANY PVT. LTD.
NEW DELHI-110059

ISBN-13 : 978-81-8069-914-6

First Published 2013

Published and Printed by

Concept Since 1974

Concept Publishing Company Pvt. Ltd.
A/15-16, Commercial Block, Mohan Garden
New Delhi-110059 (India)
T: 25351460, 25351794, *F*: 091-11-25357109
E: publishing@conceptpub.com, W: www.conceptpub.com
Editorial Office: H-13, Bali Nagar, New Delhi-110 015, India.

Cataloging in Publication Data--*Courtesy:* D.K. Agencies (P) Ltd. <docinfo@dkagencies.com>

Singh, M. Kennedy.
Socio-economic and cultural dimensions of entrepreneurship in North-East India /M. Kennedy Singh.
p. cm.
Includes bibliographical references (p.) and index.
ISBN 9788180699146

1. Entrepreneurship—India, Northeastern. 2. Economic development—India, Northeastern. 3. Social change—India, Northeastern. I. Title.

DDC 658.42109541 23

Dedicated

to

The Loving Memory of My Father

Late Shri M. Ibohal Singh

Preface

The issue of entrepreneurship development has long puzzled policy makers, administrators, social scientists in India and the discussion is enduring on the functioning of entrepreneurship development programmes, the direction of their socio-economic and technological transformation. In search of various alternatives to help the rural poor in India and the world to come out of poverty, especially of the developing world, the movement of entrepreneurship development emerged as one of the highly praised and almost across the world notable interventions for poverty reduction and self-employment among the rural educated people since some decades back. Apparently, there have not been sufficient works to show these sketchy claims.

In India the moment of entrepreneurship development has got its momentum especially in the last two decades or so. During these decades, constant efforts were given attention on identifying the potential entrepreneurs, training, motivating, etc. In fact, the term "Entrepreneur" became popular among the young generation as a way to elevate themselves from poverty and unemployment. The main spotlight of all government policies was also on the development of the "First generation entrepreneur". Eventually, the movement was enhanced by initiating a separate wing to provide financial assistance for development of entrepreneurship and giving series of training programmes in entrepreneurship development for various target groups like women, technocrats, graduates, ex-servicemen, handicapped, economically and socially backward classes, artisans and craftsmen, etc. at different states in the country.

The earlier studies carried out by Anthropologists and other Social Scientists among various communities have constantly pointed out various problems of entrepreneurship development and also offered various suggestions for bringing better results. In fact,

Entrepreneurship Development is considered as a way for creating new venture for earning livelihood or a new scope for self-employment or as an option for generating employment to eke out the problem of unemployment in the rural world. It needs to take a multidimensional approach to study for better understanding of the ground realities. Consequently, various models and numerous strategies have been suggested by different committees and scholars for eradication of unemployment and upliftment of poor and needy people. Yet problems have not been solved. Due to globalization, decentralization and rapid demographic and social change have taken place; there is an urgent call for an in-depth study of the present issue. Moreover, Indian rural and tribal backward society represent a fascinating variety of culture and their local customs, traditions and practices that play important role in the entrepreneurship development progress. Hence, entrepreneurship development cannot be treated as stereotyped phenomenon. It varies from one region to another due to difference in terms of geographical and socio-cultural settings.

Considering the present situation in North East India, entrepreneurship development in this region becomes more complex due to the problems like insurgency activities, tribal conflicts, extortion by militants, frequent economic blockade and road bandh in the National Highways, the perennial issues of corruption, struggle for getting loans, etc. These problems became a major obstacle for entrepreneurship development in the region. Therefore, such issues deserve a special call to capture the dynamics of entrepreneurship development as a pivotal concern of the present development process. In this environment, this book examines the profile of the potential entrepreneurs, socio-cultural imperatives of entrepreneurship development, the functioning of entrepreneurship development organizations and the socio-cultural and technological changes taking place due to entrepreneurship development in the region. This study has received wonderful support and co-operation from various individuals.

M. Kennedy Singh

Acknowledgements

I would like to express my deep sense of gratitude and heartfelt thanks to Prof P. Venkata Rao, my supervisor, for his guidance, helpful suggestions, constant support and patience throughout my research work. Without his intellectual stimulation and guidance, this work would not have come to fruition. His constant encouragement and parental support during my crucial hours of research work will always remain in my heart.

This is also an occasion to thank my teachers in the department who had taught me, placed me in a position to significantly look at things, analyze them and made me feel at home in anthropology. I am thankful to Prof. R. Siva Prasad, Prof. K.K. Misra, Prof. N. Sudhakar Rao, Dr. B.V. Sharma, Dr. George Tharkan, Dr. M. Romesh Singh, Sir Md. Abdul Munnaf for their support and encouragement during the course of this work.

I am indebted to Dr. Kondiaha, Former Director General, National Institute for Micro Small and Medium Enterprise (NIMSME), Hyderabad, for his intellectual comments on my research work. As an external expert during the interaction for my UGC - Junior Research fellowship to Senior Research fellowship upgradation, he has given me the wider view of research work in my research area.

I am grateful to Dr. Prem Bahadur Singh (IAS), Director, Centre for Rural Studies, NIAR, Lal Bahadur Shastri National Academy of Administration, Mussoorie, for his constant encouragement in my academic endeavour. I also thank all my faculty members and supporting staff of CRS, NIAR, LBSNAA, Mussoorie who always co-operated with me by their constant help, love and affections.

I heartfully express gratitude to the people of Kakching for their immense co-operation during the course of my field-work.

And I will be failing in my duty if I do not thank the entrepreneurs of Kakching, Manipur for their readiness to furnish information.

I am most grateful to the UGC, New Delhi for giving me a research fellowship in August, 2006, without which I would have more financial problem in carrying out the research work.

I am thankful to my seniors, juniors and my friends for their support and encouragement in finishing this work. I specially would like to thank Tayai Dr. Romesh, Dr. Anil Kumar, Dr. H.C. Behara, B.K. Srinivas, Madhukar, Depak, Appa Rao, Anand, Padma, Lalit, Bipin, Boinao, Premchand, Suresh, and others whose names I might have missed.

I am very thankful to Abongpa Sh. Heiton Singh, Abongpa Tonungshi Singh, Mayanglambam Madumangol Singh, Oja Laishangbam Mohondas Singh, Oja Mayangbam Naran Singh, Sh. Mangijao, Paboung Bormani, Baji Kokngang, M. Gridhari Singh for their valuable and kind information.

I am thankful to Baba N. Ibotombi Singh and Ema Sana Devi for their encouragement and moral support during my research work. I am thankful to Echeman Tabahal, Echama Tamphamani, Echea Chaoba, Echea Bino, Echea Memcha and Echea Shangai for extending support during my crucial hours. Also my special thanks are due to Ebai Modhuchandra, Ebai Manikchand Singh, Ebai Krishnamohon Singh, Ebai Sajan Singh, Ebai Rameshwor Singh, Ebai Praveen, Ebai Jotin Singh, Ebai Basanta, Saolin, Surchand, Rosilline, Robert, Gandhi, Indira, Kamala, Tadon Godhadhor Singh, Tadon Purnima, Premchandra, Chandra, Roshan, Nabachandra, Robin, Tajou Raghu, Mr. Sanjoy Singh, Mr. Durgadas Singh for giving all the possible help for my research work.

My heartfelt thanks to my beloved parents who nurtured me from the cradle and brought me to this stage. I am thankful to my wife Menaka for her constant encouragement and support that have always supported me in each and every moment of my life. My special thanks to my loving daughters Mannjita and Nikkita for their blissful affections during their forlorn moments.

Last but not the least; I extend my heartfelt thanks to Concept Publishing Company (P) Ltd., New Delhi for publishing my work promptly in stipulated period.

M. Kennedy Singh

Contents

Glossary

Apokpa	Clan god
Atiya Guru Shidaba	Supreme God
Bamon	Meitei Brahmin
Chagem	A favourite curry of Meitei
Chak	Rice
Chuni	Processed sugar juice
Chini	Sugar
Chaitharol Kumpaba	Royal Chronicle
Chong	A huge white umbrella used at a Lai temple
Emoinu	Goddess of wealth of Meitei
Engkhol	Household vegetable garden
Ima	Mother, address for an elderly women
Itheikbong	Irrigation canal
Jagoi	Dance
Jatra Jumbi	Main post of the house
Kei	Family Granary
Keithel	Market
Khamlangba	Ancestral village god
Korbat tumba	Traditional water container
Koumjin	Beginning of the year
Koummai	Ending of the year
Koumyai	Middle of the year
Lai	Meitei deity
Lai-khurumpham	Place reserved for prayer
Lai-mapu	A temple keeper
Laimaren Sidabi	The Goddess of earth
Laipao	An oracle by a *Maibi*
Lairembi	Meitei female deity
Lai Una Thetpa	Avoidance of outsiders
Lamjel	Race
Langtheri	Herb used for ritual ceremony
Leikai	Locality
Loi	A Meitei outcaste

Loushan	Lending of agricultural land
Loushi	Wet or floodea agricultural land
Luhongba	Marriage
Maiba	A male scholar/priest
Maibi	A priestess
Mandap	Religious hall
Marup	Voluntary association
Mayang	A non-Manipuri
Mukna	Traditional wrestling
Nahutpa	Ear piercing
Namungba	Avoidance of outsiders
Ngareima	Goddess of fish
Pakhangba	Ancestral god of Meitei
Phouoibi	Goddess of rice
Phamel leipak	Better quality of clay
Piba	The head of lineage
Sagei	Lineage
Sagei Apokpa	Ancestral deity
Sagol-kangjei	Polo
Salai	Clan
Sanamahi	Household deity
Senmit	Prediction
Singju	Traditional vegetable mixture
Tairen	Herb used for sprinkling water at Lai haraoba or rituals
Tingthou	A type of wild grass
Thongal	Gate for houses
Thumleima	Goddess of salt
Tulsi	Basil plant; used for rituals
Tulsibung	Altar with a basil plant
Umanglai	Forest rod
Yaosang	Spring festival or Holi
Yek	Name of sub-clan
Yotsungba	Iron smelting
Yumleng	Row of houses
Yumnak	Name of the lineage
Yumsaba	Construction of house

List of Tables

1
Introduction

Entrepreneurship in recent times has become an important area of study. It is considered to be a solution for creating wealth, generating employment and providing new and better goods and services. Developing the spirit of entrepreneurship among the young has become vital because the government cannot provide jobs for all kinds of unemployed youth. In addition to this, the corporate sector will provide limited jobs only to the best and that too without any job security to their employees. Entrepreneurship is simply finding new opportunities to do things better and then seizing the opportunity. With changes like globalization, deregulation, open competition and technological change taking place, our society is becoming an entrepreneurial society. In an entrepreneurial society, individuals face a tremendous challenge in their life.

An entrepreneur is one who innovates and initiates something new. But this may not always be true, practically in less developed or developing countries, where an entrepreneur is often an imitator. Jeremy Boissevain (1997) in his article "Small European Entrepreneurs" mentioned that Entrepreneurs are those who manage enterprise for the pursuit of profit, in the course of which they innovate. And successful entrepreneurs are usually regarded as having self-confidence, achievement orientation, perseverance and resourcefulness. They must be willing to accept risk, to work hard and to save. They must also possess the ability to network – that is, to maintain and cultivate a range of useful contacts.

Sometimes, entrepreneurship has been considered as a quality which can be acquired by an individual and is a function of various factors like psychological, socio-cultural, economic etc. It is evident from the studies conducted by Schumpeter (1961), McClelland (1961), Pareek (1967), Nandi (1973), Rao *et al.* (1975), Akhauri (1977, 1978), Cantillian (1955), Lucy Mair (1984), Adam Smith (1984), Geertz (1967), Firth (1967), Barth (1960), Singer (1967), Epstein (1964), Nafziger (1975), and others that these factors play a key role in the development of entrepreneurship.

Entrepreneurship Development in Manipur

Manipur is situated in the extreme corner of North-eastern India. It has two distinct areas of hills and valleys. The area of plains or valley is located in the centre of Manipur surrounded by hills. Manipur is industrially very backward in the context of the backward N.E. regions of India with a per capita income far below the All India average. In addition to these, there are not enough industries to keep pace with the rapid growth of population and to deal with the growing problems of unemployment, poverty, lack of housing, medical care, insurgency, political unrest, etc.

However, there are two kinds of small industrial units in Manipur viz. SIDO (Small Industries Development Organization) and non-SIDO. In the SIDO group, there are Small Services Establishments (SSEs) units such as colour photography, x-ray, xeroxing, automobile workshop, etc. But the non-SIDO units are those not in the reserved items such as knitting, embroidery, blacksmith work, carpentry and handicraft items, etc. For these, the DIC (District Industries Centre) provides all services and facilities to entrepreneurs at one place so that they may set up small and village industries. These services and facilities include identification of a suitable scheme, the preparation of feasibility reports, arrangement for the supply of machinery and equipment, provision of raw materials, credit facilities and input for marketing and extension services, quality control, research and entrepreneurial training, etc. And all DICs give various kinds of training programmes to the entrepreneurs without which industries that are bound to play an active role in the growth process. Entrepreneurial motivation and training are the most important factors that help accelerate the pace of industrial development by inducing people to undertake risk-bearing activities.

In Manipur, the main objective of conducting this Entrepreneurship Development Programme (EDP) is to motivate young and promising entrepreneurs for self-employment after the successful completion of their training programme conducted by the government and non-government organisations. The trained entrepreneurs are provided with different incentives/facilities by the state government to assist them in the developmental process. However, there is a lack of awareness among the educated youth about entrepreneurship opportunities. The socio-psychological attitude and economic environment among the rural people towards entrepreneurship has also been a hindrance to entrepreneurial development. There is not much coordination among organizations and institutions like District Industries Centres, Industrial Consultants, Small Industries Service Institutes, National Small Industries Cooperation, All Manipur Entrepreneurs Union, banks and financial institutions which are involved in entrepreneurship development in the region to ensure a better impact of programmes. The Prime Minister Rozgar Yojana (PMRY) that has already been implemented in the state may be linked with EDP to achieve greater success in promoting first generation entrepreneurs in the hill region as well.

Problems/Constraints of Entrepreneurship Development

It must be recalled that continued dependence on agriculture is a living testimony to the primary character of the rural economy of Kakching. Modernization of life and tempo of living may be duly enriched through a sound process of industrialization and rural development. However, the economy of Manipur is largely influenced by the imperatives of the fundamental backwardness i.e., the handicaps imposed by the geo-physical location has become one among the major constraints for development. It has also possible departure from the national strategy for development. Special programme of action are undertaken for the backward sector of the economy in the state.

However, it is not a surprise that the small scale units in Manipur experience the disadvantages of shortage of power supply, absense of Foreign Direct Investment etc. Thus, on the whole, we need to have a critical examination regarding the performance in the industrial sector in the right perspective in order to have a way for further industrial growth in the region. Besides these, the market of the small scale and tiny products depend only on the local buyers whose preference is undergoing a change due to the emergence of a new trend of expansion of economic activities beyond national and state boundaries. In addition to these, the new temptations to buy competitive goods are considerably fostered by the performance of the Indo-Myanmar-Border Trade.

Needs of Entrepreneurial Development Programmes

Nowadays, Entrepreneurial Development Programme (EDP) is an effective human resource development programme in the country. This helps in removing unemployment, promotion of household entrepreneurial activities and small-scale units, development of industrial regions, overall economic development programme etc. Entrepreneurship development programme is more necessary in the case of first generation entrepreneurs. They may not become successful unless a proper training is received. So, they need a continuous process of motivation for their entrepreneurial activities. However, motivation is not an inherited but a personal quality. Through formal education, knowledge can be acquired. Entrepreneurs can solve many of their problems provided proper training is given to them. But, by joining in an entrepreneurial development programme, one cannot solve all these problems. It only gives confidence to the entrepreneurs and make them to face and solve variety of problems. However, entrepreneurial development is a systematic and organized effort. At present, it becomes catalyst for developing industry and economic programmes. It is believed that through EDP, entrepreneurial skills of an individual can be developed, his outlook towards organizing entrepreneurship can be changed and his ideas can be converted into action.

Besides these, increasing unemployment is the chronic problem of the region as well as most of the developing countries. In such situations, EDPs can help the unemployed people to opt for self-employment and entrepreneurial careers. Several programmes such as National Rural Employment Programmes (NREP), Integrated Rural Development Programmes (IRDP), PMRY, DIC etc. are in operation in India. These special schemes focus on the poverty alleviation and also try to solve the problem of unemployment in the region. Entrepreneurial development programmes have become an important way for utilizing the vast unexploited human skills and to channelize them into accelerating the process of industrialization. Entrepreneurship development programmes are responsible for emerging entrepreneurial opportunities in various fields like electronic, handloom, food technology, packaging, carpentry work, motor cycle and lorry workshops, piggery, poultry and dairy, etc.

Several institutions are engaged in conducting entrepreneurship development programme in India. Government of India at an early stage realized the importance of promoting new ventures particularly household entrepreneurial units, small-scale industries as a means of self-employment as well as employment generation. Small Industries Development Organization was setup at the apex level to provide technical inputs and guidance to small industries. Khadi and Village Industries Commissions were established to promote village industries. In 1984, Government of India set up National Institute of Entrepreneurship and Small Business. At the same time, IDBI and other financial institutes set up Entrepreneurial Development Institutes of India (EDI). With the same objective NIESBUD and EDI have been conducting various researches in entrepreneurship development programmes and imparting training to entrepreneurs. Other organizations, like State Bank of India (SBI), Entrepreneurial Motivation Training Centre in North-Eastern Region, Indian Institute of Entrepreneurship (IIE), Guwahati,

National Institute for Micro Small and Medium Enterprise (NIMSME), Hyderabad, etc. are imparting training to entrepreneurs in India.

Above all, the state and the central level promotional agencies have announced a series of fiscal and non-fiscal incentives, concessions and facilities for attracting new entrepreneurs to set up tiny, small, medium and ancillary industries in their region.

Entrepreneurship and Economic Development

In our society, entrepreneurs play a role in the field of economic development. According to economists, entrepreneurship and economic growth will take place in those situations where particular economic conditions are most favourable. Economic historians have classified economic system into different stages. They claim that every society passes through different stages in the course of development. Adam Smith (1949) used the sequence of hunting, gathering, pastoral, agricultural, commerce and manufacturing. Marx (1844) classified economic history into the stage of Feudalism, Capitalism and Socialism each respectively representing Thesis, Antithesis and Synthesis. The most systematic definition of economic development was given by Schumpeter (1967) who places the innovation in the centre of the whole process of economic development. The entrepreneur locates ideas and put them into effect in the process of economic development.

Entrepreneurship development—why social and cultural capital is important?

Social capital and cultural capital have influence on the development of entrepreneurship. These factors of social organization facilitates co-ordination and cooperation among the people of Manipur especially values and norms of reciprocity influencing in one's social networks. Social capital tries to explain the importance of using social connections and social relations in developing entrepreneurial activities. That is why, social capital, or resources accessed through such connections and social relations, is critical (along with human capital, or what a person or organization actually possesses) in achieving goals for individuals, social groups, organizations, and communities. Among the people, the term social capital is a way of conceptualizing the available intangible resources of community, shared values and trust upon which we draw in daily life. It can also be considered that the norms and networks that enable collective action among the communities as an important ingredients/components of entrepreneurship development. It brings out the close relationships within the society and customs that shape the quality and quantity of a society's social interactions. Subsequently, increasing evidence shows that social capital is pivotal component for societies to prosper economically and for development to be sustainable in the region. By social capital, we mean, it enhanced social relationship and strengthen social organisation in a positive manner. It brings effectiveness and sustainability by building the community's capacity to work together to address their common needs, fostering greater inclusion and cohesion, and increasing transparency and accountability.

However, cultural capital has different dimensions that act as a social relation within a system of exchange. It includes the accumulated cultural knowledge that confers power and status. We can consider, cultural capital are forms of knowledge, skills, education, any advantages a person has which give them higher status in society, including high expectations. For example, we provide our children with cultural capital, the attitudes and knowledge that make the educational system a comfortable familiar place in which they can succeed easily in the society. Cultural capital is embodied in the individual. It is both the inherited and acquired properties. Through socialization, parents or other family members of the community transmitted cultural, and traditions bestow elements of the embodied state to another like a gift.

Moreover, in every society social institutions are the building blocks of development. These institutions, i.e. traditional and modern, at the community, local, regional and national levels and in the public and private sectors are the vehicles through which social change and social action occur for development in the society. Social capital is the network of horizontal connections which leads to mutual commitment and trust within the community, family, etc. This enables people and their institutions to function effectively. To be successful, entrepreneurship development needs to both strengthen institutions and enhance the social capital on which they depend. And social capital is based on group membership, relationships, networks of influence and support in the society.

As according to Bourdieu (1983), it is mentioned that social capital is the aggregate of the actual or potential resources which are linked to possession of a durable network of more or less institutionalized relationships of mutual acquaintance and recognition. Here, the central idea is that 'social networks are a valuable asset'. It is also suggested that interaction enables people to build communities, to commit themselves to each other, and to knit the social fabric. Hence, it brings a sense of belonging and the concrete experience of social networks and the relationships of trust and tolerance that can be involved. It becomes trust between strangers and trust of a broad fabric of social institutions. Ultimately, it becomes a shared set of values, virtues, and expectations within society as a whole. Without this interaction, on the other hand, trust within the society decays. At certain points, this situation begins to manifest itself in serious social problems and becomes a threat to their development.

In order to apply the concept of social capital at a practical and operational level, it can be broken down into five key dimensions: (1) *Groups and Networks*—collections of individuals that promote and protect personal relationships which improve welfare; (2) *Trust and Solidarity* – elements of interpersonal behaviour which fosters greater cohesion and more robust collective action; (3) *Collective Action and Cooperation*—ability of people to work together toward resolving communal issues; (4) *Social Cohesion and Inclusion*—mitigates the risk of conflict and promotes equitable access to benefits of development by enhancing participation of the marginalized; and (5) *Information and Communication*— breaks down negative social capital and also enables positive social capital by improving access to information. These dimensions capture both the structural and cognitive forms of social capital.

Entrepreneurship and Social Change

Social change is a continual process wherein the structure of society undergoes transformation under endogenous and exogenous pressure. Modernization is a process of change of a particular type, which is attributed to the growth and institutionalization of new roles and group structures based on concomitant norms of modernization. Marx (1904) in his interpretation of historical materialism not only expresses the history of class struggle, but beyond that formulates a theoretical framework, in which he describes how the mode of production determines the relations of production which ultimately determines the pattern of social relationship. Others who have studied the causal factors of social change are Veblen (1922), Ogburn (1964) who emphasized the crucial role of technology in the process of social change, as technological development is both the cause and effect of industrialization and occurrence of changes.

Besides these, Entrepreneurship is an important ingredient of socio-economic development and the dynamic entrepreneurs are considered to be the agent of change in the society. Growth and development of industries, therefore depends on the supply of right type of entrepreneurs with respect to the existing socio-economic and cultural environment. However, due to the low achievement motivation, passivity to the environment, lack of command over resources and lack of financing support, there is short supply of entrepreneurs in the backward areas especially in North-eastern states of India.

From this point of view, for the development of entrepreneurship, it requires to infuse achievement motivation to break the passivity among the common people through favourable social atmosphere. In addition to these, the lack of financial resources by the majority of population due to lower per capita income is the important ingredient among the problem of entrepreneurship development.

Entrepreneurship and Technology

The science of man's origin and the development of his culture, known as "cultural diffusion", is associated with different methods of economic, political, religious or social organization. Occasionally, a particular fortunate combination of interest, leaders or methods of organizing different activities leads to technological revolutions. It ultimately leads to technical invention of very economic value. People see the advantage of the new techniques and adopt them when they first learn about them. However, the kind of technological adaptation has a series of barrier to change like psychological, social and cultural barrier of changes. As cited as an example, countries like China knew about many of the technical developments in the West for centuries yet were not eager to adopt them until the present century. According to Adam Smith (1977), the more remarkable is the experience of Middle Eastern countries, which are closer to the West. During the entire period when the West was developing technologically and economically at a rapid rate, very few Western methods or techniques managed to "diffuse" by trade into the Middle East. In contrast, Japan adopted Western technological advances at a very rapid rate once it came in contact with Western ideas.

However in India, technological adoption is a continuous phenomena and it is in an accelerating rate with each passing years. The rural entrepreneurs are increasingly in touch with urban centre through radio, television, relatives who have migrated to cities, and improved education in their own villages. With perceived opportunities and supportive condition, they make realization of success in their entrepreneurial activities through the adoption of new technology. According to Scottish economist Adam Smith (1723-1790), the invention of better machines and equipment was responsible for the greater increase in productivity and material welfare. Dozens of technological improvements, such as the wire cable for mines, and the improved techniques for refining iron which made rail roads possible made production more efficient and increased profits. These profits could be reinvested in the business, leading to more technical improvements and further increases in productivity. But, economists also stressed the importance of technological development in the late 19th century when its effects could be seen even more clearly. The German political philosopher, Karl Marx (1818-1883) stressed the importance of technology as a determining force in history. Technology, Marx claimed, would hasten the class struggle, because the Capitalists would instal machinery were replacing workers and forcing them to live on lower wages. Thus, the workers would eventually attempt to protect themselves by seizing power.

The role of entrepreneur made the key force in economic development. Schumpeter (1883-1950) believed that an economy did not grow "naturally" or even steadily, but rather was pushed forward in sudden bursts of activity by key men, who wanted to promote new goods and new methods of production, or to exploit a new source of material or a new market. Due to such improvement in technology, there is division of labour or the specialization of productive function that leads to—

1. an increase in skills among workers.
2. a reduction in the time necessary to produce commodities
3. the inventions of better machines and equipment.

Entrepreneurship and Organizational Behaviour

Entrepreneurship and Organizational behaviour are complementary terms in the development of entrepreneurship. Organizations have been in existence, since the dawn of civilization, but modern organizations differ from the earlier ones in several respects. Modern organizations are large in size and complex in nature and meet a great variety of individual and social needs. The number of organizations has also increased tremendously. They are engaged in such a diversity of tasks that organizations in the past were generally small in size, whereas modern organizations are entities of scale. In the earlier organizations, direct contact between the employer and the employees were possible. But the modern organizations, on the other hand, have too many levels to permit such contacts. As modern organization involves huge investment and complicated technology, their management and operation is a complex affair. Every level needs assistance from diverse specialist. Working harmoniously, co-operatively and productively for the mutual benefits of all is not an easy task in the midst of such circumstances. This is in contrast to organizations in the past, most of which were simple in nature, using simple techniques of functioning. Elaborate rules and regulations were not needed for their governance.

Also the entrepreneurial activities represent the interests of all participants such as, suppliers, shareholders, managers, workers, customers, etc. in a business organization. There is a system of working in all organizations. Organizations have built-up hierarchical levels, a chain of command, rule and procedures, communication networks etc. This ensures that the superiors know what is expected of the subordinates and the subordinates know what is expected of them so that they do not make unnecessary demands upon each other. Likewise, further division of work take place and each individual performs a job he is specialized in. Thus, task specialization and hierarchical levels lead to differentiation. Each of these functional parts of an organization deals with a different part of the environment and develops a cognitive point of view that reflects its adaptation to that part of the environment.

In accordance with recent development of the study on entrepreneurship development, it needs to give emphasis on human behaviour and social relations. This creates a context within which trust and cooperation can be developed among the entrepreneurs to enhance entrepreneurial activities. As according to Cle Lesger (1997), society becomes more complex and the conduct of entrepreneurs is embedded within a network of social relations.

Within this network, there is distinction between relations with parties that are directly involved in the transaction of their entrepreneurial activities. Therefore, stable relations with suppliers and customers becomes the main entrepreneurial strategy and the backbone of their firm.

In addition to this, each and every entrepreneur participated in a number of overlapping network of social relations. These overlapping networks of social relations may be regarded as a self-regulating mechanism in which rewards and sanctions promoted or discouraged certain types of entrepreneurial behaviour. So, trust and reputation are the key notions in regard to social networks. A good reputation is also indispensable in the creation of social capital. Social capital becomes an important aid in the acquisition of wealth, power and prestige. Moreover, social capital inclined towards opportunism and risk taking that enables the market economy to develop and survive. In long run, socially accepted behaviour is probably also the best strategy to preserve social capital to enhance the entrepreneurial activities.

Review of the Literature

There have been several studies on entrepreneurship developments. It was Cantillian (1755) who coined the term "Entrepreneurship" in French. The term "Entrepreneur" was variously translated into English as "Merchant", "Adventurer", or "Employer", though the precise meaning is "the undertaker of the project". In the 16th Century, the Frenchmen who undertook military expedition were also referred to as "Entrepreneur". John Stuart Mill (1848) popularized the term in England. According to the *Social Science Encyclopaedia* by Adam Kuper and Jessica Kuper (1985), the term "Entrepreneur" seems to have been introduced in economic theory. Economists, sociologists, psychologists and other social scientists have increasingly recognized entrepreneurship as a profession in recent time.

Different scholars studied the development of entrepreneurship from different perspectives. The review of the literature has been categorized thematically into different sections based on their nature of studies like historical aspect, economical aspect, social aspect, and cultural aspect etc.

Studies based on Historical Aspect

There are also many studies on development of entrepreneurship in India with the historical perspective. Such studies give a clear picture of how the early entrepreneurs set up their social networks for their business purpose. Dwijendra Tripathi (1984) in his edited book "Business Communities in India: A Historical Perspective" has highlighted development of entrepreneurship in Indian History. It also highlighted the various perspective of different scholars studying in different communities like Nurul Hasan's (1979) study of Mughal period entrepreneurs in the 18th Century, Seth N.R.'s (1979) study on Indian business communities, Ashin Gupta's (1979) on Indian Merchants during the period 1500-1800 A.D., Sharma G.D.'s (1979) on the Marwari communities, Grawal J.S. (1979) on Business communities of Punjab etc.

Dwijendra Tripathi (1984) highlighted that ethnicity, language, religion and regional affiliations are the basic characteristics which seem to have been used to divide businessmen into various categories giving the typical example of class character of the Gujarati business community. Sinha Dipendra (2003) in his article "The Rise of Entrepreneurship in India" gave a picture of the history of entrepreneurship in India. It also highlighted the bottlenecks of the development of entrepreneurship, future of entrepreneurship in India. In the article, he commented that Indians have never lacked the spirit of entrepreneurship.

Regarding male and female entrepreneurship, there is a myth that entrepreneurship is a matter of inheritance, in-born quality, is a monopoly of few sections of population and is internalized before an entrepreneur is born. Unlike men, women are equally endowed with psychological qualities and managerial abilities that are essential for successful entrepreneurship. It is also highlighted that through proper training, the entrepreneurial qualities can be acquired and developed in individuals.

Studies based on Economic Aspect

According to the economists, development of entrepreneurship is associated with economic growth. In the studies, various scholars like Schumpeter (1934), Cantillian (1955), Colin Clark (1957), and Bishwanath Ghosh (1988), etc. have highlighted the different economic stages of economic development relating to the development of entrepreneurship.

According to the Schumpeter (1934), the entrepreneur is the prime mover in economic development, and his function is to "innovate", or "carry out new combinations". He distinguished five types of innovations (1) the introduction of new goods (or an improvement in the quality of an existing goods); (2) the introduction of a new method of production; (3) opening of a new market—in particular an export market in new territory; (4) the "conquest of a new source of supply of raw material or half manufactured goods"; (5) the creation of a new type of industrial organization – in particular the formation of a trust or some other type of monopoly. Moreover, Schumpeter emphasizes the role of the entrepreneur as a source of change.

In the view of Cantillian (1755), the entrepreneur is one who is generally not an owner of capital, i.e. not necessarily working with his own or borrowed capital. Later its meaning has undergone changes and others defined it according to the economic and social conditions prevailing in their societies. Bishwanath Ghosh (1988) in his book *Entrepreneurship in India* highlighted the role played by small-scale business entrepreneurship in the development of the country. He commented that most of the industrial and business activities start small and with market and opportunities and vision of the entrepreneur, it grows into a large industry. He also classified Indian entrepreneurs into various types like rural entrepreneurs, farm entrepreneurs, artisan entrepreneurs, merchant and trader entrepreneur, tribal entrepreneurs, and women entrepreneurs, etc.

C. Hari Narayana Rao and Dr. Ch. Uma Mohan (1988) mentioned in their article "Grass Root Entrepreneurship and Rural Industrialization" that the success of rural entrepreneurship depends not only on the drive and initiatives of the rural folk but also on the provision for adequate financial assistance, supply of raw material, machinery and equipment and the stupendous task of providing the marketing assistance. Plaschka and Welsh (1990) suggest that the development of entrepreneurship is the result of co-ordination of internal components (like, individual characteristics of employees, financial resources and firm characteristics such as system of production, organization and marketing, etc.) and external components (like, government, taxes, laws, regulations and free trade policies, location infrastructure and the existence of enterprise zones, the availability of skilled labour forces, governmental loans and grants, etc.).

Studies based on Social Aspect

Different scholars also have carried out several works on the development of entrepreneurship from the socio-cultural aspects. They had formulated theories like Weber's theory of protestant ethic (1958), McClelland's theory of achieving society (1961), Cochran's theory of cultural value and social structure (1971), etc. The studies discussed the influence of culture, social norms, values, etc. on the development of entrepreneurship in different societies. Max Weber (1958) pointed out the "resistance to change" and "the restriction of the caste system and highlighted the traditionalism of Indian entrepreneurs which was reinforced by the caste structure and Hindu religious values and other cultural factors. In fact, McClelland's theory of "achieving societies" can be seen as a development of Weber's Protestant ethic in which an intermediating psychological motive is introduced. However, this approach is strongly opposed by many prominent scholars like Berna's (1960) study on the manufacturing enterprise in Madras and Coimbatore, M. Singer's (1966) study on the successful business community in Madras city, Nafziger's (1975) study on the higher caste entrepreneurs of Vishakhapatnam, etc. They found that the religious values and the caste system have no hindrance on the development of entrepreneurship.

Other studies like Levine (1985), Geertz (1963), Barth (1960), Schumpeter (1934), etc. show that the actions of entrepreneurial activities have an effect on the social organization of the communities. Levine (1985) explored the nature of the relationship and social change on the entrepreneurial fishing community of New Zealand. And the earlier work of the economist Schumpeter (1934) stressed the entrepreneur's role in changing and improving society through the creation of new combination of production factors. It is because the mobilization of factors of production takes place in a socio-cultural milieu, wider questions concerning the condition of entrepreneurial activity and associated socio-cultural changes must be addressed.

The development of entrepreneurial activity directly or indirectly brings socio-economic changes in society. In fact, entrepreneurs are considered to be an agent of change by the scholars like Epstein (1964), Broehl (1978), Nash (1965), etc. Epstein's (1964) study of the contrasting villages in South India describes social change in one village, which was primarily dependent upon the provision of irrigation to the neighbouring village; entrepreneurial opportunities were exploited by relatively few individuals. Similarly, in *The Golden Road to Modernity*, Nash (1965) alludes to the concept in only a few sentences and appears to describe only on individuals who could be called an entrepreneur. Firth (1965) in his, *Themes in Economic Anthropology* suggested that anthropologists should study entrepreneurs more widely in primitive, peasant and industrial societies, even, in relation to the complex problems of business administration. And he feels that they should remain aware of the way in which "structural" and "institutional" differences may modify the meaning of the term. Wayne G. Broehl (1978) in his book *Village Entrepreneur: Change Agents in India's Rural Development* commented that the entrepreneur is a highly respected word in the developed world. It conjures up visions of active, purposeful men and women accomplishing a wide variety of significant deeds. The entrepreneur is an important change agent in every society that bridges the gap between plan and reality. In fact, his study is among the private fertilizer distributors who enterprise as the wholesaler in the south Indian village in Karnataka.

Abner Cohen's (1969) study on the Hausa businessmen who control the north-south trade both in meat and in kola nuts in Nigeria. It also examines the assertion that the Hausa leaders lack the innovative qualities of their Yoruba neighbours. The study of Marris and Somerset (1971), "African Businessmen" in Nairobi collected individual histories and found that they have a typical course, but, except in so far as they were predominantly Kikuyu, they could not be described as coming from a particular dis-esteemed group.

Raymond L. Owen (1976) in his article *The Anthropological Study of Entrepreneurship* gives a review of the general approaches of the anthropologists who have taken to the study of entrepreneurs and also some of the modification in the approach which may be necessary in both rural and urban setting. He comments on the effective theory of the economic growth that will appear only when the social process and the take-off approaches are joined in a simple framework analysis. He also commented that the study of entrepreneurs by anthropologists has been relatively confined to micro-scale studies of tribal and peasant societies in which other academic disciplines have had only a marginal interest.

Lucy Mair (1984) in her article *Enterprise and Entrepreneur* gave a description of an entrepreneur as an innovator or an individual who makes improvement in technique of some new method. She highlighted that entrepreneur has a role not only in the capitalist societies but also in the non-industrial societies. Hadimani R.N. (1985) in his book *Dynamics of Industrial Entrepreneurship* presents in-depth analysis of the relationship of sociological factors like caste system, the form of religion and level of entrepreneurship etc. But Paranjape (1987) in his article *Entrepreneurial Background and Performance* highlighted that entrepreneurship is an area that has been very much neglected in academic studies in India. He also highlighted the relationship between entrepreneurial background and entrepreneurial performance. He also attempts to scrutinize an environmental factor, which affects a vigorous display of entrepreneurship.

Moreover, there are some other studies carried out in the backward and tribal areas Madhusudan Trivedi (1991) in his book *Entrepreneurship Among Tribals,* Pande, G.S. (1998: 179-188) in his article *Entrepreneurship Development Among the Disadvantaged and Tribals*, Pande, G.S. (1998) in his article *Entrepreneurship Development Among the Disadvantaged and Tribals* etc. shows that entrepreneurial studies in such areas needs to keep primary importance to analyse the historical experience of the forest people in their existing socio-cultural and environmental setting. Madhusudan Trivedi (1991) in his book *Entrepreneurship Among Tribals,* commented that the study of entrepreneurship among the tribal is a relatively neglected field of enquiry in social anthropology. He made an in-depth study of the experience of Bhils in their recently adopted entrepreneurial efforts and he also analysed the historical experiences of the forest people in their endeavour to earn a livelihood. Khanka (1994) in his study highlighted the long striving for achieving rapid and balanced regional development through entrepreneurship in the backward areas. It has been considered as an effective instrument in the programme for reducing inter- and intra-regional balance in economic development. Pande, G.S. (1998) in his study highlights the drawbacks of the large-scale industries like Hindustan Aeronautics (Sunabeda), Sugar Factory, Ferro-silicon and J.K. Paper (around Raygada) that have not benefited the tribal. B.C. Mitchell (2004) in his article *Motivation of Entrepreneurs: A Case Study of South Africa* in the journal of entrepreneurship, examines the motivation of entrepreneurs in starting business in the socio-economic milieu of South Africa.

Studies based on Cultural Aspect

Various studies have been carried on religious and cultural values and its impact on the development of entrepreneurship. Many scholars like Singer's (1966), Berger Brigitte (1992), Janet Landa (1992), Don Lavoi (1992), Jan I.J., and Stein K. (2004), etc. highlighted that culture has a role to play in the development of the entrepreneurship. Singer's (1966) study of the nineteen very successful Indian industrialists in Madras highlights the relation of economic rationality to religious values, demonstrating religious ideas and rituals do not have to change much to accommodate economic rationality. His study calls into question such studies as that of Max Weber which attempts to predict the reception of economic rationality according to religious values.

Berger Brigitte (1992) in his edited book *The Culture of Entrepreneurship* shows that in certain circumstances, entrepreneurship produces its own culture. The book explores the cultural dimensions of modern entrepreneurship that is closed to groups of people. It is also mentioned that any culture is available to any group at any time provided external conditions like social values, practices and norms permit and encourage new patterns of entrepreneurship. Don Lavoi (1992) in *The Discovery and Interpretation of Profit Opportunities: Culture and Kirznerian Entrepreneurs* presents a sophisticated and systematic explanation of the creative process of discovery and interpretation that are integral to entrepreneurship. He argues that entrepreneurship necessarily takes place within culture, which is utterly shaped by culture, and is fundamental in interpreting and influencing culture.

Regarding the notion of the unsuitability of Indian tradition to industrial entrepreneurship was dwelt on in studies conducted on Indian businessmen in 1950s and 1960s (Berna 1960; Hazelhurst 1966; and Fox 1969 etc.) In this view, the cultural disposition and subsequent commercial orientation of Indian businessmen with a trading background was supposed to have turned the highly developed profit motivation of Indian entrepreneurs. But they were not towards productive investment of significant scope but towards consumption and less risky and more immediately profitable fields of economic activity. Partly basing himself on McCrory (1956), who carried out a study in 1950s among owners of small industrial firms in north-Indian city, James Berna (1960) argued that the Indian entrepreneurs with background in trade are "Opportunistic business with very short time horizons", interested only in fast turnover and quick profits, completely unconcerned with technology, unwilling to invest more than the bare minimum in fixed capital, and still preoccupied far more with trade than with industry. Richard Fox (1969), who studied *Banias* in another small north-Indian town, also argues that these businessmen were more willing to accept smaller profits as long as they covered essential expenses, rather than to invest more profitable long-term enterprises in which they risked losing their investment.

Barth, F. G., (1960), in his edited book, *The Role of the Entrepreneur in Social Change in Northern Norway* reports on a series of studies of entrepreneurship in contrasting ecological niches in sparsely settled North Norway. According to Barth, the crucial features of entrepreneurship are largely a matter of degree and emphasis; that are: (1) the entrepreneur's more single minded concentration on the maximization of one type of value, "profit", (2) the more experimental and speculative, less institutionalized character of the activity of the entrepreneur, who must act in terms of a deductive prognosis of results rather than as may the incumbents of institutionalized status, accumulated experience which give empirically founded expectation of results, (3) the entrepreneur's greater willingness to take risks exemplified by his (i) committing a greater part of his total assets to a single venture (ii) putting trust in his own deductive reasoning as against common opinion, and (iii) delighting in gambler's odds where other actors might entertain a conservative, exaggerated fear of the risk of loss (1963: 7-8)

The study of the entrepreneurship by Clifford Greetz (1963: 1-27), of the two Indonesian towns, in his book *Peddler and the Princes* describes the term entrepreneurship in terms of the adoption of new techniques. It helps to depict the situation in highly urbanized and industrialized environments, where anthropologists, economists and members of other disciplines are no longer aware of each other. He also equated "Development" with

"Modernization". In his study, he observes the Javanese town "Modjokuto" with the number of bazaar traders selling goods casually to customers and haggling over prices. There had always been many competitions with the Chinese people who started entrepreneurial work. A few of these adopted more Western methods of trading, setting up shops, maintaining stocks, charging fixed prices. Most of them were members of the trade reformist "Masjumi Movement" which make rather orthodox religious virtue of the systematic and untiring pursuit of worldly ends. But in the Balinese town, Tabanan, the entrepreneurs were petty princes who had lost their political power after the withdrawal of the Dutch and the revolution that followed it.

Some of the studies explored the cultural embeddedness of ethic enterprises and the role of cultural values, attitude etc. for the development of entrepreneurial activities (Janet Landa 1992; Jan I.J., and Stein K. 2004; Muthayya B.C. and Loganathan 1990; Cle Lesger 1997, etc.). In *Culture and Entrepreneurship in less Developed Societies: Ethnic Trading and Network as Economic Organisation*, an article by Janet Landa (1992) confirms the cultural embeddedness of ethnic enterprises. Sorting out the viability of various economic approaches for the continued success of ethnicity homogeneous middleman groups such as the Chinese in South East Asia, the Indians in East and Central Africa, the Lebanese in West Asia and the Jews in Medieval Europe. She demonstrated how cultural factors allow a particular group to succeed and reinforce the group homogeneity. Jan I.J., and Stein K. (2004) in their article *Sub-Cultures and Entrepreneurship: The Value of Social Capital in Tanzanian Business* attempt to argue how the sub-cultural characteristics affect the acquisition of entrepreneurial resources at a specific location and also to see how the same influence on the development of social capital. He used a case study methodology to study the entrepreneurs involved in the wood business in the coastal town of Tanga, Tanzania.

Muthayya B.C. (1990) and Loganathan (1990) highlighted the cultural and psychological factors influencing the entre-preneurship in rural areas. It is mentioned that most people in rural areas are engaged in the traditional occupations which are land-based and, therefore, had developed an orientation to think of their occupational life in terms of interaction with land and whatever it can produce. Therefore, gradually an attempt has to be made to diversify large sections of the rural people who are guided by traditional culture in their occupational choices to occupations in the non-traditional areas like small scale, cottage and household industries, etc.

Cle Lesger (1997), in his article *The Visible Hand: Views on Entrepreneurs and Entrepreneurship in Holland, 1580-1850*, highlighted the performance of the Dutch economy. He also mentioned that it seems a miracle and a threat that such a small country i.e. the Dutch, was able to play a prominent role in the international economy and on the European political scene. He also made a distinction between formal and informal institutions. The difference between them is gradual. Informal institution comprises taboo, common law and traditions but formal institutions comprise written law. As society becomes more complex, informal rules no longer suffice, they have to be increasingly backed up or even replaced by formal rules. So, informal and formal institutions are the only mechanisms for governing entrepreneurial behaviour. And the conduct of entrepreneurs is embedded within a network of social relations.

In fact, the innovation process is flexible and that there are alternative path of development. However, products and processes emerge in particular form, rather than others, primarily because of general political and economic choice (Veronica M. 1987; Dave Elliott 1987; Kenneth Lancks 1991; etc.). Veronica in her study "Enterprising Innovation: An Alternative Approach" argues that the capability of governments to introduce new socially-oriented technologies, altering traditional lines of technological development, is often less restricted by object factors, such as competitiveness on international market than commonly assumed. Kenneth Lancks (1991) in the study "Training for small business creation (Lesson from experience)" explored that in promotion and encouraging the use of new technology in the developing countries are not in a position to take risks or seek out information or alternative technologies. He suggested that such entrepreneurs need not be highly creative in technology, strategy or good operation practices. As for example in small shops such as welding services, bicycles repair, shoe repair, retail clothing, etc. are imitative and, as has been shown in the franchising industry, can adopt formats similar to those successfully practiced elsewhere.

Mark Lazerson's (1997) article on *Entrepreneurship in Italy* highlighted that although, Italy has one of the largest economies in the West, its economy is still heavily based on family owned and operated firms. This is true for both small shops and huge Italian multinational corporations, such as the *Fait Corporation*, still under the control of the founding *Agnelli* family after nearly 100 years, and *Pirelli and Benetton*, both tightly controlled by their eponymous founding families. Above all, small entrepreneurs are also mainly depending upon networks of friends and families for loans and to established firms with relatively small capital requirements.

Jeremy Boissevain (1997), in his article *Small European Entrepreneurs* explores some of the interrelations between small European entrepreneurs and their social and cultural contexts. It also examines some of the ways in which differences in cultural background influence the activities of entrepreneurs. He also mentioned that family affair is the most important characteristics of small enterprises. Huang Ping (1997) in his article *New Private Entrepreneurs in China: Family Relations and Social Connections*, highlights that in Chinese society for centuries, social and personal connections are considered as crucial factors for developing entrepreneurship. But such family, kinship relations and personal relations were officially considered to be "Out of date" and were replaced by the "revolutionary" (professional) relations under the unit system. This paper argues that it is social networks, including both family and personal relations, which are the key to understanding the newly-emerged individual and private entrepreneurs.

Sameer Sharma (2004) in his article *Entrepreneurship Development in Networks of Weaver Cluster of Pochampalli* explores the needs of networking among the weaving entrepreneurs of Pochampalli in Andhra Pradesh to help potential entrepreneurs-producers to overcome the constraints with size, promote technology development and develop their ability to compete in local and regional market.

Sang-Bok-Han (1997), in his article *Local Level Entrepreneurs in Rural Punggi, Korea: Economic Behaviour and Lifestyle* have several case studies on rural entrepreneurship in Korea, but most of them have focused on the careers of successful individual entrepreneurs in sectors such as agriculture, fisheries and forestry. He analyzed the entrepreneurial career of fisherman who brought about social change in a southern Korean Island fishing village. This paper describes and analyses the characteristics of Korean rural entrepreneurs with regard to their economic behaviour and lifestyle. But, Soundarapandian, M. (2001) gives an illustrative account for development of entrepreneurship. He highlights the shortcomings of the State and Central Government in developing the entrepreneurship as there is a wide disparity among the cities, state capitals and the district areas. Hence, it is felt necessary to establish required facilities to village and small industries under one roof.

Observation from the Review of Literature

From the above review of literature, the following observations can be made regarding the dynamic of entrepreneurship development:

1. The entrepreneurial spirit is not lacking among the people of the country, irrespective of their religion, caste, community and region, etc.
2. There is the overlapping social and cultural networking among the entrepreneurs for creating the entrepreneurial atmosphere which is influenced by social norms, values, customs, beliefs, ethos, etc. So, it becomes a self-regulating mechanism.

3. The entrepreneurship development strategy of the region should be placed on development of entrepreneurship among the people as human resource development that will ultimately resolve unemployment, economic problems, social problems and also bringing the widening of social network.
4. The entrepreneurial and managerial needs, the nature and extent of their support system, action programmes for entrepreneurship development in the backward region should be encouraged.
5. In developing entrepreneurial activities, the most important problems among the rural entrepreneurs are the accessibility of capital investment, supply of raw materials, marketing problems, etc.

Apart from the above factor, some of the factors that have been pointed out, few observations can be drawn from the studies of Manipur. Due to geophysical condition, the region has been facing many other problems like shortage of power, supply of raw material, improper marketing facilities, etc. Besides these, the state has different ethic groups who expertise in various traditional occupations which contribute important part in entrepreneurship development. Such activities are also needed special attention for the research since traditional occupations are historically linked with socio-cultural habitation of the group.

Theoretical Framework

Interestingly, studies on Indian entrepreneurship over the past few decades have employed different theoretical perspectives. It is due to the reason that India, being the second largest sub-continent in the world having different geo-physical environment, has diverse socio-cultural factors that prevails the growth of entrepreneurial activities among the people of various region. Considering such multi-ethnic and multi-cultural communities, it needs for new approaches that have a better understanding of entrepreneurship development in the country. Mario Rutton (1994), in his article *The study of Entrepreneurship in India: In Need of a Comparative Perspective* highlighted the different perspectives in studying the Indian entrepreneurship i.e., cultural perspectives, structural perspectives and comparative perspectives (integrated perspective). He discussed cultural perspective as the dominant approach to the study of Indian entrepreneurship in the 1950s and 1960s. This approach was inspired by Max Weber's (1976) Protestant ethic thesis and compatibility or incompatibility of Hindu religious values and other cultural factors with industrial entrepreneurship in India. And the structural perspective, dominant approach in 1970s and 1980s, which was mostly based on Marxist theories of Capitalist transformation that emphasized macro-economic or political factors to explain the development of Indian Entrepreneurs.

However, Weber (1958) pointed out "resistance to change" and "the restriction of the caste system" and highlighted the traditionalism of Indian artisans, which was reinforced by the fact that caste structure was an obstacle to occupational mobility and socio-economic changes. Weber's analysis of Hindu Society (1958), argued that the spirit of enterprise was inhibited among the indigenous population of India by the religious philosophy of resignation embodied in the doctrine of *Karma* and by the rigid social organization of the caste system and the joint family. It can also be noted that according to this cultural perspective, these negative elements were viewed as important factor in explaining India's retarded entrepreneurial activities. Weber had also categorically emphasized the traditionalism of Indian Artisans. He commented that Caste System was an obstacle to occupational mobility and socio-economic change among the people in the country. Besides, D. McClelland (1961) was also inspired by Weber's notion that religion, norms and values, behaviour and economic life are all interconnected. He highlighted that achievement motivation is of critical importance to successful entrepreneurship which is more or less absent in the Indian entrepreneurs. However, such views are criticized by Scholars like M. Singer (1972), D. Tripathi (1992), etc. M. Singer challenged

Weber's thesis by arguing that Hindu industrialist in Madras compartmentalize their religious lives and their business activities. He also argued that joint family organization play a positive role in industrial entrepreneurship.

However, the structural perspective is based mostly on theoretical views of Marxist persuasion. It tries to criticize the cultural approach, and the modernization theory. Such criticism is due to its lack of understanding of the exploitative relations between developing countries and the economically advanced countries, both at present and in a historic perspective. In addition to these, Ray (1992) also commented that the decisive factor was not so much their cultural disposition or religious mentality. But he pointed out that their social network and the strategic positions they had carved out for themselves early on by virtue of acting as the collaborators of the Europeans in the Asian trade. That is why, Indian entrepreneurship have failed to develop their entrepreneurial activities, not by their "traditional" orientation, but by the "colonial policy" and the process of de-industrialization. It also pointed out that imperialism by very nature was exploitative.

The present approach combines both the cultural and structural perspective. This fresh approach highlights how political, economic and cultural processes interact within the historical process of capitalist development. It also tries to explore through a comparative analysis that needs to take into account the wide diversity in the form of business organization and development of entrepreneurship within and between the urban and rural areas. It is also suggested that the study needs to look for the condition that promote or inhibit the growth of entrepreneurship rather than a stereotypic study. By interacting with local structure and culture, the study tries to account both similarities and differences in entrepreneurial behaviour among the entrepreneurs at various timings and at different places. In addition, it will bring more in-depth knowledge about entrepreneurs in different socio-cultural set-up of entrepreneurship.

Moreover, this theoretical approach to the study of entrepreneurship development is to look at the activities of individual entrepreneurs as an actor within a socio-economic and cultural system in the region. It also tries to examine their contribution to social and economic life of their society and the changes through innovations of new technologies and organization of new social relationship in the society. Here, the primary importance for the study will also be the kind of socio-cultural and economic re-orientation through historical analysis that has been taking place when a social group or individual transforms itself into a class of business entrepreneurs from the so-called rural/urban life in Manipur.

The Key Research Questions for the Study

Considering the above discussion, the present study tries to attempt the following broad questions in order to make a comprehensive study of the social and cultural basis of entrepreneurship development, social relationship and organizational behaviour among the entrepreneurs in developing entrepreneurial activities, socio-cultural and technological changes resulting from the development of entrepreneurship, and the role and contributions of NGOs, voluntary organizations, government agencies etc. Following are the key research questions:

- Are there any historical, chronological and religious antecedents to the development of entrepreneurship in the region? As a corollary, to what extent, cultural and religious associations are engaged in the development of entrepreneurship?
- To what extent and in what ways, entrepreneurs are bound by social relationship while developing their entrepreneurial activities within and outside their communities?
- How do the attitudes, interests, meanings and values influence the organizational behaviour pattern of the entrepreneurs in Manipur?

- Why do they initiate this new venture? In other words, do these initiatives merely aim at searching for livelihood or mutual co-operation, belongingness, etc.?
- What are the identifiable traits of the indigenous entrepreneurs and modern entrepreneurs?
- What is the role of entrepreneurship development organizations? What are the major constraints which entrepreneurs face in developing entrepreneurial activities? How do they encounter and cope up with such kind of constraints?

Statement of the Problem

The study takes a balanced view of cultural approach and structural approach. It tries to comprehend the dynamics of entrepreneurship development with a fresh approach that combines both the cultural and structural perspective by looking how political, economic, social and cultural processes interact with the historical process of entrepreneurship development in the study area. The earlier studies, carried out by Anthropologists and other social scientists among various communities, have constantly pointed out various problems of entrepreneurship development and offered suggestions of bringing better results. Based on various studies on entrepreneurship development, efforts have been subsequently made to improve the entrepreneurial activities by providing various kinds of provisions and schemes. However, unfortunately, the people have not been able to derive sufficient benefits from the process of planned development and schemes provided by the government. It is also true that entrepreneurship development in the country cannot be considered as stereotyped phenomenon as it varies from one region to another. Thus, it is very important to study in different parts of the country through micro level study to gain better understanding of various problems, issues and concerns of entrepreneurship development.

From the review of literature, it is found there are less number of micro level anthropological studies except some studies like

Geertz (1967), Firth (1967), Barth (1960), Singer (1967), Epistine (1964), Nafziger (1975), Lynch (1976), etc. Moreover, the anthropological studies in entrepreneurship among the rural and tribal areas are comparatively less, except some studies like Abner Cohen (1969), Pande G.S. (1998), Madhusudan Trivedi (1991), etc. The economists and the management scholars carried out most of the earlier studies on the development of entrepreneurship. Such earlier studies gave less emphasis on the socio-cultural dimensions in their studies. In spite of all, there are also many constraints for development like the lack of proper transport and communication, credit facility, etc.

However, there are very less number of studies on the entrepreneurship in Manipur. It is important to study the development of entrepreneurship since the problems of the development of entrepreneurship vary from one region to another. So, the study tries to understand the nature and functioning of entrepreneurship, the socio-economic profile of entrepreneurs and the social changes taking place due to the development of entrepreneurship in the study villages. Most importantly, the study will try to find out the social and cultural basis like morals, values, ethos, attitudes, and networking in their entrepreneurial activities. The study will also try to examine their social networking and organizational behaviour among themselves, development of entrepreneurs with new entrepreneurial technology and adoptive behaviour of entrepreneurs with the emergence of new technology.

Definition of the Terms Used in the Study

The term "Entrepreneurship" in the present study refers to the practices and activities started by an individual or a group of people for earning, with the capabilities of adopting or imitating new ideas to the rapid changing situation in the tribal or rural backward areas. The study regarded entrepreneurs as those who attempted to achieve something by utilizing their vision, drive and talent. However, the degree of these characters may vary from person to person.

For the study, Entrepreneurs are classified into two types:

Traditional Entrepreneurs are those who practice or do activities which are undertaken by a person, a community, a group, etc. that have been inherited from their long tradition along with their cultural values, customs, laws etc. from generation to generation. The new generation people organise the traditional activities like bamboo crafts making, weaving, piggery, poultry, firewood and timber selling etc. and make a way of earning from it. These activities are practiced as a secondary source of their livelihood.

Modern Entrepreneurs are those who practice or do activities which introduce modern technologies like rice mill services, van services, tractor services, etc. as a venture in the tribal and rural backward society by adopting or imitating a new way of earning for their livelihood. Such venture may be due to individual's decision or due to the influence of the development programmes, etc. by giving proper awareness or trainings. It may also be due to the influence of the family and friends who stay in the cities and towns. Sometimes, these may be an experimental practice by putting the individual's skill and reasoning against the challenging and unusual common opinion.

Objectives of the Study

Considering the above points, following are the objectives of the study :

1. To study the socio-economic and cultural profile of entrepreneurs;
2. To examine the social and cultural basis of entrepreneurship development;
3. To study the social relationship and organizational behaviour among the entrepreneurs;

4. To examine the functioning of entrepreneurship development programmes in the study area; and
5. To understand the socio-cultural and technological changes resulting from the development of entrepreneurship.

Methodology

The present study was conducted in Manipur. The state has various indigenous and traditional entrepreneurs. They have distinct and traditional way of enterprising and networking for organizing and maintaining themselves. Based on this, Thoubal district was selected for the present study. Within the District, Kakching block has been selected for the study. Entrepreneurial units were scattered un-uniformly among the different *leikais* (wards) of the study area, Kakching. Personal contact with the help of key informants and other knowledgeable persons helped in identifying the entrepreneurs in the study area. It was found that there were altogether a total of 137 entrepreneurs available in the study area who engaged in different entrepreneurial activities. It was divided into two major entrepreneurial types as per the operational definition for the study like Traditional Entrepreneurs and Modern Entrepreneurs. Among the total entrepreneurs, 64 entrepreneurs were engaged with traditional entrepreneurial activities and 73 belong to modern entrepreneurial activities. However, some of the entrepreneurs were engaged in more than one entrepreneurial activity and they are highlighted as a special case in the study.

The present study is based on intensive field-work conducted at Kakching. Thus, the study is a micro level study. The study adopted both qualitative and quantitative methods for the collection of data. Initially, a pilot survey was carried out over 3 months, i.e. January-March 2007 in this area. This was facilitated the designing of the study tools. After this, an intensive field-work for a period of 9 (nine) months from September, 2007 to May, 2008 was carried out. For the collection of data from the field, various anthropological tools and techniques like entrepreneur's schedule, case studies, interview, key informants, group discussion, observation, etc. were employed. However, secondary sources of information have also been used as and when necessary.

After establishing rapport with the people, it brought an understanding and transparency between the respondents and the researcher regarding the purpose of the study while collecting data from them. Key-informants were chosen for collecting in-depth knowledge of the entrepreneurs regarding the religious knowledge, morals, values, belief and networking etc. which were directly or indirectly influencing in developing the entrepreneurial activities among the younger generation. This also helped in collecting the primary data regarding the information about the entrepreneur's habits, attitudes, opinions, social participation, cultural background, ritual activities associated with the entrepreneurial activities etc.

Entrepreneur's schedule was employed to collect the first-hand primary data from the field areas. This was specially organized with a list of items of information to be filled-up by the respondents. By employing this, various categories of data were collected relating to entrepreneur's socio-economic and cultural background of entrepreneurs like age, sex, marital status, education, religion, caste or social class, income, occupations of respondents and their parents, opinions, belief, expectation, social participants, social and economic support system in developing the entrepreneurial activities, etc.

During the study, both participant observation and non-participant observations were employed. This helped in systematic cross-checking of information. Preliminary data from observation provided the insights and clues necessary for developing interview questions, case studies, etc. It provided the further checking and monitoring of field information like attitude towards, the owner and the client, and the master and their workers, marketing networks relating supply of raw materials and products, and other activities involved in the transaction of their entrepreneurial activities that was necessary for evaluating data gathered by the specialized techniques. Careful observations were made from the information collected through clues developed from interview and key informants regarding clear understanding of the lifestyle of entrepreneurs, customs and manners, interpersonal relations, group dynamics, leadership role, managerial role, risk taking behaviour, innovativeness, socio-cultural and technological changes resulting from the development of entrepreneurship, etc. Observation were conducted at their working places or offices for the cross- checking of information about the role and the contribution of NGOs, Voluntary Organizations, and Government Institutions for entrepreneurship development. It also gave a clear understanding of how the organization and agencies carried out their activities. Most importantly, it helped to identify how potential entrepreneurs were selected. Moreover, the personal or social networking within the entrepreneurs and the official was also observed.

For the study, unstructured and open-ended interviews were carried out regarding their socio-economic and cultural background, occupational background, social mobility, etc. This was carried out so as to get the in-depth data and majority of them at their working place, either offices or industries or business centres. This provided a good opportunity to observe the entrepreneurs at work, the type of individual management and their interaction with workers and also with other people etc. This was followed up with an open discussion regarding how they perceived the entrepreneurship and to be being an entrepreneur, the kind of ritual functions, religious sacrifices and sentiment that favours or hinders in developing entrepreneurship. This was also opened to common people to bring the true picture of general conception and in-depth information from the field.

An attempt was made to prepare case studies to facilitate the understanding of socio-economic and cultural profile of the entrepreneurs. It helped to collect the holistic and meaningful characteristic of real life events. The case study method was used for exploring and analyzing socio-economic and cultural milieu of entrepreneurs, households and the institutions dealing with entrepreneurial activities. It explored the factors like education, family background, kinship relationships, ritual functions participated by the entrepreneurs, social relationship within the family, relatives and friendships, etc. which were influencing in developing the entrepreneurial activities.

Life history method was also employed in order to find out the historical and chronological information of the entrepreneurs while developing the entrepreneurship. The richness and personalized nature of life histories afforded vividness and integration of cultural information that were of great value for understanding particular lifestyle. This life histories material were more useful for examining the patterning of general values, foci of cultural interests, and perceptions of social and natural relationship than as true histories.

Besides these, FGD (Focus Group Discussion) was also employed for collection of data as per the suitable situations and requirements.

Significance of the Study

Although several empirical studies have investigated the basis of entrepreneur in different parts of India, these studies lack the data essential for comparing the origins of entrepreneurs with that of the population as a whole, and for relating socio-economic characteristics of entrepreneurs to their success. The study tried to compare the information on the population at large related to the educational attainment, entrepreneurial and managerial experience, initial capital, access to government assistance and success of the entrepreneur.

Limitation of the study

The study has various limitations :

1. The literature and secondary data pertaining to Manipur State were not sufficiently available. So, the study has to rely more on primary data collected from the field-work.

2. The law and order situation, insurgency problem, *bandhs* and blockade in the study area made the field-work difficult while conducting field-work.
3. Collecting Information relating to investment, loans, sales, profits, etc. were the main hurdles during the field-work as the entrepreneurs were afraid of extortion by the insurgents if they happen to know their growth in entrepreneurial activities.

2

Development of Entrepreneurship in Manipur

(Cultural and Historical Perspective)

Introduction

The judgment of the extent to which the developments of entrepreneurial activities are encouraged in the backward region of North-East is very challenging. The oldest and most important household entrepreneurial activities like handloom, bamboo crafts, wooden crafts, piggery, poultry etc. are very common in different sections of the society. Such kind of entrepreneurial activities have been associated with the people as a compulsion or choice for earning their livelihood due to unemployment or less availability of other earning opportunities. It may also be because of the reason that the region is always away from the different earning activities which are common in the other mainstream regions of India like in the industrial employment or non-governmental works or self-franchised business etc. The region is lagging behind in all respects of development activities. The people of the region try to cope up with the socio-economic and cultural changes by adapting their own entrepreneurial activities with the changing situations brought by the external or internal forces. These become a part and parcel of their culture and tradition.

Since the time of their forefathers, among the Meeteis, agriculture was the main economic activity of subsistence among the people in the region. Besides agriculture, different communities of Meetei at different places of Manipur were associated with different entrepreneurial activities. For instance, Meetei at Sekmai,

Pheiyeng and Andro have their traditional alcohol preparation, Meetei at Thongjao have pottery, Meetei at Moirang have fishery etc. as their traditional entrepreneurial activities. However, the Meetei of Kakching were mainly associated with the iron smelting. In addition to this, they were also engaged with handloom, wood crafting, carpentry, timber and fuelwood business, charcoal business, bamboo shoot fermentation, fishery, piggery, etc. from generation to generation.

In order to have a better understanding of the development of entrepreneurship in Manipur, it is also necessary to know people's perception on the term and concept of entrepreneurship, how people start using money, origin of market, the legends associated with the development of entrepreneurship, etc. These are the basic factors which directly or indirectly initiated the development of entrepreneurship in Manipur.

People's Perception on the Entrepreneurship Development

The Meeteis and the hill tribes of Manipur have been living together in different parts of Manipur under a wide variety of cultural arrangements and close social-networking among them. The quality of institutional role and individual personality were related to the ethos of their particular culture. Moreover, people of the region were activated by various needs in their day-to-day life. As to fulfil various needs, they have to exert power on the nature, thereby developing diverse types of institutions and organization among themselves for their livelihood. In the rural and backward areas of Kakching, people follow certain conventional and customary roles and functions for their daily lives and activities. But, sometimes specific socio-economic and cultural factors are responsible for the emergence of new roles and functions. This leads to the beginning of new activities among the people in rural Manipur. Starting various entrepreneurial activities is one among them. However, the rural people think that initiating an enterprise is difficult for them due to the unpredictable capital investment, risk in profit making, etc. They also perceived that developing entrepreneurial activities is a new venture for earning which can generate their own livelihood without depending on others.

Local term of Entrepreneurship

It is also found that there are also local terms (like *"Lalol-Etik"* or *"Karbar"*) which are closely related to the term entrepreneurship. Such terms need to be explained. As per their perceptions, *"Lalol-Etik"* or *"Karbar"* means the activity of making things, buying, selling or supplying goods or services for money especially at the market. On the other hand, it is a kind of practice that involves in any activity either for earning money or organizing any activity not only in the market places or business centres, but also at home or other places. But it is also mentioned that the word *"Karbar"* seems to be derived from other non-Manipuri languages that have been diffused from the neighbouring regions.

Myth associated with the God and Goddess and Belief system

There are also myths associated with the origin and development of different entrepreneurial activities and also the habit of saving among the people of Manipur. The Meetei people perform various *pujas* and offerings on different occasions in their lifetime. The entrepreneurs perform specific *pujas* and recitation while inaugurating their newly established entrepreneurial units. They also perform daily offering and *pujas* as per their convenience and offer charity in the name of their entrepreneurial unit so that the Almighty will forgive all their sins and give blessings for their growth and prosperity. They also have strong religious sentiments from their own religion as well as the Hindu belief system of Gods and Goddesses. Some of their traditional sentiments of Gods and Goddesses contribute to the solidarity among the entrepreneurs and their workers within their entrepreneurial activities. It also enhances the moral obligation and self-respect among the people of the region. The Meetei of Manipur worship different Gods and Goddesses viz. *Atiya Guru Sidaba, Pakhangba, Sanamahi,*

Leimaren, Phunga Lairu, Apokpa, Umanglei, etc. However, it is considered that *Atiya Guru Sidaba* is the supreme of all Gods and Goddesses. Some of the Gods and Goddesses are described as follows:

Atiya Guru Sidaba

It is believed that *Atiya Guru Sidaba* is considered the supreme of all gods and goddesses. In the mythology of Meetei, *Atiya Guru Sidaba* is described as forefather of all gods, men, animals and planets. He is also the husband of *Ema Laimaren Sidabi*, the goddess of earth. The name *Atiya Guru Sidaba* literally means "Sky Guru Immortal". It is also believed that He is the sole breeder of all that bred and personified as immortal god. He has two sons: *Sanamahi,* the first one and *Pakhangba,* the second one. The entrepreneurs of the region worship and perform rituals every year for the growth and betterment of the entrepreneurial activities. They also donate money or material for the construction or electrification of religious places in the name of Gods and Goddesses.

Pakhangba

The god *Pakhangba* is considered the destroyer of the Universe in the mythology of Manipur. Literally, *Pakhangba* means "One who knows his father". The name is also meant as "God by day time and Man by night time". Another form of *Pakhangba* is that of a snake. The mythology also tells that *Pakhangba* and *Sanamahi* were the brothers, the two sons of the supreme god *Atiya Guru Sidaba. Atiya Guru Sidaba* wanted to find out which of his sons recognized him not only as father but also as Guru. So, to test their knowledge, he took the form of a dead cow and floated down a big river. On seeing the floating dead cow, *Sanamahi (*then known as *Kuptreng)* disliked dead cow, but *Pakhangba (*then known as *Shentreng)* realized that it might be the God in disguise. *Sanamahi* asked how they could find whether this was so. As an answer, *Pakhangba* argued that it is not possible for a dead cow to move its tail. On hearing this *Atiya Guru Sidaba*, wishing to reveal himself, moved his tails. Then he took his proper form and gave *Shentreng* the new name *Pakhangba* (*Pa*—Father, *Khangba* – to know). *Kuptreng* came to be known as *Sanamahi.*

This myth ascribes a divine origin to *Pakhangba*, as well as its divine nature. Divine aspect is also shown in that worship is afforded to him by the ruling Meetei in Manipur of those times, although with considerable secrecy. It should be stressed that the worship of *Pakhangba* remains prerogative of the *Ningthoujas* (a clan) and intimately associated with the throne, so no member of other *yek* (clan in Meetei) is allowed to worship him.

Sanamahi

It is also believed that worshipping *Sanamahi*, the most important household deity will bring the prosperity and good health to family. They offer *puja* everyday in the morning before going out for work as well as in the evening after coming back from work. This helps them to motivate morally and spiritually in all respects of their activities. Literally *Sanamahi* mean "Liquid gold". He is the son of *Guru Atiya Sidaba* and *Ema Leimaren Sidabi,* and also the elder brother of *Pakhangba*. The myth is that he created the Universe, human beings, frogs, animals, plants, etc. He created man in the image of the Almighty father. The Guru introduced life into it in order to adore Him. Every Meetei family has a *Piba* (Chief of the families) whose main function is to officiate as a priest in the rituals. *Sanamahi* is propitiated on the last day of the year. The idol of *Sanamahi* is ceremoniously washed in the morning. Rice-cake offering is made to Him to the accompaniment of *mantras*. However, *Sanamahi* is worshipped together with his mother *Leimaren*, and seldom alone. In every household, a particular place is set apart in the south-west corner of the house, locally termed as *Sanamahi Kachind*. People do *puja* and burn incense and lit up a lamp before *Sanamahi* and *Leimaren*. He is the God of all those who desire life and energy and also for the removal of diseases from the family. The festivals like *Cheiraoba* (New Year of Meetei) celebrate the glory of *Sanamahi*.

Leimaren Sidabi

Leimaren Sidabi is the most important goddess worshipped by the Manipuri Meetei. She is considered to be the mother of all who can give prosperity, wealth and caring to all. The earth goddess with name *Leimaren* or *Leimarel* (the great princess) is a fascinating one. Her worship and her place in the house explicitly connect her with *Sanamahi*. According to the myth, she was originally the wife of *Atiya Guru Sidaba* and was subsequently married to *Sanamahi*. This was the punishment to her for her partiality to *Pakhangba* in advising him to walk around the Throne of *Sidaba Mapu* and bow down in order to obtain the succession. The myth is related to Kingship. *Sidaba Mapu* announced that he would appoint one among the brothers (*Sanamahi* or *Pakhangba*) who returned first after circuiting the whole world as King. *Sanamahi* started off from the southern side of the Royal Kangla. *Pakhangba*, on the advice of *Leimaren*, went round his father's throne seven times regarding it equivalent to going round the world. *Sidaba Mapu* gave the throne to him. But when *Sanamahi* returned and found *Pakhangba* ascending the throne, he was angry and tried to kill *Pakhangba*. The frightened *Pakhangba* took refuge among the *Lairembis* (Goddesses). But the angry *Sanamahi* declared that if his brother's advisors were a man he would be killed, and if a woman, he would marry her. As the *Lairembi's* include his mother *Leimaren* too, *Sanamahi* marrying his mother is explained. The place of *Leimaren* in the house explicitly connected her with *Sanamahi*. An earthern pot, full of water with a lid is kept on the platform and it is considered good to fill-up the pot with new water every Tuesday and Thursday. The presence of water in the pot symbolizes the well-being and peaceful living in the family without any attack from diseases.

Apokpa

The term *Apokpa* means "to beget or to give birth to". These domestic *Lais* are the ancestors of the immediate family circle.

They are deceased males of the previous three generations (the father, the grandfather and great-grandfather), who look after the interest of the family. Worship of *Apokpa* is carried out by each household as a closely knit group. The food for the offering consists mainly of *Kabok* (puffed rice), *Larou* (sweetened parched rice), different kinds of sweets, fruits and other different offerings. *Apokpa Khurumba* (meaning "bowing down to *Apokpa*") is observed in a series of rituals. The various offerings to *Apokpa* are buried in the house between the *Phunga* and the *Lairu*, and covered with seven layers of banana leaf. It is also observed that another cult of ancestor spirits termed as "*Kasalai*" is closely connected with the cult of *Apokpa*.

One very interesting thing in the rituals of *Apokpa* is that during the ritual offering the local ritual performer predicts the fortune of the family members and the activities they would be involved in. So, most of the entrepreneurs among the family work sincerely and are also offered with goods and money in the name of their entrepreneurial activities. This brings solidarity and group feeling within the family and enhancing the social networking in the entrepreneurial activities.

Phunga Lairu

The *Phunga Lairu* is an important place, and it has a great religious significance in every Meetei house. *Phunga* means "fireplace" and the *Phunga Lairu* refers to the fireplace in the main room of the house. It consists of a small hole and fire is kept burning in the hole using husks and other fuel like wood material. They usually keep three stones considered as *Mangang, Luwang* and *Khuman* in the fire place. Nowadays, it has been replaced by *Yotshubi,* i.e. a platform with three legs (iron rods) representing the three stones. The *Phunga* is also used in household work, like baking fishes, drying beans, and chillies to make suitable dishes. There is a ritual that *Phunga* should be kept burning in the house at least for five days at the time of formal entry to a new house for prosperity in the house.

Phunga Leiru Emoinu Khurumba (Prayer for Goddess of Wealth: Emoinu)

Hea Ema Emoinu ahongbi ahing arai kangdabi, nungthil arai tadabi, tara chakning khakna chakshoubi, yanglou yenpang tamlebi, phurak leima achibi langon chaobi leimaran phamthon karebi, emana nanaibu watta padababu pinabiu !!!

Phunga Leiru Emoinu, the Goddess of *Meetei*, is associated with every household of *Manipuris*. Irrespective of *Meetei* or Hindu *Meetei*, they all have belief in the Goddess and that ritual and *puja* offered to her will bring good fortune to their family solidarity among themselves. While conducting rituals, the local *Maiba or Maibi* (religious functionary or physician) recites the above *mantras*. They perform rituals in different timings in consultation with the local elders and ritual performers. These rituals morally help them to performing their duties. They can be categorized as below:

1. Rituals performed during	*Engga* (May-June)	for blessing of wealth.
2. Rituals performed during	*Langban* (Aug-Sept)	for blessing to beget children.
3. Rituals performed during	*Poinu* (Nov-Dec)	for blessing for long life.

Fire place of every household is considered to be a special place for the deity "*Emoinu Ahong-Achoubi*". Her divine power is considered to be very magnificent. Everyday there should be light on it and every dawn there should be the offering of incense smoke to the deity. It is also considered to be a place where the bad spirit infected from outside can be driven out by getting the light/heat from this fire place. Nowadays, most of the Meetei entrepreneurs keep photo of *Emoinu* near their money box or at their working place so that it will bring luck and prosperity to their entrepreneurial activities.

The mythological story related to the wealth and concept of saving and hospitality to customers

The mythological story of Meetei Gods and Goddesses start with the one and only supreme God *Atiya Guru Shidaba*. He is considered the supreme God who advised his son *Sanamahi* to create man, who was assumed be on earth to perform duties given by Almighty God. After the creation of man, Lord *Sanamahi* requested to *Atiya Guru Shidaba* to provide food for the human being. Then *Atiya Guru Shidaba* advised his wife, *Ema Leimaren Shidabi* the Goddess to arrange for providing all the basic needs for human being as requested by Her son. So, the Goddess *Ema Leimaren Shidabi* had an incarnation and produced three Goddesses namely, Goddess *Ngareima* (Goddess who provides varieties of fishes), Goddess *Thumleima* (Goddess who provides salt) and Goddess *Phouoibi* (Goddess who provides rice, grains, etc.). The Goddesses were ordered to perform their own duties for the welfare of the human being. Two Goddesses *Ngareima* and *Thumleima,* went to the water and Goddess *Phouoibi* remained on land and transformed herself as paddy plant for the procurement of human being. Later, Goddess *Ngareima* and *Thumleima* asked Goddess *Phouoibi* to travel the whole earth to spread their blessing to all the human being. They started travelling and later found a place called " Erei-Lok" where they had to cross a swift and steep stream. The two Goddesses tried to cross over it; but Goddess *Phouoibi* was not able to cross it and drowned in the water. Knowing the suffering of *Phouoibi*, *Atiya Guru Shidaba* came and helped her to reach the bank of the river. The incident happened due to the deceiving word of a deer that was nearby that river. So, the deer was cursed to be a symbol of bad omen and human beings consider it inauspicious to be faced by a deer while setting out for a journey. This belief still continues among the Meetei till today.

Later, *Phouoibi* met *Akoijamba* and promised to meet the following day. *Phouoibi* visited *Akoijamba*'s house but she was ill-treated by his mother. She was disheartened by the act of *Akoijamba*'s mother. Before she left *Akoijamba*'s house, she handed over a *Korbat tumba* (a type of traditional container) with a tight shield at the opening to *Akoijamba*'s mother so that he could remember that she came to his house. She also requested to *Akoijamba*'s mother not to open the shield of the container. With suspicion, *Akoijamba*'s mother opened it and suddenly, a steam like flow of rice came out from it and she was surprised and also afraid of it. When *Akoijamba*, came back from hunting, his mother narrated the story and he followed to get *Phouoibi*. On the way to *Thangjing ching*, he found her and requested to come back but *Phouoibi* refused his proposal. But they promised again to meet in the next generation as *Khamba* and *Thoibi*. So, *Phouoibi* had given a stone representing herself to *Akoigamba* to keep it in the granary. It is believed to bring growth and prosperity to the family. *Phouoibi* also advised to clear the granary before the coming of new rice and offer *Khoijuleikmam* (a kind of leaf) smoke as a symbolic arrival of *Phouoibi*. So, this cult has performed from generation to generation among the people irrespective of their belief in Meeteism or Hinduism.

This brings the tradition of not taking out all the grains from their granary and also providing proper hospitality to the customers by businessmen. They presume that every customer should be given good hospitality and only then would their entrepreneurial unit will grow and *Emoinu* the incarnation of Goddess wealth will bless them.

Origin of Entrepreneurial Activities and Myth associated with Traditional Iron Smelting at Kakching

The history of the origin of traditional iron smelting activities has been widely described in different books associated with the origin of the Kakching people. For better understanding of the process and the functioning of the iron smelting activities at Kakching, a brief account of it collected from different secondary sources are mentioned here. Literally, *"Yotsungba"* means "Iron smelting" in Manipuri. It has a long history which has been associated with the origin of the Kakching people. It can be considered the oldest of the entrepreneurial activities associated with the people of the region passing through generations after generations as part of indigenous knowledge. The technology of iron smelting which were in possession of the Kakching people is a great matter of archaeological, historical and cultural interest. Kakching and its people were the only community who were engaged in the work of iron smelting among the Manipuris. The entire transformation of the Iron Age in Manipur would be inferred from the study of the indigenous iron technology.

The tradition of iron smelting among the Kakching people can be traced out from their myths, legends, oral traditions, religious festivals, etc. So, the Kakching people's association with iron work has been an established fact of history. The local God *Khamlangba* is associated with the discovery of iron. Legends about his search for iron in the ancient land of *Takhel* (presently called Tripura), his marriage to a *Takhel* lady, his arrival at Imphal and ultimate migration to *Kereaching* (presently a place near Kakching Khullen Turel Wangma) and founding of an iron smelters' colony at Kakching is meticulously written down in the ancient *Puyas* (the King Chronical of Manipur). The deity *Khamlangba* is indeed a historical figure and is associated with rituals in the mythology of the Meiteis. Probably, he is a historical and cultural hero whose exploits in the development of iron technology has been of great significance in the agrarian development of Kakching. The fertility of the soil, the collective spirit of the Kakching people and tremendous changes in agriculture with the introduction of iron tools made Kakching a forward moving agricultural community. The food produce from Kakching, the richness of rice production to be precise, had earned for Kakching the title of "the Granary of Manipur" and it has indeed deep roots in history. The indigenous iron technology of Kakching is a salient feature of its people. The Kakching people of those days followed several procedures for the production of indigenous iron metal. They are discussed below as described by Gourachandra (1997) in his book "Manipurda Yotshung Yotsha : Traditional Iron Smelting and Forging in Manipur."

Extraction of iron ore

Generally three or four persons under a specialist (basically a knowledgeable person) with necessary equipment like spade, a long bamboo skewer, baskets and a pot go out for ore deposits. To check whether the ground contains ore-deposit or not, with a prayer to *Ibudhou Khamlangba*, they dig a small pit and the skewer is pushed down deep into the ground at two or three places inside the pit. At times little water is poured along the skewer. If the ground has deposit of iron ore, that can be heard and felt through the bamboo skewer. After the deposit is fully confirmed, they start digging the ground. The excavated earth or iron ore are exposed in the sun to dry. Ore is found in layers and different in quality. The lower layer has better quality deposit.

Cleaning

A pit with roughly 4 ft diameter, 2.5 ft depth and a base which has a gradual slope towards the centre are made. Then water is poured into the pit after which the dried iron ore with clay is thrown into it and kept soaked at least for a night. The soaked earthen ore is trodden again. By pouring more and more water, the ore is cleaned and collected. The cleaned ore noodles are then dried in the sun.

Burning

A piece of ground is smoothened and plastered with fresh cow dung and mud. On this ore-noodles are placed in layers with straw in between and burnt. It is kept for a night and on the next morning the particles of ore are collected with the help of winnowing fan and pounded. This work is usually done by women-folk. The pounded ore powder is then taken into a wooden tray measuring 12 inches in diameter and maximum slope depth of 1.5 inches approximately and smelted one "*Yotshung*". Due to the labourous work involved during iron smelting, people can extract only one "*Yotshung*" in a day. They have different measuring units like

Yotshung and *Yotkang*. *Yotkang* is the smaller unit than *Yotshung*. It is mentioned that one *Yotshung* is equal to ten *Yotkang*.

Smelting

An earthen furnace with two holes opposite to each other is erected and kept in the sun for a month or so to be dried fully. One hole would be much bigger than the other and the base of the furnace would have a gradual slope towards the smaller hole. Smaller hole is closed thoroughly with "*Phamen Leibak*" (a kind of better quality clay), forming a little convex mound inside the furnace. The point of mound is placed towards the other bigger hole roughly at a height of 3 inches from the base. A hole is made through the point of the mound for air supply from bellows. Bellows consist of two hollow wooden cylinders each with a hole at the top. Two-third of the height of the cylinders are buried roughly four inches away from the furnace at the side of the small hole. Little ore is poured into the cylinders. The hole in the cylinders and the small hole in the furnace would be connected with two fitting bamboo tubes. Each of the cylinders would be covered with cow-hide securely binding around the rim of the cylinders with long bamboo straps (*Kabow payaa*). At the centre of each cover is a hole. Two pieces of leather straps with toggles attached are passed through the holes and held. The other ends of the straps are tied to two sticks carefully buried in the ground and bent it so as to act as a spring and the cover is always kept utmost raised to it.

Burning charcoals are kept at the base of the furnace and are filled with black charcoals. The bellow-man (a person who blows air for burning) takes his stand on the cylinders placing a foot over the hole in each cover. Resting his hands on a crossbar, he raises his feet and descends alternately and continually. The feeders feed the charcoal and the ore powder into the furnace in turn. In this process, the other impurities are burnt away and molten iron gets collected at the same base of the furnace. Now, the bellow-man stops supplying air for burning and iron is extracted.

The transition from new Stone Age to Iron Age in Manipur is still one of the few chapters in its history which had not been properly highlighted so far. Indigenous method of smelting and forging iron by the people of Kakching in the ancient past would be an ethno-archaeological discovery of great cultural interest. The method of extracting iron from crude iron-ore through indigenous devices which was a speciality of the Kakching people in the early Christian era would provide an understanding of the social and cultural changes in Manipur.

Problem encountered by the traditional iron-smelter (Black-smithy)

Kakching from time immemorial had been a quiet village inhabited by a hardworking distinctive group of people. They believe that their ancestors were the follower of "*Lord Khamlangba*", a local deity associated with iron smelting and manufacture of iron implements in Manipur. Till today, the people of Kakching worship "*Ibudou Khamlangba*" with all devotion, love and belief. In quest of iron ore, they had changed their settlement from different parts of Manipur to the present place at Kakching in the beginning of 17th century. Everyone at Kakching boasts of and owes allegiance to their ancestors for the right choice of their promised land.

In the olden days the *Loi* communities settled in remote areas were given specific occupation by the then Kings according to the inherent qualities in their trade. The people of Kakching were duty bound (obligation to the then Manipuri Kings) to extract iron ore and manufacture iron implements for domestic use and for warfare as well. Out of the total product some of good quality was presented to the Kings of Manipur as tribute. People believed that they were guided by the spirit of *Lord Khamlangba* in the whole process of iron manufacture. Without his mercy, no one could expect to achieve anything in iron smelting. In this connection on iron smithy of Manipur, "*Lord Khamlangba*" was credited with the power of gifting the iron ore or resources. "One day iron ore was found near the surface, the next day it was disappeared, only to appear again as and when the capricious god chose. The presence of a deposit was detected by probing the soil with a long bamboo skewer, after heavy rain when the ground is soft. If the skewer strikes something hard, a trial excavation was made. The deposits would generally be on the surface of the pit at a depth of approximately 9 feet. Members of the team work together and the result of their labour were divided equally".

The extraordinary power of Lord *Khamlangba* is also described in the chanting of devotional prayers by the *Maibas* (the traditional ritual performer) during the "*Lai Haraoba*" the yearly festival of Lord *Khamlangba*. He is a powerful deity who could dissolve stone like salt and chew iron like eating "*Chagem*", a favourite curry of Meetei. Late N. Amuyaima, the *Pandit Achouba of Sana Konung* in his book "Kakching Khunthoklon" describes that during the time of their settlement at Thoubal, the people of Kakching could find soil similar to that of *Takhel* from where iron ore could be extracted.

The time honoured occupation was gradually given up when a complicated issue was raised by Maharaj Churchand Singh. He charged the people of Kakching with the supply of bullets made by Kakching people during "*Khonsai Lal*" or "*Khonsai War*". So, Maharaj Churchand ordered to give heavy punishment to those persons who involved in such activities against him. However, it was not true. It was a misconception of the King. The fact was that the small pieces of iron were made to be fixed at the fishing net locally called "*Ell-lic*". But the King assumed it as bullet. Again just before and after the World War II, industrial products appeared in the markets in Manipur in large scale. People did not find it profitable to continue the time consuming process of iron smelting with limited resources of iron ore available in the locality. However, the efforts of hard-working people of Kakching in iron work will go down in the history of Manipur.

Origin of *Keithel* (Market) and entrepreneurship development

The development of market has brought many changes in the socio-economic and cultural lives of rural people in Manipur. Without the development of market the entrepreneurial activities in the region might have been much slower. Basically, market is the site of the economic life of the community. In their forefathers' days, market was the only place where people could gather freely and exchange information. This led to the exchange of ideas and discussion for the betterment of their livelihood among the rural people. In this connection, the origin of market gives some of the explanations regarding the development of entrepreneurial activities in the region.

In Manipur, the origin of *Keithel* is not clearly known; but the practice of market has been there down the centuries. It is also mentioned that the origin of *Keithel* is as early as the origin of Manipuri civilization as it has been mentioned in many of the folk tales of Manipuris. In fact, *Keithel* (Market) is a place where exchange or transaction between the buyers and the sellers took place. It may also be regarded as the place where the balanced reciprocity is carried out. This also gives a clue of the introduction of the concept of money in society as money became a medium of their exchange for goods and services.

Literally, *Keithel* is a synthesis of two words, i.e. *Kei* and *Thel*. The term "*Kei*" means the store house, and "*Thel*" means displayed or kept open for buying and selling. Such places are used not only for the exchange of goods and services but also for getting information of the current events. It can be considered as the support system and the backbone of their socio-economic organization.

Besides these, in Manipur, *keithel* plays an important role in developing different entrepreneurial activities too. The uniqueness of Meeteis in Manipur is the "*Nupi Keithel*", the market places specially reserved for women for selling different varieties of goods like rice, fish, vegetables, monkey rice, fruits, clothes, iron implements, etc.

The women's market in Manipur has a very distinctive position because women control trade and it affects and contributes to the whole economy of the state. It might be very rare in other parts of India that large ensemble of women manages the local market.

From historical period, Manipuri women performed both household chores as well as outside work besides taking active part in various affairs of the state.

Legends associated with the origin of Market at Kakching

The people of Kakching have inhabited in a very compact site surrounded by the agricultural land, lakes and hills on four sides. Kakching is also known for its good production of rice and other vegetable products over generations. Surrounded by many small villages like Keirak, Wabagai, Tentha, Tekcham, Pallel, Unapal, Phunal, Wangjing, Khongjom, etc., Kakching has been one of the popular centres for the marketing of their products.

The origin of Kakching *Keithel* (market) has a long history. It was started during the reign of *Maharaja Khagemba*, the then King of Manipur. During those times, there were no markets in the southern part of Manipur. People had to go to *Khwiramband Keithel* in Imphal for buying and selling their products. They used to go by walk from different parts of Manipur to *Khwiramband Keithel*. Sometimes, people travelled in groups on bullock-carts. They sometimes used water navigation to reach Imphal from different regions of Manipur. In those days, roads were very bad and there were bushes around. There were frequent attacks by the wild beasts like tigers, bears, etc. while travelling to the main market from their villages. Local dacoits were also very common. Still, the people of the region had to travel long distance for the sake of buying something or the other. They sometimes took breaks on the way in some of the villages and camp one night there itself if they were not able to reach Imphal in one day. All these were problems to the rural people in different regions of Manipur.

In those times, people could not establish any market place without the wishes and will of the king. It was also considered that if the blessing of king was not there, there would be no progress in their market and there would be less gathering in the *Keithel*. That is why, there was always the necessity of *Maharaja*'s blessing. Moreover, there is also the custom of taking some clay from the palace after the announcement of King's approval of initiating the market. If the people of the region found the place not suitable for running market, they could shift to the new place but the custom of collecting some clay from the former market was compulsory. Again, they have to place the collected clay at the proposed market site for inauguration of the new market. It was followed by the rituals and *pujas* to bring good fortune.

Leishangthem Leishangchaoba was the legendary hero of the establishment of Kakching *Keithel*. He was the first to approach the then Maharaja of Manipur. Kakching *Keithel* is the gift of *Epu Leishangchaoba* to the Kakching people. His contribution to the people of the region is immense. It is needless to mention that the emergence of such a market place brought all the turning points in the rural life of Kakching and its surrounding villages. This kind of development in market also leads to the emergence of different types of entrepreneurial activities for the sustenance of rural people in the region.

Origin of Money and Currency in Manipur

The beginning of using money brought a significant change in all socio-economic spheres of Manipur. The use of money leads to easy transaction of goods and services among the people in the region and ultimately enhances the development of entrepreneurial activities as it became an important aspect of the new generation. This becomes the prime source for the motivation for different entrepreneurial activities with different people of the neighbouring regions. However, the origin of money in any society is always associated with a history and it is also very debatable. Most of the people assumed that money is invented in any society (or borrowed from another society) when trade increases and barter system becomes increasingly inefficient for the exchange of goods and services amongst the people. The more the practice of trade increases, the more the difficulty to find out what exactly people want for their goods. Therefore, money becomes an important and valuable item that could be exchanged for anything and so it becomes an effective medium of exchange when trade become important. This leads to satisfying both the buyer and the seller in their exchange.

It has been mentioned by the aged people that, from early king's period Manipur had its own currency, made by them. Till today, the origin and starting of using currency in Manipur is not yet clear. This may be because of the less availability of historical written accounts. However, there are two ways of tracing out the origin of money/currency in Manipur Kingdom. First, the use of money that is mentioned in old book, Puya, "*Numit Kappa*". This Puya is claimed to be written in the 2nd to 3rd century, a notion which is also debatable. Second, through the mythological stories and oral traditions of the Manipuris which have been handed over generations after generations.

Meetei *Maibas* and some scholars mentioned that during the reign of *Nongda Leiran Pakhangba* (33 A.D.), there was the presence of money in the kingdom. (Mutuwa Jhulon). According to them, the currency during those times was made up of bronze metal. It looks like the plate, big in size, very thick, and there is no mark on both sides. It has also been mentioned that there were the use of currency during the reign of *Leiningthou Khagemba* (1597-1652 A.D). Much earlier than this, they have also mentioned the use of currency in different periods of Manipuri Kings like *Ura Konthouba* (568-658 A.D). Till today, this is the oldest currency used by Meetei's that had been found by scholars. Later, there were many different currencies during the time of different Meetei Kings, like *Ayangba, Leiremba, Chalamba, Khagemba, Paikhomba, Kulachandra,* etc. Till the reign of *Kulachandra Maharaj* (1890-1891), the then king of Manipur, the Meetei had their own currency. Later, during the reign of *Maharaja Churchand Singh* (1891-1941), the king stopped making their own currency and started using Indo-British currency due to the influence of the British Empire in the region. The king started collecting the tools and equipment which was once used in making currency from the *Aheibam* group (a particular family group who were engaged in producing currency in those times in Manipur with the advice of the then kings). And also, the then king ordered to collect and exchange those old currencies (which were made by Meetei Kings) from different parts of the Meetei kingdom so that they could use the new currency in the Kingdom.

However, certain communities like the *Chakpa* group, preserved the unused indigenous currency with certain cultural sentiments and refused to surrender such indigenous currency to the king. They used such indigenous currency during their last rites by keeping it under the forehead and the feet of the dead body. There still is the tradition of keeping the indigenous currency among many of the *Meetei* communities in Manipur and also Meeteis in neighbouring states like Assam, Tripura, Bangladesh, etc. especially in the house of family *Pibas* (the head of the lineage). There is still the tradition of keeping the indigenous money inside the *Lubak* (traditional basket) of every household in Manipur representing Lord *Sanamahi* and *Ema Leimaren Shidabi*. Even the *Maiba* and *Maibi* of Meetei still use such indigenous currency while performing the *Shenmit Yengba* (an indigenous and traditional way of predicting the future or fortune telling).

It is also mentioned that there were different contacts of Meetei's with other kingdoms like Assam, Shan province and Pongs of Burma. They termed the Meetei kingdoms differently as per their convenience like *Mugali* by Cashar, *Makhali* by Assam, *Kashea* by Shan's, etc. This reflects the connection and ties by Meetei Kings with other neighbouring countries in terms of trade, solidarity, etc.

The currencies made of bronze were marked only on one side, and the other side was kept plain. They made straight corners and line mark/prints to beautify the currency. In fact, there are 5 different types of marks/prints in the currency like, (1) to print the beginning letter of the King who produced that currency, (2) to print "Shree" instead of King's name, (3) to print the Lord's name in the kingdom, (4) to print the full name of the King who produced it, and (5) to print the short cut mark/symbol, etc.

General background and the stages for the entrepreneurship development in Manipur

To the outsiders, i.e. to the mainstream Indian, the name of Manipur has become almost synonymous with the fascinating dance and issues of insurgents in the region. The origin of the entrepreneurship or other different traditional economic activities is lost in obscurity; but its roots can be traced back into the ancient history of Manipur. However, the history of different entrepreneurial activities in Manipur can be broadly divided into three developmental stages. Typically it can be broadly divided as follows:

1. Pre-British Period
2. British Period
3. The present phase or the third phase.

The first stage began with the dawn of Manipur history and lasted up to the Pre-British period i.e., till 1891. This period can be regarded as the golden age of all the traditional entrepreneurial activities like handloom, crafts, and other household industrial activities in Manipur. This is so because, the limited outside contact and the bulk of increasing domestic demand for textile that had to be met by increasing domestic supply only. One well-known feature of this period was that every house becomes a production centre of either one or the other goods and the bulk of the products were meant for self-consumption purpose. They sold out the surplus product in the market. In those days, handloom of Manipur was very prominent. Cotton was the main raw material, though wool and silk were also used. Another feature was that the period was dominated by "Loin-looms" for the purpose of manufacturing handmade textile goods.

The second period which can be termed as the British Period began with the defeat of Manipur in the Anglo-Manipur war in March 1891. In the initial days of British rule, Manipur handloom and handicrafts and other business activities continued to flourish.

Despite the topographical isolation and transport bottleneck, small entrepreneurial activities still continued to flourish. But the important international events which took place in the twentieth-century left deep imprint on the entrepreneurial activities in Manipur. The first event was the outbreak of World War I (1914-1918). Although this event affected Manipur only indirectly, it left a lasting impact on the handloom industry in Manipur. Further setback to Manipur household industries was again caused by the outbreak of the World War II (1939-1945). The war necessitated the British Government to construct new roads and also improve the existing transport and communication system in Manipur. It also brought about a change in the attitude and belief of the people. It marked the end of the partial isolation of Manipur from the mainstream land. Improved means of transport and communication brought the heavy influx of imported machine made textile, goods, and other consumption materials, etc. This influx crippled the indigenous Manipuri handloom, handicrafts, etc. but also brought new dimensions in the development of other entrepreneurial activities in the region.

The present phase or the third phase began with the independence of India on 15th August, 1947 and with the merger of Manipur into the Indian Union on 15th October, 1949. During this period, numerous steps have been taken by the government to revive the past glory of household industries in Manipur. Economic considerations also necessitated the government to encourage various entrepreneurial activities as well the agricultural activities in the region. It is so because handloom and handicraft industries continue to be one of the most important household industries in Manipur. In the absence of industry in Manipur, the majority of the people depend on agriculture for their livelihood. But as agriculture is only a seasonal occupation in Manipur, it become imperative to develop other entrepreneurial activities to provide employment to the rural masses. It also becomes essential to develop entrepreneurial activities to provide full-time employment to the people.

Paradigm shift in the entrepreneurial activities of Manipur

Rural entrepreneurship in Manipur have been making a significant contribution to rural development by way of increasing rural entrepreneurial activities and productivity and also by improving the human resource base in the rural and backward areas of Manipur. In a state like Manipur, the rural entrepreneurship requires less capital and simpler technology. It is also suited to the existing socio-economic environment of the region especially for the managerial and organizational ability available in rural areas. In these regions, it is not always possible to absorb the growing number of unemployed and underemployed people in agriculture or government or private jobs.

However, it depends not only on the drive and initiative of the rural people but also on the provision made by the financial agencies and government institutions for the development of entrepreneurial activities, supply of raw materials, machinery and the marketing facilities organized by the agencies and other voluntary organizations. So, the development of entrepreneurship initiates various economic activities when the entrepreneur finds the suitable environment of work with the sense of security and self-confidence. They are always bound by the high risk in running their entrepreneurial activities. The support systems available are very minimal and have to be utilized wisely. Once the support resources are exhausted, it is hard-life and struggle for running their entrepreneurial activities. The Government agencies, NGOs, voluntary organizations, etc. are encouraging to initiate any kind of entrepreneurial activities by which people can earn their livelihood.

In due courses of time, there is rapid growth in the number of small and household entrepreneurs in Manipur over a period of few decades. In the rural and backward region of Manipur, people become entrepreneurs due to many personal and socio-economic reasons which can be noted as follows:

1. The rural people who take up their entrepreneurial activities

as a big challenge to satisfy some of their personal or individual satisfactions like self-employment, uplifting status in society, novel experience, earning their livelihood, etc.

2. The unemployed youth who become entrepreneurs would like to utilize the knowledge gained through their education.
3. Educated youth become entrepreneurs due to economic needs for their livelihood.
4. Young generation people take it up as a family occupation for generating their income.
5. Most of the rural people initially take it as leisure time activity and ultimately become a source of earning.
6. Jobless youth are forced to choose some business activities as an alternative goal or self-employment.

Different entrepreneurial activities at different regions

In the rural and backward regions of Manipur, substantial elements of entrepreneurship in agriculture and allied activities are being shifted to off-farm or non-agricultural activities. These shifts involve public programmes that control the awareness programme and other training centres run by the NGOs, VOs, and other Government agencies for the development of entrepreneurial activities in the region.

Many people who were engaged in agricultural activities as their primary subsistence economy has been shifted to different entrepreneurial activities in due course of time. Such entrepreneurial shifts are a part of the structural change in today's rural agricultural society of Manipur.

They are frequently exposed to new technological innovations. Such technological and structural revolution perhaps brings change among the rural people. It brings changes in the organization and operation of production process and lifestyle of the rural people in Manipur. In addition to these, the Manipur Government agencies and extension services, vocational institutes and micro-credit institutes were established to serve the needs of the numerous household based entrepreneurs. Unique privileges were granted to entrepreneurs to help them to grow bargain effectively with other corporates or other big enterprises which are mainly run by the non-Manipuris like Bengalis, Assamese, Biharis, Gujaratis, etc.

In Manipur, developing traditional entrepreneurial activities and new occupational activities formation processes have become a trend among the new generation. Despite various problems on regional variations in entrepreneurship, the contextual approach to entrepreneurship development has been discussed from different perspectives. In fact, different entrepreneurial activities in the region are much more relevant among themselves and their social and cultural relationships always support development.

The relationship between entrepreneurship development and other socio-cultural factors in the region is an interdependent one. It can be described as a system of interrelatedness among the factors that influence the individual entrepreneurs. As for the rural people at Kakching, socio-cultural and environmental factors include, in particular, the social and professional backgrounds and the social networks of the potential entrepreneurs, the belief system among particular society, ritual practices associated with the entrepreneurial activities, etc. In addition, personal factors include entrepreneurial motivation, demographic factors (age and sex) as well as personality traits (e.g. efficiency and the willingness to take risks), psychological or moral supports within the family or friends, etc. These factors play a pivotal role in developing the ideas of initiating various entrepreneurial activities within the society.

Every entrepreneur tries to search their opportunities in the region and such entrepreneurial activities in a particular region determine the entrepreneurial activity of the rural and backward areas of Kakching. Moreover, the rural people usually start small entrepreneurial activities where they were born and have work. In addition to this, promising young entrepreneurs are very well established in their career, life and communities, which foster the starting of new business anchored in a local environment. It can also be argued that the entrepreneurs have a positive impact on entrepreneurial attitudes and activities. The role model of the successful young generation entrepreneurs effects to the rural entrepreneurs and their inter-villages networking for development of entrepreneurship.

3

Socio-economic Profile of Entrepreneurs

Introduction

The study on entrepreneurship development needs a close examination of the socio-economic and cultural environment of the people and also of the potential of the state or region within which the study is located. The development of entrepreneurship depends on the availability of resources and the presence of basic infrastructure necessary for carrying out certain tasks. Hence, before proceeding further, here is a brief account of the geographical and socio-economic environment of the state of Manipur.

Manipur is one of the seven sisters of the North-Eastern Region of India. The state is having an international boundary of about 352 km. long stretch of land with Myanmar in the south-east and 502 km. long border with the adjacent states of Nagaland on the north, Cachar District of Assam on the west and Chin Hills (Myanmar) and Mizoram on the south and the south-west and Surma Tract and upper Chindwin of Myanmar (Burma) on the east. It is an isolated hill-girt state stretching between 92°58′E to 94°45′E longitudes and 23°50′N to 25°42′N latitude.

Geographically, Manipur has an area of 22,327 sq. kms. which constitutes 0.7 per cent of the total land surface of India. Ninety per cent of the total geographical area of the state i.e. 20,089 sq. kms. is covered by hills, the remaining area is a small valley covering only 2,238 sq. kms. and accounting for only one-tenth of the total area of the state. The state of Manipur could be divided into two regions viz. hill and valley. The valley lies in the central part of the state and hills surround the valley. The average elevation of the valley is about 790 m above the mean sea level and that of the hills is between 1500 m and 1800 m. The hill comprises of five districts : namely (i) Senapati; (ii) Tamenglong; (iii) Churachandpur; (iv) Chandel and (v) Ukhrul, while the valley consists of four districts, viz. (i) Imphal East; (ii) Imphal West; (iii) Bishnupur; and (iv) Thoubal. The valley areas of Manipur have two constituent parts like Imphal Valley in the heart of the state and Jiri Valley in the west beyond the pale of hill ranges bordering the Cachar District of Assam. The districts are further divided into sub-divisions. There are altogether 38 (thirty eight) sub-divisions.

The state is landlocked and it does not have any waterway connection and effective transport system (except a railhead at Jiribam in the south-western border). The state is connected by air with Guwahati, Delhi and Kolkata. There are three National Highways like NH-39, NH-53 and NH-150 which connect the state with the rest of the country. NH-39 links Imphal with the railway head of Dimapur in Nagaland at a distance of 215 kms. to the north, NH-150 with Mizoram and Nagaland, and NH-53 with Silchar in Assam towards the south-west.

According to 2001 census, the population of the state is 22.9 lakhs and the sex ratio of the state as a whole has improved from 958 females per 1000 males in 1991 to 974 females per 1000 males in 2001. This can be seen in details as shown in Table 3.1.

Table 3.1 : District-wise population and area (2001 census)

Sl. No.	*District*	*Population*	*Sex ratio (Female per 1000 male)*	*Density of population (per sq. km.)*	*Decadal growth in % (1991-2001)*	*Area in sq. km.*
1.	Imphal West	4,44,382	1004	856	16.69	519
2.	Imphal East	3,94,876	991	557	19.49	709
3.	Thoubal	3,64,140	998	708	23.87	514
4.	Bishnupur	2,08,368	993	420	15.26	496
5.	Chandel	1,18,327	981	36	66.62	3313
6.	Ukhrul	1,40,779	916	31	28.82	4544
7.	Churchandpur	2,27,905	944	50	29.85	4570
8.	Tamenglong	1,11,499	922	25	29.23	4391
9.	Senapati	2,83,621	951	87	36.09	3271

The population of valley districts accounts for about 59 per cent as compared to about 41 per cent of the hill districts. Density of population varies from 415 to 847 among valley districts and 25 to 116 in the hill districts as against 107 for the state. Thus, the valley districts are densely populated while hill districts are sparsely populated. The decadal growth rate of population of the state during the period 1991-2001 is 24 per cent as compared to 21.35 per cent at all India level. This is as against a growth rate of 29.29 per cent during 1981-1991 periods. It has an unbalanced population distribution of 14.12 lakhs (61.55 per cent) people living in the valley which constitutes only 1/10 of the total geographical area of the state and 8.82 lakhs (38.48 per cent) thinly dispersed in the hill areas which constitutes 9/10 of the total area of the state. Nearly 74.89 per cent of the population lives in the rural areas. Table 3.2 gives growth of population in the state during 1971 and 2001.

Table 3.2 : Growth of population in the state during 1971 and 2001 (in Lakhs)

Sl. No.	*Year*	*Population of Manipur*	*Rural*	*Urban*
1.	1971	10.73	9.31	1.42
2.	1981	14.21	10.45	3.76
3.	1991	18.37	13.32	5.05
4.	2001	22.94	17.18	5.76

Source: Government of Manipur, 2008, Economic Survey Manipur (2007-2008), Directorate of Economics & Statistics, Government of Manipur, Imphal.

Brief introduction to the study area

The study was conducted at Kakching (a small town having 28,724 population) in Thoubal district of Manipur state. The study area is densely settled. In the middle of the study area, Imphal- Sugnu State Highway passes touching the heart of the Kakching Bazar. The settlements in the southern part have a tendency to locate along the transport arteries e.g. Keirak, Wabagai, Langmeidong, Elangkhangpokpi, Waikhong, Kakching Khunou, Sugnu, etc. Different small lakes (*Pat*) with their adjoining swamps are generally devoid of settlements, due to their frequent inundation during the rainy season. The eastern part of the area is sparsely settled, and small settlements can easily be noticed which may be due to its late expansion of the new settlement especially like Irum Mapal etc. Generally, settlement exhibits circular patterns which are situated along the agricultural field.

Kakching is situated 45 km. away from the capital city, Imphal. It is surrounded by small hills from East to South to West, the Laiching hill on the East, the Lairenshibi, the Nonjubi hills on the South and the Mahadeva hill on the West. The Indo-Burma International Highway runs through the eastern edge of the Town and the Leingang Lake is between the highway and the airfield. The Sugnu State Highway divides the Township into two halves – Kakching Wairi on the North and Kakching Khullen on the South. The Chumnang Lake on the foot of the Mahadeva Hill, once a beautiful boating site, is now almost extinct. It has been made on an arable area. Small villages viz. Irengband, Mairenbam, Hawairou etc. look like floating islands in the Northern paddy fields. The biggest lake of the area is Loushi Pat. Hill cutting scheme under the Bharat Sevak Samaj brings a complete change from the original picturesque of the lake. Water from the lake has been drained away to Kharungpat and hence the lake becomes an arable ground except its interior portions. The Sekmai is the only river flowing through the heart of the town. Irum is another river which is dried up. The southern portion of it is becoming a good paddy field and fishing industry is fast developing in its Northern portion.

About the people

The native population of Kakching town is mainly belonging to Hindu-Vaishnavite sect and Meitie community. In addition, a small proportion of them belong to Christian religion. Historically, the native people were engaged in iron smelting activities. But now their occupation is diversified. During 1990s, major part of the population got Scheduled Caste status (*Loi*). Kakching exhibits the largest concentration of *Loi* families in Thoubal district. Sekmai, Kakching Khunou, Waikhong and Sugnu are other Scheduled Caste settlements in Manipur. Lois speak a separate dialect. They are getting special facilities for their social and economic upliftment.

The total population of this Municipal Town, according to the census of 2001 is 28,724 (Male – 14,156 and Female— 14,568). It is expected that its population in near future will be very high since the influx of outsiders is increasing. The present township comprises five parts— two in Wairi and three in Khullen. The major leikais are — Sumak Leikai, Makha Leikai, Mayai Leikai, Laithagol, Moirangthem Leikai, Ningthou Leikai, Turen Wangma, Khunyai, Ningthoujan, Salam, Senapati, Shougaijam, Sabal Leikai, Khullakpam Leikai, etc. The inhabitants of a Leikai do not belong to the same *Sagei* (Clan). In certain Leikais, however, one or two *Sageis* dominate the others in number.

Kakching Municipality area is approximately 1722 acres and that of the cultivated land is about 6631.74 acres. It is an important agricultural town. The Chandel district covers the eastern and the southern parts of the boundary, on the north there is the *loushi pat* (Lake) and Irengband Village. It is 785 metres above the sea level. The annual rainfall is 1000 to 1500 mm.

The Sekmai River runs through this town. It is one of the most important rivers in Manipur as it runs northwards and gives water in and around Kakching town and makes paddy fields fertile. The people of Kakching are very industrious and they produce the highest percentage of foodgrains in Manipur and therefore Kakching is called the Granary of Manipur. The existing irrigation and water supply system was constructed many years ago. Therefore, the triple or double cropping is practiced in only a small area of the cultivable land. Still the production is higher than that of any other parts of Manipur.

Myth behind the Migration and network among Kakching People

The people of Kakching made their first settlement at Uripok (now at Imphal) and later on shifted to Thoubal. There is a saying that during its settlement at Thoubal a small section had been split away and came to be known as Kakching Kamang. The reasons why they had abandoned their earlier settlements were not known. However, it was presumed that the two sites might not be suitable for their profession—smelting of iron and blacksmithy. *Khamlangba* (ancestral god) was their legendary hero. Their subsequent settlements were at Keirak and Karching.

Finally, Kakching Kunou was also split away from its parent group. The Heiram khunja (the original inhabitants of Kakching) were already merged into this new group. During the period of last 300 years, people coming both from East and West merged into this group. Others of *Ningthouja* clan, who took up blacksmithy as their trade also gradually joined them through intermarriage. It was this intermingled or combined group that later on came to be known as Kakching.

Besides, Kakching was also associated with many historical events. Kakching was the site of many battles in the raids and encounter between Manipur and Burma in the 18th and the 19th centuries. During the Second World War it served as an important war base. A clear evidence of it is the big airfield still lying in the Eastern portion of the Township. The Anglo-Manipuri War of 1891 was also partly fought at Kakching. The Kuki Rebellion of 1918 made it an important base. On the instruction of Sir Surchand Singh, Maharaja of Manipur, Shri Angou, the king of Kakching had constructed a war barrier at Unapal near Pallel. Among the historical events that took place at Kakching mention may be made of Bamon Wathok, Illikki Wathok, Maharani Nganbi Loukol case, Tikka Senkhai, Amang Aseng etc. — all against feudal remnants.

Due to the main dependence on the irrigation locally known as *Ethei Khong* for their agriculture, the people of Kakching have social entrepreneurial group which controls the irrigation system in the area. It has been handed over generation after generation among the Kakching people. The network of drainage system saves it from flood and the well planned irrigation scheme and public tanks from draught. Generally, the *Itheikhong* or the irrigation canal runs along either side of the main road. Since the time of its settlement, February is observed every year as the month of repairing the roads. Separate funds have been raised in each *Yumleng* (a row of houses) for the purpose. The brick culverts are constructed and repaired out of the fund. The custom of helping each other is still popular. No beggar is yet seen. Common funds are raised for the construction of houses for higher education of their children, for trade and business, purchasing of vehicles, paddy fields, cattle, fertilizer, utensils, marriage and *sradha* ceremony, etc.

Moreover, Kakching has its share in the slow progress of Manipur in the field of industry. The original professions of the people of Kakching were blacksmithy and cultivation. Iron-smelting was a popular activity of the people till the third decade of the century. Iron ore of high quality was found in the eastern paddy field of Kakching.

Namungba (Avoidance of outsiders entering the village)

Namungba is literally mean not allowing outsiders to enter into the village (i.e. people who is not from the village). It is still carried out once in a year but the norms are relaxed to some extent. It is the symbolic representation of the internal security and mutual cooperation among the people of the village. It is also considered as the period of celebration of rituals and conducting some development activities of the village. In the earlier days, it was so strict that anyone from the village was not allowed to go out of the village and the outsiders were not allowed to enter the village. During those days of *Namungba*, they kept freshly chopped branches of trees at the gate of the village as the symbolic representation of avoidance of outsiders. So, it is also known as *Lai Una Thetpa.*

During the reign of *Meetingu Mayampa* also known as *Maharaj Garibniwaz*, the then king of Manipur, during 1709-1748 A.D. declared Vaishnavism as the state religion and subsequently he ordered the people to adopt Hindu religion. This had contributed considerably to the political and cultural ethos of the region and somewhat encouraged Hinduisation in the kingdom. With the advice of the Hindu missionary, Santidas Goswami, the old manuscripts of Meetei were burned that is what in Manipuri called "*Puya Meithaba*". After that, the King ordered to avoid traditional Meetei cult and also forest God festivals. However, the then King of *Kakching* requested the Maharaja to perform some simple rituals to the forest God of *Kakching*, the *Ebdou Khamnangba.* "He" is the God and the founder of *Kakching* people. But the then king of *Kakching* also made a request to the King of Manipur regarding the outsiders' avoidance of entering the village during that ritual period. With the advice of the Maharaja, they performed *Lai Una Thetpa,* i.e the *Namungba.* On the first day of *Lai Una Thetpa*, people offer simple bread made from *shingju* (traditional vegetable mixture), *tal* (traditional bread made from baked soak rice powder) and three eggs. The village priest can predict the good and bad situation of the village at different seasons in a year, i.e. during *Koumjin* (beginning of the year), *Koumyai* (middle of the year) and *Koummai* (ending of the year). The priest test it through breaking the three eggs which is offered to the God. On that particular day, every house of the village will offer *Tal* to their house God and Goddess. They also cling some pieces of it at the doors of the house. At the evening, every household strike the winnowing fan and goes out till their *thongal* (household gate) that symbolizes the driving out of evil sprit and ill fate from their house. While beating the winnowing fan, they have to shout some words which are as follows with their meaning in English:

Thokoo Talloo	Get out Drive out
Thokoo Tallo	Get out Drive out
Leikhom Lakpi	Mud catcher
Thokoo Tallo !	Get out Drive out

During that ritual ceremony, the people of *Kakching* secretly performed forest God Festival with traditional dance, traditional wrestling (*Mukna*), race (*Lamjel*), and Manipuri *Polo* (*Sagol Kangjei*).

Religion

Religious ties and trade have its links from the past. The followers of four distinct religions, i.e. Hindus, Meities, Muslims and Christian are identified with their different institutions such as Temples, Laisang, Mosque and Church, respectively. The Meities represent a section of Hindus or non-Hindus who had intended to revive their cultural tradition before adopting Hinduism. Thus, the area has an amalgamation of Manipuri-Hindus, Meities, Muslims and less concentration of tribal population. Hence, religion has a deep root in Vaishnavism/ Hinduism, Meiteism, Christianity and Islamic identity. Hindus believe in the Radha-Krishna cult and worship the idols of Radha-Krishna in their temples. The Meiteis worship the local deities more vigorously. Nowadays, some people started following Christianity.

The people are simple minded, gentle and courageous. The famous temple of Sree Sree Govindaji of Palace compound is the centre for Vaisnavism in Manipur. The cleanliness of the Meitei houses is exemplary.

Family Structure

The family is the basic unit of social and economic organization of the people of Kakching. The family structure among the population under study is predominantly joint family. Both the parents, children—married and unmarried live together and participate in family activities. However, there are also nuclear families but they have a strong bond between the families of their brothers, who live close to each other and share their feeling. They often help each other while any of their family members are in trouble.

Social organization

The people of Kakching belong to Loi community. In Kakching, only the Loi community are inhabiting. In course of time, non-Manipuris (*Mayangs*) are also living at Kakching area. The people of Kakching are organized into functional groups on the basis of blood tie. It is divided into *Salai* (Clan). The *Salai* (Clan) is further divided into *Yek* (Lineage). *Khuman* is the largest Clan and is followed by *Ningthouja* or *Mangang*. Each *Salai* is again sub-divided into a number of lineage or local kin-groups. It is found that the composition of lineage varies greatly ranging from a single family to many families. This is due to the reason that some families have migrated from other villages and settled at Kakching.

Beyond kinship based relations, every family voluntarily becomes a member of the village level association. At the time of death of a person, all the people, irrespective of religion, comes to share the suffering of the bereaved family and every family of the village contribute a fixed amount of cash (e.g. Rs. 10 or 15) and rice (i.e. 1 kg or 2 kg). It is a kind of institution that looks into other's internal matters relating to village administrations, mutual helps, etc. Such kind of traditional institution is called *Marup*. However, there are different types of *Marup* existing among the people. They are *Yumsha Marup* (House construction), *Luhongba marup* (Marriage contribution), etc.

Distribution of Property

The Hindu law of inheritance prevails in Manipur. The property of a person including household land is equally distributed among his sons after he expires. Normally, daughters are not considered for this purpose. But in some extreme cases such as fathers having only daughter or only one daughter among the sons, have given equal property to all of them. However, the kind of distribution of property depends upon the head of the family with the consent of their offspring.

Settlement Pattern

Their forefathers left a well planned town. The biggest road which passes through the centre of the village is locally known as *Sugnu Road* as it reaches till Sugnu (the most southern part of Manipur). This road is also economically very important as all the economic activities and transportations are carried out through this road only. Besides the Sugnu Road, the village has seven other main roads running east-west. Smaller roads, all motorable, running north-south meet the main roads. In between two *Leiraks* (lanes), the houses are arranged in proper rows facing the Sun rise. This makes the settlement more beautiful.

The settlement is composed of houses and household garden. The settlement is divided into dwelling compartments called *Engkhol.* Each such Engkhol is meant for a household or more. The compartments are well fenced with bamboo and tree bushes. Vegetable gardens or kitchen gardens are found in the compartment. There are dwelling houses and animal sheds in the homestead compound. Cows, pigs, ducks and fowls are reared. Each homestead compound has a gate which is well maintained.

Economic activities at Kakching

The main economic activity at Kakching is agriculture. In addition, people are also engaged in piggery, fishery, poultry, dairy, carpentry, foundry, goldsmithy, ironsmithy, bamboo craft, wooden craft, charcoal business, fuelwood business, handloom etc. as well as other small business. Besides these, they are also practicing horticulture. The major crops are paddy, sugarcane, potato, groundnut, mustard, monkey rice, etc. in wet and dry land. They get an additional income by growing fruits like mango, guava, pomegranates, almond etc. The forest provide timber and grass for the construction of houses, wood for fuel, brooms for getting additional income, bamboo for making bamboo baskets, etc.

Manipur is very different from the other states of the north-eastern region in all socio-economic and cultural aspects of life. Even though, the state has some small scale entrepreneurs, there are very few persons who have entered medium scale sectors. Most of the large scale entrepreneurs are from outside the state of Manipur. The development of entrepreneurship in the rural backward areas of Manipur is comparatively less. However, many young educated persons are eager to initiate entrepreneurship. The growth patterns of entrepreneurship at Kakching are very closely associated with the socio-economic situation in the region. So, there is a need to study the entrepreneurial effort at Kakching and the factors which have contributed to the development of entrepreneurial activities.

Age of the Entrepreneurs

The age of the entrepreneur has a role to play in starting enterprises. Among the people, youth are more adventurous for new things. The old-aged persons try to adjust with the traditional environment around them. Young generations are more motivated and easily adjusted to the changing life of Modern world. The young people are more educated and have different experiences. They have frequent contact and exposure with the towns and city people. These frequent interactions enhance the relationship and exchange the idea of developing entrepreneurial activities. This leads to enhance organizing ability among the youth in the region.

Table 3.3 shows the age-wise information of the entrepreneurs in the study area. According to the data, the age groups of the entrepreneurs are categorized into five sections as for the convenience of analysis. These age groups are as follows:

> (i) age between (16-30) years, (ii) age group of (31 - 40) years, (iii) age group (41 - 50) years (iv) age group of (51 – 60) years, and (v) age group (61 and above) years.

Table 3.3 : Age group of the entrepreneurs

Sl. No.	*Age group of entrepreneurs (yrs)*	*No. of entrepreneurs*	*% of the entrepreneurs*
1.	Between 16–30	11	08.03
2.	31 – 40	60	43.80
3.	41 – 50	37	27.00
4.	51 – 60	28	20.44
5.	61 and above	01	0.73
	Total	**137**	**100**

Table 3.3 indicates that 11 (08.03%) entrepreneurs are in the age group of (16 – 30) years, and 60 (43.80%) entrepreneurs are under the age group of (31 – 40) years. These groups contribute the majority of the entrepreneurs. And 37 (27%) entrepreneurs are under the age group of (41–50) years. However, 28 (20.44%)

entrepreneurs are above the age group of (51 – 60) years and the age group of (61 and above) years contribute only 1 (0.73 %) entrepreneurs.

This shows that majority of the entrepreneurs are mainly from the age group of (31 – 60) years and 11 entrepreneurs from the age group of (16–30) years also initiated entrepreneurial activities in the study area. This is due to the reason that the educated young people are more willing to take up new ventures to earn a better livelihood.

Year of starting enterprises

It is interesting to examine the period during which the entrepreneurs from different occupational background made an entry into the entrepreneurial activities. In the study area, most of the entrepreneurs are from different occupational backgrounds like agriculture, unemployed, employee, etc.

Table 3.4 depicts different years of commencement of entrepreneurial activities by different entrepreneurs. The data regarding the year of commencement of enterprises are divided into various groups with regard to the year of entering into entrepreneurship development like entrepreneurs entering before 1992, entrepreneurs entering between the years (1993-97), entrepreneurs entering between the years (1998-2002), and entrepreneurs entering between the years (2003-2008).

Table 3.4 : Year of starting enterprises

Sl. No.	*Year of starting enterprises (years)*	*No. of entrepreneurs*	*% of the entrepreneurs*
1.	Before – 1992	50	36.50
2.	1993 – 1997	24	17.52
3.	1998 – 2002	34	24.81
4.	2003 – 2008	29	21.17
	Total	**137**	**100**

It is observed from Table 3.4 that 50 (36.50%) entrepreneurs have started before 1992. During the period (1993-97), 24 (17.52%) entrepreneurs started the business from different occupational background. 34 (24.82%) entrepreneurs started during the period (1998 -2002) and 29 (21.17%) entrepreneurs started during the period (2003-2008).

From the following analysis, it is seen that most of the entrepreneurs are from the agricultural background. They are either illiterate or educated cultivators. But there is a rapid increase in the number of entrepreneurs who belong to educated cultivators. This shows that large number of entrepreneurs are from the educated background.

Entrepreneurs' Educational Background

The formal education not only helps in the acquisition of required skills for a job but also give way for different occupational opportunities. Education is becoming the source of developing new skills for earning. The formal education enhances to increase the supply of entrepreneurs by making available skills and more contact with outside urban people. Such good network is necessary for entrepreneurial endeavour. Therefore, education is always looked upon as a means to improve one's socio-economic status in society. In the study, different entrepreneurs emerge from different educational backgrounds. The educational backgrounds of entrepreneurs are categorized into 5 different groups according to the level of their study. They are as follows :

(1) *Illiterate:* Those who cannot read and write but run some kind of entrepreneurial work as a means for earning income.

(2) *Educated till Matriculation or Below Matriculation:* These groups of people are those entrepreneurs who studied below matriculation like primary level, high school level etc. and did not continue further studies.

(3) *Undergraduate:* This group of people is those who have

passed matriculation and studied till class XII. After the studies, they have started entrepreneurial activities.

(4) *Graduate and Above* : This group of people is the highest educated categories of people among the people who initiate entrepreneurial work after their completion of graduation or above. They are more influential in all the activities in their communities. But the number of this group is very less.

(5) *Technical* : These are the group of people who got some technical training from the neighbouring towns. In fact, they were not in the formal institutes as diploma holder but as trained in an informal way. For example, the mechanic in a motor parts repairing workshop, cycle workshop, electronic repairing shops etc.

Table 3.5 depicts the entrepreneurs' level of education at the time of entry into entrepreneurial venture. It gives detailed information of the educational status of the entrepreneurs. It is observed from the Table 3.5 that out of 137 (100%) entrepreneurs, 13 (9.50%) entrepreneurs are illiterate and the rest 124 (90.50 %) entrepreneurs are literate.

Table 3.5 : Entrepreneurs' educational background

Sl. No.	*Educational status*	*No. of entrepreneurs*	*% of entrepreneurs*
1.	Illiterate	13	09.50
2.	Up to Matric	42	30.65
3.	Undergraduate	39	28.46
4.	Graduate and above	41	29.93
5.	Technical	2	01.46
	Total	**137**	**64 (100)**

Among the educated entrepreneurs, 42 (30.65%) have studied up to Matric level and below Matriculation. This category of people constitutes the highest number of entrepreneurs. And 39 (28.46%)

entrepreneurs are undergraduate. However, 41 (29.93%) entrepreneurs are graduate and above, and 2 (01.46%) of the entrepreneurs have already got the technical knowledge from the neighbouring town.

From the analysis, majority of the entrepreneurs are educated. The educated entrepreneurs are mainly involved in those modern enterprises like running rice mills, saw mills, van for school going children, tractor for agricultural purposes, etc.

Occupational Background of the Entrepreneurs

In the course of the field study, information was collected on entrepreneur's occupation before starting their entrepreneurial activities. Different people from different economic and occupational background of the study area are emerging as the young entrepreneurs. The occupations of entrepreneurs are classified into the following categories:

(1) *Agriculture:* Agriculture is the primary occupation of entrepreneurs before initiating enterprises. It refers to those who have taken up agriculture as their full time occupation and who are owners of agricultural land. These groups of people primarily depend on agriculture for the subsistence. Among them, agriculture is the primary occupation of the people from generation after generation. They produce paddy, maize, potato, mustard oilseeds, tubers, pumpkin, chilly, mango, etc. Nowadays, some of them take up different entrepreneurial activities as source of their earning.

(2) *Employment:* It includes those who are employed in some private or government organization or institution. In the study area, these groups of people are considered as economically supportive for organizing entrepreneurial work. These people get money regularly from their monthly salaries and have extra income from their agricultural field.

The government employees also continue practicing their agricultural work by hiring labour so that it will enhance the annual income. Besides these, they have initiated entrepreneurial activities to earn extra income in the family.

(3) *Educated Cultivators:* It includes those who are educated but did not get any job from the government, private institutions etc. So, they start to earn their livelihood adopting themselves to the agricultural activities as the parents are no longer able to support their children after their studies. The unemployed educated youth have many pressures from their family for getting jobs, earning to support their old parents, etc. However, some people start new way of earning by imitating from their friends and relatives who have entrepreneurial skills in the neighbouring towns and city. They have more contacts with the neighbouring urban people as they have interacted with the town people during their studies in town.

(4) *Business:* This category refers to those who are engaged in trading and other allied business activities to earn for the family. They are engaged in different entrepreneurial activities like fuelwood and charcoal business, dry fish fermentation, bamboo shoot fermentation, etc. Such business have different timing for collecting the raw material at different season when the raw materials are abundantly available in their local surrounding either from the surrounding hills or neighbouring villages. For instance, the tender bamboo shoot have to be collected from different hill villages before the raining season and sold after properly fermented at their home. It is also needed more physical labour in carrying out the whole processes. So, they have more practical knowledge for organising entrepreneurship and also they are aware of the business skills. Even the old generation people perceived that starting business is always associated with risk taking and needs skills to get more profit. The data relating to the entrepreneurs' occupation before starting their entrepreneurial activities are presented in Table 3.6.

Table 3.6 : Occupational background of the entrepreneurs

Sl. No	*Occupational background of the entrepreneurs*	*No. of entrepreneurs*	*% of entrepreneurs*
1.	Agriculture	34	24.82
2.	Unemployed (Agri)	60	43.80
3.	Employed	06	04.38
4.	Business	37	27.00
	Total	**137**	**100**

It is observed from Table 3.6 that agriculture is the primary occupation before starting their entrepreneurial activities among the majority of the entrepreneurs in the study area. Out of 137 entrepreneurs, 34 (24.82%) entrepreneurs are from the occupational background of cultivator, and 60 (43.80%) are educated cultivators who practice agriculture to get livelihood. These groups of people are having their own land with an average of 1.5 acres for cultivation. They grow paddy during the rainy season i.e. May – November and also cultivate potato, mustard oilseed, onion etc. from December to April. Paddy cultivation is mainly for their domestic consumption but potato and mustard oilseeds are used both for consumption and for selling in the market. Besides these, they also cultivate sugarcane as the cash crop grown in the hill slopes. Villagers sell boiled sugarcane juice at the rate of Rs. 130 – 180 per mustard oil tin (approximately 14 kg). It also gives good annual income to the family. However, employees constitute a very less number of 6 (4.38%) entrepreneurs.

Entrepreneurs' Income Status

Entrepreneurs' income status is one of the important components for the process of economic growth. Better financial status of entrepreneurs facilitates entrepreneurship. The financial strength creates a sense of security against fear of failure. This section deals with the study of the economic background of entrepreneurs just prior to their entry into entrepreneurial activities. Annual earning of entrepreneurs from various sources before starting the enterprises is taken as economic status of the entrepreneurs.

Table 3.7 : Entrepreneurs' income status

Sl. No. Annual income (Rs.)	Before starting		After starting	
	No. of entrepreneurs	% of entrepreneurs	No. of entrepreneurs	% of entrepreneurs
1. Below 12,000	06	04.37	00	00
2. 12,000-20,000	43	31.39	21	15.30
3. >20,000-30,000	57	41.60	64	46.70
4. >30,000-above	31	22.64	52	38.00
Total	137	100	137	100

Table 3.7 presents the annual income of entrepreneurs at the time of starting their enterprises and after starting of their entrepreneurial activities. Taking both the entrepreneurs belonging to the traditional and the modern entrepreneurial activities, Table 3.7 reveals that out of the total 137 entrepreneurs, 6 (4.37%) of the entrepreneurs earned an annual income below 12,000 before starting their entrepreneurial activities. And 43 (31.39%) entrepreneurs have an annual income ranging between Rs. 12,000–20,000 before starting their entrepreneurial activities. These groups of entrepreneurs are usually investing in micro entrepreneurial activities like running small shop, starting piggery, bamboo shoot fermentation which can control investment in their hand. However, the number of entrepreneurs belonging to this income group decrease to 21 (15.30%) entrepreneurs and shifted to the higher income group. Among the entrepreneurs, 57(41.60%) of the entrepreneurs have an annual income between Rs. >20,000–30,000 and 31(22.63%) of the entrepreneurs earn above Rs. 30,000 and above before starting their entrepreneurial activities as both of these groups engaged in higher capital invested entrepreneurial activities like readymade shops, rice mills, oil mills, van service, etc. After initiating their entrepreneurial activities, there is an increase in number of entrepreneurs among the higher income groups, i.e. 64 (46.70 %) entrepreneurs from 57 (41.60%) entrepreneurs and 52 (38%) from 31 (22.63%) of income groups Rs. > 20,000 – 30,000 and Rs. > 30,000 – above respectively. From the above analysis, it is observed that entrepreneurs are entering into entrepreneurial

activities from various income groups of the study sample. Due to the development of entrepreneurial activities, there is increase in number among the entrepreneurs in the higher income groups.

Case Study— Role of income/Assets

Mr. Naorem Samsundar (Tongba) Singh (38 years) is a married man. He has completed his intermediate and started helping his family by working in the agricultural field. He is a very warm hearted and generous person. He works very hard and started saving money. He had 2 acres of wet land. He thought that if he starts van service in the village for those school going children and for the emergency purpose he will be benefited. He sold out 1 acre of his wet land at Rs. 1lakh and 15 thousand for buying a second hand van from Guwahati. He spent Rs. 95,000 for the van and started his earning. He also invested Rs. 15,000 from his saving for construction of garage and other expenditures like servicing of van, changing of old seat covers for his van etc. He started van service for the school going children. The parents are happy for his work which helps the small children who have been suffering during the summer and rainy seasons. He also provides emergency service like taking patients to the hospitals, delivery cases etc. for the villagers at a reasonable rate. He is also supplying drinking water (home delivery in his locality) at the rate of Rs. 200 per 500 litres. It is in demand during the summer season as the water supply department failed to provide drinking water for the past one and half decades in spite of repeated demand by the people to the government.

After the establishment of entrepreneurial activity, Mr. Samsunder Singh earn approximately Rs. 35,000 per annum. Before starting his van service, he got an annual income of only Rs. 25,000 from his agricultural field. As he sold out 1 acre of wet land, he got approximately Rs. 16,000 per annum from the agricultural field. In addition to this, he gets Rs. 30,000 per annum from his van service. Now, he is happy about his earning and he is planning to reinvest his earning by venturing a grocery shop so that he can earn extra income with the help of his wife, Mrs. Lata Devi.

Nature of Enterprises

In the study, information was also collected on the nature of enterprises with references to the need of capital investment and labour that required for the entrepreneurial activities. The natures of enterprises are classified into two categories: (1) Capital intensive; (2) Labour intensive. It is shown in Table 3.8.

Table 3.8 : Nature of Enterprises

Capital intensive		*Labour intensive*	
Type of ES	*No. of EP*	*Type of ES*	*No. of EP*
Van Service	03	Piggery	04
Tractor Service	02	Poultry	03
Tata lorry service	01	Firewood/Timber/Charcoal	05
Computer work/print/DTP	04	Weaving/Handloom	07
Pharmacy and Medical Lab.	02	Seri-products	01
Stationery and small shops	06	Carpentry/Furniture work	09
Rice mill service	05	Progressive farming	01
Oil mill service	01	Agri-implement shops	01
Saw mill service	03	Shoes knitting	05
P.C.O./Tel. Service	02	Wood carving	04
Press	05	Bamboo craft and broom	03
Electronic servicing	02	Gur making	02
Parlour	01	Tailoring	03
Cycle workshops	02	Embroidery/wool knitting	04
Motor, Tata, Maruti etc. servicings	04	Foundry	01
Hardware store	01	Betel nut and betel leaves	03
Photo servicing	01	Bamboo shoot fermentation/ Mushroom	02
Cinema halls	02	Dhup making	01
Oil Pump	01	Dairy farming	02
Bakery	01	Iron/Blacksmithy	02
Brick-field work	04	Dry fish fermentations	01
Everest tile	01		
Jewellery shop	05		
Iron and steel work	05		
Clothes and readymade shops	08		
Tyre repairing	03		
Total	**73**		**64**

(i) *Capital Intensive*: Capital intensive are those entrepreneurial activities which need more capital while initiating and running the entrepreneurial activities. It is very difficult to initiate these kinds of enterprises in rural areas. Only a few people can initiate such type of entrepreneurial activities like running tractor service for tilling the agricultural field, running school van service, running rice mill for husking the paddy, etc. It is also very risky to initiate such types of entrepreneurial work in rural areas as there is shortage of money for investment in their business. Among the sample, there are 73 entrepreneurs who initiated such activities. They are the pioneers among the entrepreneurs who introduce new kind of venture to earn their livelihood by taking more risk in their work.

(ii) *Labour Intensive*: Labour intensive are those entrepreneurial activities which need more labour besides the capital investment to carry out the new way of earning. In such type of entrepreneurial work like piggery, poultry, weaving, firewood supply, etc., entrepreneurs are bound to do more physical work and there is less burden of capital investment to organize their entrepreneurial work. In most of the cases, they have to devote their time in managing or operating the entrepreneurial activities. In the study area, there are 64 entrepreneurs who initiated such activities.

Case Study— Low Income/Labour Intensive Entrepreneurs

Mr. Ingocha Singh is a 36 years old married man. He is a graduate from Kha Manipur College, Kakching (Manipur University). He got married with Mrs. Lalita Devi from Kakching Turel Wangma. He has one daughter and one son who are studying in class II and K.G. I respectively. After his graduation, he tried in Manipur Police as Assistant Sub Inspector through one of his friend from Imphal. He paid Rs. 20,000 for the post by selling out half acre of his paddy field. His brother who is in the Indian Army, asked him to start his own business life instead of joining any employment in active service as there is no one to look after their family.

He started thinking to rear pigs. His wife Lalita is very convincing and she proposed him to start piggery as a new way of earning. He bought 3 piglets (2 male pigs and 1 female pig) each of which had cost Rs. 700 at that time. He had spend Rs. 300 for the construction of pig-shed. He has specially nurtured the female for procuring the piglet. The following year, the female pig produced 8 piglets and expanded his piggery farm. Later on, his luck favoured his hard work. Now-a-days, he is doing other entrepreneurial work like supplying firewood as well as a small pan-shop by which they can earn extra income during the free hours in afternoon and night. His contacts and friends circle increased due to his success in the entrepreneurial work. He is satisfied with his work now.

Financial assistance

In general, the entrepreneurs depend mostly on family for financial assistance while a few entrepreneurs get help from different sources like friends, relatives, banks, etc. However, majority of the entrepreneurs are getting their financial assistance from the family by selling their land property. The entrepreneurs also invest the capital from the family income or by selling cattle, parents' pension money, etc. Sometimes, they mobilize additional resources from friends and relatives. So, capital investment for initiating the entrepreneurial activities is one of the crucial factors that is faced by the entrepreneurs in the region. Their main source of income is from agriculture and some allied activities. Some of the families also depend mainly on seasonal agricultural labours, and other available odd jobs. The youth of the new generation are eager to initiate the new venture even if they have some shortage of capital investment. These educated youth are not able to get any job due to the unstable political situation in Manipur. But they need to give financial support to their old parents. So, they are looking for earning money by starting some kind of small business activities.

Table 2.9 highlights the sources of capital investment of different entrepreneurs who are engaged in different entrepreneurial activities.

Table 3.9: Sources of Fund

Sl. No.	*Source of capital investment*	*No. of entrepreneurs*	*% of entrepreneurs*
1.	Family	93	67.88
2.	Friends/Relatives	22	16.06
3.	Banks, other financial institutions, etc.	22	16.06
4.	Others	14	10.22

Table 3.9 shows that out of 137 entrepreneurs, 93(67.88%) entrepreneurs are financed by family, 22 (16.06%) entrepreneurs are financed by the friends or relatives, 22 (16.06%) entrepreneurs are financed by the bank. 14 (10.22%) entrepreneurs reveal that they get the financial assistance from other sources like borrowing money from moneylenders, *Marup* (a traditional financial organization), etc. Most of the entrepreneurs mentioned that family gives moral as well as financial support to the entrepreneurial activities. However, financial resources are the ultimate solution of the entrepreneur. It is very difficult to get any financial assistance from anyone other than family members and friends. It is because of the fact that the study area is economically backward with very low annual income other than agriculture. Agriculture is the main source of their annual income. This occupation does not give sufficient economic support to the family. They also depend on the moneylenders. But the moneylenders give money at an interest rate of Rs. 5-8 per hundred per month which requires gold deposit of nearly an equal amount or the land *Patta* as security. Sometimes, the interest rates for borrowing money from the money- lender are hiked up to Rs. 10-13 per hundred a month (without keeping gold of nearly equal amount or the land *Patta* for security). Such cases are only those who need money for emergency purposes. Even though the moneylenders get high interest, sometimes they are reluctant to give money as they fear about the repayment from the borrower.

However, only few people are getting loans from the banks and other government financial assistance institutions. Even the official channel for giving loans from the bank is also very problematic to the common man as they cannot follow all the complex rule and regulations prescribed by the government. The government and non-government agencies ask the applicant who applied for loan to put guarantor (who should be a government employee) in favour of the applicant while applying for the loans. But it is very difficult to find the guarantor itself. And the job holders are also not willing to be a guarantor as there is a chance of recovering money from his or her salary, if the beneficiary fails to pay back the amount taken as loan.

Case Study—Importance of Family Support

Mr. N. Premchandra Singh, 33 years, is a graduate from Manipur University who studied in the Kha Manipur College, Kakching. His father, Mr. N. Niranjoy Singh is a retired prominent teacher in District Institute of Educational and Training Centre. After completion of his studies, he tried his level best to get a job with the advice of his elder brother and sisters who are working as a government employee in Imphal. But he did not get any job in the government sector. He was frustrated and started helping his father in their agricultural activities. He decided to start a new venture with the help of his father's retirement money. So, he convinced his father and brother to invest in his idea of starting entrepreneurial activities instead of paying money for job to the Minister and Officers. His parents gave an approval for his suggestion of initiating a grocery shop. Later, he started investing and he also managed all the necessary arrangement for his new venture. He now earns nearly Rs. 25,000 per year. But the only problem is that there are many people who always kept credit for long time. And also, there is the frequent unavailability of getting the supply from Imphal, so he adjusted by depending on the locally available wholesaler.

Entrepreneurs' Capital Investment

Capital investment is a major task for the entrepreneurs to organize from different sources. It requires to motivate his support group, that is, his family, relatives and friends, etc. It needs to give confidence to them about the plan of their entrepreneurial activities and the possible outcomes. At the same time, it requires lots of skills to handle the customers too as he will be newly in the venture and competing with the already existed businessmen who are already well established and having good network with many customers. Different entrepreneurs invested different amount as per their needs and requirement according to their entrepreneurial activities. This is shown in Table 3.10.

Table 3.10 : Entrepreneurs' Capital Investment (starting their entrepreneurial activities)

Sl. No.	*Range of capital investment (Rs.)*	*No. of entrepreneurs*	*% of entrepreneurs*
1.	Up to 10,000	06	04.38
2.	10,000 - > 40,000	26	18.98
3.	40,000 - > 70,000	33	24.09
4.	70,000 - > 1,00,000	30	21.90
5.	1,00,000 and above	42	30.65
	Total	**137**	**100**

Among the entrepreneurs who come up from low income group start with small investment like in piggery, poultry, weaving, etc. Only six of them invested up to Rs. 10,000. However, many entrepreneurs invest more as per the needs and the types of their activities. Maximum number of the entrepreneurs, i.e. 42 (30.65%) invested 1 lakhs and above. They are involved in the entrepreneurial activities like Cinema halls, brick field, Tata Lorry service, van service, hardware shops, etc. Such entrepreneurial activities need more capital investments. There are 30 (21.90%) entrepreneurs who have invested an amount of Rs 70,000-1,00,000 in the entrepreneurial activities like the rice mill service, oil mill service, motor vehicle services, press, etc. Such types of entrepreneurial activities need physical labours as well as financial capital. On the other hand, 33 (24.09%) entrepreneurs have invested Rs. 40,000 –

> 70,000/ and 26 (18.98%) entrepreneurs have also invested Rs. 10,000 - > 40,000 in their enterprises. Entrepreneurial activities like small shops, embroidery and wool knitting, meat shops, PCO, etc. needs small investment.

Parental Occupation of Entrepreneurs

The parental occupation may influence the choice of entrepreneurial activity. The family background of entrepreneur influences the occupational choice. But in the rural backward areas, the situation is different from the urban people. Most of the people are from the agricultural occupation. Along with agriculture, they are engaged in other activities for extra income from the sources like traditional bamboo craft making, weaving, piggery, poultry, etc. Among different varieties of baskets made from bamboo are baskets for keeping vegetables locally termed as *Polang,* basket for measuring grains locally termed as *Thumuk,* big basket for storing grain locally termed as *Kot,* basket for covering utensils locally termed as *Chakolup* etc. These items are supplied by the surrounding neighbouring tribal people to the valley people for their business. These people are also engaged with the fishery during the rainy season as well as in some low land region. However, horticulture contributed handsome income to some of the people in the study area. But due to the impact of Greater Nagaland Issue, the hill people claimed that the entire hill belongs to them and the valley people have no right to utilize it even if the valley people have *patta* issued by the Government of Manipur. The tribal people inhabited on the hilly region resist them and gave warning to the valley people through their local insurgent groups, so that; the valley people who are engaged in horticulture are reluctant to continue their horticulture activity in the hilly slope. This becomes one of the main problems of the valley dweller. In due course of time, the people of rural backward areas are slowly changing to different types of occupations like animal husbandry, fishery, small shops, etc. Eentrepreneurs' parental occupations are shown in Table 3.11.

Table 3.11: Entrepreneurs' parental occupation

Sl. No.	*Entrepreneurs' parental occupation*	*No. of entrepreneurs*	*% of entrepreneurs*
1.	Agriculture	93	67.88
2.	Business	34	24.81
3.	Employee	09	6.56
4.	Technician and others	01	0.72
	Total	**137**	**100**

It is observed from Table 3.11 that the parents of 93 (67.88%) entrepreneurs belonged to agriculture and the parents of 34 (24.81%) entrepreneurs are engaging in different small business activities like pan shops, pharmacy, tea stalls, stationery shop, etc. However, the parents of 9 (6.56 %) entrepreneurs and 1 (0.72%) entrepreneurs are employees and technicians respectively.

Family Type

Family is the basic unit of social and economic organization. Family plays a major role in organizing any entrepreneurial activities in the rural life of Manipur. In the study area, the number of joint families is comparatively more than the nuclear families. Most of the married couple depend on their family. There is co-operation in the joint family to organize different entrepreneurial activities. Table 3.12 shows the detailed information of the family types associating the entrepreneurial activities in the study area.

Table 3.12 : Family type

Types of the family	*No. of entrepreneurs*	*% of entrepreneurs*
Nuclear family	92	67.15
Joint family	39	28.47
Extended family	05	03.65
Divorce and others	01	0.73
Total	**137**	**100**

As per Table 3.12, it is shown that out of the total 137 entrepreneurs, 92 (67.15%) entrepreneurs belong to the nuclear family, 39 (28.47%) entrepreneurs belong to the joint family, 5 (3.65%) entrepreneurs belong to extended family and only 1 (0.73%) entrepreneur belongs to divorce family type.

Family relations

Among the rural areas in Manipur, family connection is one of the peculiar social relationships. The family connections give solidarity among the people of different communities. It leads to close friendship within the communities. They exchange goods and services during their needy hours. The people depend on the family specially for selling their goods to the market, education of their children, etc.

Due to the development in communication system through telephone or other means of communication, the gap between rural and urban people becomes narrow and they often visit each other during marriage, ritual ceremonies, festivals, etc. This leads to bring a strong solidarity among the people. Such friendship makes each other for mutual corporation in organizing any entrepreneurial activities. Due to these close interactions, the rural people start adopting or imitating entrepreneurial activities with the help of their friends in the neighbouring town. The city people extend their support morally as well as economically for initiating entrepreneurial activities. Such types of family connections are very essential for those people who run entrepreneurial activities in the rural areas of Manipur.

Religion

Majority of the Meetei in Manipur follow Hinduism. It was during the reign of Maharaja Bhagyachandra, they have started following Hinduism. But, they were once following their own traditional belief system, the so-called Meeteism. During those days, after harvesting their crops, they were performing ritual offerings for their ancestors (*Ushop katpa*). They still follow both Meeteism and Hinduism.

Table 3.13 : Types of Religion

Sl. No.	Religious group	No. of entrepreneurs	% of entrepreneurs
1.	Hindu	106	77.37
2.	Meetei	30	21.90
3.	Christain/Muslim	01	00.73
4.	Others	00	00.00
	Total	**137**	**100**

Most of the entrepreneurs are following Hinduism or Meeteism. There are 106 (77.37%) entrepreneurs following Hindu belief system. And 30 (21.90 %) entrepreneurs follow Meetei cult which have been handed from their forefathers as an indigenous belief system. Even majority of the people who belongs to Hinduism also retain the traditional belief systems. There is only one entrepreneur who belongs to the Muslim community. He is an inhabitant of Sorah Village, which is the neighbouring village to Kakching, hardly 7 km. away from Kakching Bazar (see Table 3.13).

Rural or urban background of the Entrepreneurs

It is believed that people with urban background have a greater exposure to the environment of entrepreneurship than people with rural or hilly background areas. In most of the cases, the urban people have better knowledge. These people have more chance to exploit opportunities in the entrepreneurial activities. So, they can easily dominate the rural people who are newly exposed to the new ventures of earning.

In the study area, the entrepreneurs are from the rural background except few people from outside the village. The native entrepreneurs maintain good relationship with the outside entrepreneurs who are engaged in marketing. The entrepreneurs from the neighbouring towns/non-Manipuri (like Bihari, Assamese, etc.) carried out electronics work like repairing of T.V., radio etc. and modern house construction work. They have more experience in working. They frequently visit the city if necessary and they take the material to their home for the repairing of the radio, television, etc.

Migration

In Kakching, there are very less number of people immigrated from other villages or outside states. However, some people who are in government service from other villages have immigrated to Kakching. And also some people who got married to the Kakching ladies have also immigrated due to the rapid development at Kakching, i.e. in terms of communication, transports, educational facilities, marketing facilities, etc. as compared with the neighbouring villages.

Manipur has always been backward for a long period particularly for entrepreneurial activities. Entrepreneurs from outside the states settle in the neighbouring town and start controlling the business activities. In general, it is usual in the case of industrially backward rural region that the entrepreneurial units are started by entrepreneurs from different states like Gujarat, Bihar, Punjab etc. As such enterprises succeed; the local people are also slowly starting to imitate the business skill. This can be constructed as a sort of "Imitative entrepreneurship". It is also possible that for a long time, the entrepreneurial activities in the rural and the hilly backward areas of Manipur will be dominated by entrepreneurs from urban area. This is due to the less economic opportunities for local entrepreneurs.

Motivating Factors for the Development of Entrepreneurship

Motivating factors play a crucial role in developing any entrepreneurial activities in the region. Basically, people have rural simple mindset and to motivate for any new activities takes time for them. But, due to the changing socio-economic and cultural environment, the rural mindset is also rapidly changing. This change in their rural mindset gave a way to motivate for the new entrepreneurial environment among the rural people in Manipur.

There are many factors which motivate a person to enter into entrepreneurship. These factors can be divided into two categories like the internal factors and the external factors. The internal factors include personality of the individual, ability to take risk, leadership quality, managerial role, innovative skills, etc. and the external factors like incentives to set up the new units, awareness programme conducted by the government, influence from the family or friends etc. Some unemployed educated people started the entrepreneurial activities in order to get a social status as well as earning for their livelihood. In the study area, people give respect to the individuals who start the entrepreneurial ventures rather than going for the agricultural activities. The educated youth try to work in different ways of life rather than following their forefathers' occupation. Sometimes, the educated unemployed youth who work for the agricultural activities are misjudged by the people as their neighbours and friends expect a lot from them. Even these young generations are influenced by the neighbouring urban friends to adopt entrepreneurial work if they do not find the job.

Among all the motivating factors, family and friends play an important role in starting the entrepreneurial activities. And also, they understand the socio-political condition of Manipur, where there is no scope for the opening of new jobs by the Manipur Government. This ultimately leads to think the new venture for their earning rather than looking for job. To apply for a job in Manipur is another major problem as most of the government and non-government officials are corrupt. So, the new generation youths want to start a new way of living without depending on the government for job by self-employing themselves as running rice mill, tractor service, van or jeep service, telephone service, cycle workshops, piggery, poultry, weaving, etc.

Case Study— Motivating Factors: Relative's Advice

Mr. M. Ibopishak Singh, aged 36, is the father of two sons. He studied till class X in Kakching Higher School, Kakching. After his class X, he left study and had joined in the local printing press for earning. After working for 6 years, he asked for increasing his monthly salary. But, the owner of the press refused to increase the salary. Then he left for other press. He enquired all the printing presses about the salary but the owners of other printing presses were also not willing to give the expected amount for his work. He was very disappointed.

Later, he thought that he would be very happy if he could help himself without depending on others. By knowing his situation, his father-in-law advised him to buy a Jersey Cow which is very popular for giving milk. At the same time, he consulted to his uncle who is the Veterinary Doctor about the plan. With the advice of his uncle and his father-in-law he bought a cow with Rs. 9,000 and started keeping hope for his livelihood. Besides this, he also worked at his agricultural field during the season and tried to supplement his earnings. As time passed, his cow reproduced a female calf and his happiness found no boundaries since the female calf was also an addition for his dairy farm. His cow produced 8-10 litre of milk every day and he earned Rs.100-120 per day during the high milk yielding period. Now, his female calf also becoming mature and he has two cows for his small dairy business. He is looking forward for the development of his dairy farm. He recalls the importance of his father-in-law's and uncle's advice and without their motivation to him; this dairy unit would not be there.

4

Social Relationship and Organizational Behaviour among Entrepreneurs

Entrepreneurship is often identified with the creation of new business ventures or with self-employed individuals by initiating various entrepreneurial activities. These activities are indeed expression of entrepreneurial behaviour among the rural people of Manipur. Entrepreneurship, however, is a much broader phenomenon. Whether starting a new business or enterprise, or deciding which way to take for earning, individuals are always opening their mind for the possibility of changes that may improve their lives, even if in very small ways. In every society, all individuals are potential innovators or imitators of someone's success who are seeking new and better way to do things. Thus, starting a entrepreneurial activity needs a characteristic human behaviour like the identification of new end-means frameworks. We can also consider that it is a timeless human phenomena present in all places and cultures of every society irrespective of regional or cultural difference. So, it always needs to take multidimensional view on the development of entrepreneurial activities in the region, especially, where there are various ethnic groups with different socio-economic and cultural environments.

At the same time, classic theorists as diverse as Adam Smith, Karl Marx and Max Weber have debated the role played by cultural values in stimulating economic activity. Since, entrepreneurship is widely regarded as an engine of economic growth; which dimension of culture contributes to the development of entrepreneurship is a very important question to be analyzed. (Thomas M. Begley and Wee Liang Tan, 2001, 537). The understanding of social and cultural capital benefits are not just to realize the source of benefits. It also tends to conflate group membership, intra-group exchange, benefits of membership. It also emphasizes on long term investment in durable networks for their activities. As according to Nan Lin (2001), social capital and cultural capital play a significant role in organizing the social network and social ties that ultimately influences on the development of entrepreneurship. The social ties may influence on other agents (e.g. recruiters or supervisors of the organization) who play a crucial role in decision making (e.g. hiring or promotion) involving the actor. Some social ties, due to its strategic locations and position (e.g. authority or supervisory capacities), also carry more valued resources and exercise greater power on organizational agents' decision making. Social ties and their relationship to individual may be conceived by the organization or its agent as certifications of individual's social credentials, some of which reflects individuals' accessibility to resources through social networking and relations – his or her social capital. So, social relations are expected to reinforce identity and recognition. Being assured of and recognized for one's worthiness as an individual and as a member of a social group sharing similar interest and resources, not only provides emotional support but also public acknowledgement of one's claim to certain resources. (Nan Lin, 2001, pp. 19-20)

However, Bourdieu (1986 : 248) sees capital in three guises: as economic capital, as cultural capital and as social capital. For him, social capital is made up of social obligations or connections. It is the aggregation of actual or potential resources which are linked to possession of durable network of institutional relationship of mutual acquaintance and recognition, or in other words, to a member of a group. Capital, in this form, is represented by the size of the network and the volume of the capital (income, cultural and symbolic) possessed by those to whom a person is connected. Nevertheless, social capital is a collective asset shared by members of a defined group, with clear boundaries, obligation of exchange and mutual reorganization. Bourdieu mentions social capital as a product of members group as a form of capital possessed by members of a social network or group. Through connections among the members, the capital can be used by members as credit. In this sense, social capital is a collective asset endowing members with credit, and it is maintained and reinforced for its utility when members continue to invest in their relationship.

Influence of social networking and group feelings on entrepreneurship development

Among the rural people of Manipur, traditional mindset of rural people prevails in their day-to-day life and their social environments. They have the notion that they are initiating their entrepreneurial activities as they are not able to get any government jobs which ultimately forced them to start such a new venture. Nowadays, such logics or mindsets are slowly weaning away from them as parents encourage the young people to make their living of their own. In addition to this, the individuals' employment choice and their innovation are closely associated with the influence of the social capital of the existing society. The social networks are also crucial factors in the decision making like whether to become entrepreneurs or not. In fact, developing entrepreneurial activities does not take place all of a sudden; rather it is embedded in networks of social relationship either within the family or friends or peer groups in their society, etc.

By observing and interacting with other, entrepreneurs acquire information and skills, and learn how to find competent employees and inputs at affordable price, obtain financial support, and find potential buyer. The environment they live in and the relationships they develop influence their decisions and legitimize their activities. In fact, when choosing an ambiguous entrepreneurial environment, individuals tend to base their decisions on social indications and that participation in social networks is a crucial element for entrepreneurs. Throughout the development of entrepreneurial process, interactions and social networking are very important. And the social networkings of potential entrepreneurs are usually referred to as the entrepreneur's social capital. Such social relationships influence and motivate them to initiate new ventures irrespective of having high risk factors in organizing different entrepreneurial activities like piggery, poultry, bamboo shoot fermentation, dry fish fermentation, etc. in those rural environments.

The entrepreneurs at Kakching and the surrounding villages have strong obligations and expectations among themselves that depend on the trustworthiness of their social environment. They help each other in terms of financial assistance, exchanging information, etc. in organizing their entrepreneurial activities. Moreover, social capital may also link to the exchange of labour (among the families or relatives, etc.) in carrying out major activities. So, the existences of good behaviour among the entrepreneurial groups are very necessary especially during their crucial hours.

However, the influence of social capital in entrepreneurship development especially in rural and backward areas has complex concepts, including trust and social networks, culture, belief system, etc. As the workers in their entrepreneurial activities come from different families, they are always cautious about their habits like drinking, playing cards, influence of insurgencies, etc. Most importantly, they are very much afraid of workers who are from outside Kakching. It is due to the reason that the rural areas of Manipur are becoming the easy shelters for the insurgents. Many entrepreneurs also get extortion/demands of money from different insurgent groups. These factors ultimately bring personal relationship as its roots in the development of individuals as entrepreneurs for different entrepreneurial activities. In this connection, social organization relating to the social relationship among individuals and also the shared norms and values associated with them becomes a pivotal factor in developing entrepreneurial activities. Such relationships can be organized into two sub-groups like :

1. Social resource in the society that lies in the social ties

that an entrepreneur has with other entrepreneurs for developing their entrepreneurial activities.

2. The social structure that collectively links among the entrepreneurs, workers and customers with cohesiveness, thus facilitating the achievement of entrepreneurship development.

Considering the main contributors to social capital, the aggregate or collective responsibility of the actual or potential resources is one among the pivotal component. They are linked to possession of a durable network of more or less institutionalized relationships of mutual acquaintance or recognition. Therefore, it considers social capital as an attribute of the individual rather than of the social structure and adopts an idiosyncratic (individual-centric) view in which individuals access social relationship through their social networks. It is also considered as an individual resource for organizing any entrepreneurial activities in the region like Kakching where people know each other through their activities. Among the people, they have strong kinship relationship and it is always difficult to hide their business activities from their neighbour. This becomes one reason for which they need strong solidarity among them.

Organizing entrepreneurship in rural areas of Manipur

The nature of the entrepreneurship and its types of organizing and networking pattern in rural areas is different from the urban life in Manipur. In the rural areas of Manipur, establishing an entrepreneurship is difficult as most of the entrepreneurs are the first generation entrepreneurs. They have little knowledge about the entrepreneurial activities. At the same time, they face many problems at the initial stage like arranging raw materials, capital investment, marketing skills, etc. It is quite often that it takes a long duration to set up one entrepreneurial unit. It involves planning by considering the available resources in the area. The rural entrepreneurs always need to have strong relationship with their family as their family members are the helping hand in developing their entrepreneurial activities. They also have to keep good relationship with their local people. They should keep good image to their neighbouring families and friends so that entrepreneurs will get moral help from them. This also helps entrepreneurs to avoid the interference from militants in developing their entrepreneurial activities as insurgents always have keen interest on collecting money forcefully from the people who starts new activities, as militants consider the local entrepreneurs as financially better than the common people. Their neighbours and friends will come and extend help either in negotiating the ransom demanded by the militants or to put off the issue completely. Thus, entrepreneurs usually are compelled to keep low profile in their working place to avoid unwanted attraction from various militant groups function in and around Kakching. At the same time, rural entrepreneurs need to have strong relationship with their neighbouring villagers for developing their entrepreneurial activities. For instance, Mr. M. Mukundo Singh has bamboo-shoot fermentation unit. He keeps good relationship with the hilly people specially Purum village, Khonggam village, Lamkang village, etc. as they are the only main sources of raw material for his bamboo-shoot fermentation business. It always requires having strong solidarity and trust with the hilly villagers. Such a strong bond with the neighbouring villagers helps in developing his entrepreneurial activities. Sometimes, the social conflict among the hilly people and the valley people drastically affect his entrepreneurial unit. During the conflicts between the hilly people and the valley people, all supplies of raw material from the hilly villages stop without any reason. He suffers great loss in his business. And also, the consent of their neighbouring people is necessary as the process of fermentation of bamboo-shoot produce bad smell. So, there are chances of complaints from the locality about their entrepreneurial activities. Organizing entrepreneurial activities are more accomplished in the social interaction among the people within or outside their locality as they have trust on the people who are well-known to them. However, some entrepreneurial activities like piggery, meat shop, etc. need to have a suitable place for its establishment. For example, one cannot build a piggery unit anywhere he/she likes because it might hurt religious sentiments of the people in the locality. One should avoid establishing their units near religious places like Hindu temple, *Apokpa Laishang*, etc. Thus, organizing entrepreneurial activities is socially and culturally embedded and regional specific. They need to consider all aspects while selecting their entrepreneurial activities.

Emergence of entrepreneurial activities among the rural people

In developing new entrepreneurial activities at Kakching, proper selection of the types of entrepreneurial activities is essential. In the initial stage of establishment, more initiatives are required in carrying out their business. For instance, Mr. Chaoba Singh has a cinema hall at Kakching. He came across many hurdles in establishing his cinema hall. In his initial days, he faced many problems like arranging electric power, film supplier contact, managing his employees, avoiding demands from the insurgents, etc. This phase of development is very important for the survival and stability of the entrepreneurial activities in their rural environment. As most of the neighbouring town's entrepreneurs are the competent for them as the neighbouring town entrepreneurs start their enterprises if they happen to get the opportunity in the area. So, the local entrepreneurs have to maintain their strong foundation for the survival of their business which they can expand later. They need to consider the available resource for maximum utilization without putting much investment so that it will give maximum output.

In rural areas of Manipur, most of the modern entrepreneurial activities (like computer works, PCO, etc.) are very new. So, organizing such kind of entrepreneurial activities becomes very difficult and challenging. Procedures for managing resource consumption are developed and they have to plan before establishing their entrepreneurial activities. The individual human and social assets become increasingly important in the organization of their entrepreneurial activities. Organizing such entrepreneurial activities may add new experience and train people. It is also required to transfer their knowledge among the workers.

Moreover, the organizational processes and routines are improved, and more developed as they grow more. Some organizing activities are associated with the development of internal knowledge transfer by learning from their seniors who have been associating with the work for long, and specialization of labour within the workers is also necessary while other activities involve external interactions in implementing product/marketing strategies, acquiring new resources, and extending network among the entrepreneurs in the region. The new ventures are focused on surviving in the short term, and achieving performance in the long run, although the organization may become stable or decline with the changing social environment. It is due to the reason that most of the entrepreneurs face the problem of lack of capital investment while initiating their new venture. For instance, Mr. Joykumar Singh, born at Kakching Sumak Leikai, hails from a middle class family of five children. He is the second child born to his parents. After B.A. degree, he could not continue his studies further due to the poor economic condition of his family. He decided to set up an enterprise to earn his livelihood and help his father to maintain the family. Apart from financial compulsion, he had a desire to be on his own. And also, he was influenced by the EDP (Entrepreneurship Development Programme) conducted by DIC (District Industries Centre, Thoubal) to start an enterprise of their own. His family also responded positively when they learnt his decision to do business. At the same time, his parents were worried about the financial risk he was taking in order to start new enterprises. After discussion with his parents, he decided to start a PCO with Xerox and lamination facilities at Kakching. Mr. Joykumar Singh got a loan of Rs. 1 lakh sanctioned from DIC under the PMRY (Prime Minister Rojgar Yojana) scheme. While setting up the new unit, he faced the problem of inadequate finance, delay in getting the loan sanctioned. At the same time, he also faced problems of frequent power cuts, and unavailability of machinery spare parts locally, technical assistances, etc. Moreover, the technical adjustment to such new machines was the most difficult problem to handle for him. For every technical problem, he has to manage the technicians from Imphal. These technicians also demand more money as they have to come from Imphal city. Sometimes, the technicians were reluctant to come to Kakching due to the law and order problems in the area. Gradually, he adjusted himself to run his entrepreneurial unit.

Among the entrepreneurs, the challenges of establishing new entrepreneurial activities especially which are technological base enterprises are more complex. New entrepreneurial activities face various difficulties associated with their liability of newness and size, influencing perceived legitimacy in the eyes of external constituents. Such problems also affect a new organization's ability to obtain resources like organizing computer training centre, medical laboratory, etc. Competitive threats may challenge new entrepreneurs to stick to or modify its vision, while decisions regarding resource allocation, marketing of their products, and development into unique assets present additional dilemmas.

Case study: Challenges in developing new entrepreneurial activities

Moirangthem Muktamani Devi, an educated lady from Moirangthem Leikai Kakching, hails from a lower middle class family. Her father expired when she was very young. Her mother brought her up along with other three children by doing some petty jobs. Her mother used to collect old unused silver utensils (materials) from door to door and send them to the local dealer.

After she got married, her father-in-law did not give financial help to support their family. So, they started living in a separate house. Her husband was a small contractor who did not have a regular income. To support the family income she worked as an agricultural labour. But that too was not enough to manage the family as it gave only seasonal employment. Her sister-in-law used to knit woollen hats and Muktamani learnt the art of knitting different items from her.

Muktamani used to go to the local cobbler to mend her children's torn shoes very often. She used to sit near the cobbler and observe carefully how he had stitched and mended the shoes. She developed an idea that she could make shoes by knitting if she had the sole. One day she unstitched one of the torn shoes of her daughter and she knitted over the old sole. In doing so she consulted with the cobbler and was able to produce beautiful knitted shoes. She felt that there was an immense scope for knitted shoes and fixed up her mind to set up a shoe factory. She knitted some shoes to their neighbour to attract their attention. In the initial period of her work, she spent lot of time to find out whether people will be interested in her product. Some people commented that her products are not stylish and it will not be durable too. She worked hard to popularize her new products with lot of personal interest. Her skill became more refined over a period of time.

Later, Mrs. Muktamani Devi started the enterprise by investing Rs. 20,000 and could earn about Rs. 1000 per month. In 1993, she participated in the Entrepreneurship Development Programme organized by NECON (North East Industrial Consultants, Agartala). It created more confidence in her. In 1995-96, she got a loan of Rs. 30,000 from Khadi Board and she had upgraded the unit by this financial support. Then she got many invitations to participate in exhibitions inside as well as outside the state. Since then there has been a lot of demand.

Mrs. Muktamani Devi attended another EDP in January, 2000, which was conducted by IIE (Indian Institute of Entrepreneurship, Guwahati). Since the quality of her shoes was good, the business got stabilized. She started earning about Rs. 20,000 or more money per annum. Now she sells her products locally, through dealers and mainly by participating in trade fairs and exhibitions. Her marketing efforts have elicited enquiries from various quarters. However, success did not come to Muktamani very easily. It was not easy to market something new and unique. It was sheer perseverance and hard selling that built Muktamani's business.

She has the satisfaction of providing employment to ten persons. And Mrs. Muktamani Devi is also an excellent employer to her workers. Though many entrepreneurs have found it difficult to manage labour in her locality, she had no such difficulties. She has convinced her workers that if production increased all would be benefited. As an incentive to reduce wastage in production and maintain quality, she has also introduced some sort of production linked incentive scheme. Muktamani leads an active life looking after her business and being a role model to budding entrepreneurs.

Entrepreneurship Development and Local environment adaptation

Local social networks, norms, and trust among the communities facilitate coordination and cooperation for mutual benefit among the entrepreneurs in developing their entrepreneurial activities. The goodwill available to individual entrepreneurs or groups lies in the structure and content of the entrepreneur's social relations. It enhances the relationships and social networking between individuals and their surrounding social environments that facilitate good responses and thereby create social value for developing their entrepreneurial activities.

It also refers to the kinds of relationship people develop when experiencing social interaction. It involves trust, respect, friendliness, and trustfulness, which in turn, affect the quality of the mutual understanding and social relationships and the availability of resources, information and knowledge through networking within the social unit. It also provides shared representations, interpretations, and systems of meaning among parties within the communities. Hence, it can act as an available resource capable of creating interdependencies and of producing trust thereby reducing transaction costs for running their enterprise and encouraging sustainable cooperative behaviour among entrepreneurs. So, within the group or communities, mutual trust is generated from others' awareness. And the future benefits depend upon current honesty or on efficient enforcement mechanisms among the entrepreneurs in the local environment. For instance, Mr. Khongnemba Singh is a hardworking, soft hearted and a very enterprising man. He started his brick farm in his paddy field near the Irum Mapal, Kakching. In the initial year, he could not sell his product profitably, but this did not disappoint him at all. Later, he enhanced the quality of the brick through experiences. Moreover, in due course of time, the workers also have gained skill to produce more quality product in their work. Most of the workers are from the surrounding villages like Keirak, Irengband, Pallel, Sora, etc. He developed good relationship with his workers. He spent most of his time with them during working days. He gave incentives during festivals like *Ningol Chakouba, Durga Puja, Cheiraoba,* etc. He always maintains close and friendlier relationship with his workers. He also respects all his workers irrespective of age, economic status and religion. He kept trust in them and asked them to consider work as their own. Such type of co-operative behaviour and encouragement helped in developing his entrepreneurial unit.

Social networking among entrepreneurs, workers and customers

The main discussion is the social networking among the entrepreneurs with their workers, customers, etc. It also deals with different entrepreneurial units having different organizational structure that have a bearing on employees' attitude and behaviour.

Many of the rural entrepreneurs lack the skill of organizing their entrepreneurial unit in a more formalized way. However, some of the new entrepreneurial units have transformed their units into more adaptable and productive ways in the existing rural environment. They learnt the organizational structure within the entrepreneurial unit that concentrates on how job tasks are formally divided, grouped, and coordinated among the workers and with other entrepreneurial units too. It is mainly focusing on the activities which entrepreneurs organized in their working capabilities and their production. Sometimes, entrepreneurs allow their workers or employee's to take part in decision making for the progress of the unit. For instance, Mr. Mukesh Singh runs his piggery unit for the past five years with his local uncle, Mr. Kanta Singh. Mr. Kanta Singh, as helper, took all the responsibilities when Mr. Mukesh is not available in the piggery unit. In his absence, Mr. Kanta also takes care of the supply of their pigs to the Pallel, Lanmeidong,

Tera, etc. So, Mr. Mukesh Singh is very happy to be with him in his piggery unit. Some of the elements of the organizational structure observed from the study are as follows:

Expertise

Most of the earlier entrepreneurial units in rural entrepreneurial activities lacked specialization in their activities. Workers were engaged in different activities while functioning their work. However, with the advancement in their working organization, workers are assigned to do a specific, repetitive task which they are familiar with. For instance, consider a person who is specialized in designing Almirah or cot or assembling the final product in furniture entrepreneurial unit—someone will provide him with the raw material for his needs. Again those who are specialized in supplying raw material (finished) for assembling the final product always assist him. This leads to avoid loss of time and also avoid extra wastages of the materials. It also brings group solidarity among the worker.

The essence of work specialization within the entrepreneurial unit is that, rather than an entire job being done by one individual, it is broken down into different steps, each step being completed by separate individual. So, it helps the workers to get the chance of specializing in doing part of an activity rather than the entire activity. Most of the young entrepreneurs saw this as a means to make the most effective use of its employees' skills. And employee's skill at performing a task successfully increases through repetition. Less time is spent on changing tasks, on putting away one's tools and equipment from a prior step in the work process, and on getting ready for another. Equally important fact is that the training for specialization is more efficient from the organization's perspective.

Departmentalization

It is an interesting process which is observed from the workplace at different entrepreneurial activities. Once the activities are divided through work specialization, the workers need to group these jobs together so that common tasks can be coordinated. The main basis of it is the grouping together for common goals. This makes the entrepreneurs to organize among their workers into different units like accounting, manufacturing, purchasing, making of their products, etc. This functionally seeks to achieve more goals oriented by using common skills among the workers within their entrepreneurial unit. As mentioned by the workers from the Ratan's Jewellery works, Mr. Ratan Singh, the proprietor, mentioned that his jewellery work is divided into two different sections like the selling section and the manufacturing section. In the selling section, he assigned Mr. Kumar and Mr. Tomchou. They are B.A. degree holders. They maintain good relationship with the customers as well as they are good in accounting work. However, in the manufacturing section, most of the workers work together. The skilled and trained workers took major works in making high cost ornaments.

It becomes easier and less expensive to find and train workers to do specific and repetitive tasks than to do a broad range of diverse tasks. In such cases, productivity could be increased by enlarging rather than narrowing the scope of job activities. In addition, some entrepreneurs observed that by giving employees a variety of activities to do and by allowing them to do a whole and complete job, and putting them into teams with interchangeable skills, they often achieved significantly less output with lesser employee satisfaction.

Impact of Culture on Entrepreneurship Development

Among the rural people in Manipur, well organized entrepreneurial units have a strong relationship with the socio-cultural environment in their society. To form new venture entrepreneur requires foresight and energy, passion and perseverance, initiative and drive, etc. Entrepreneurs share a predictable set of values like fixing the common price of their products, sharing and resolving problems for the common causes, e.g. extortion of money by insurgents, etc. that are different from those shared by individuals who have followed a non-entrepreneurial trajectory. Despite this evidence, it is also reasonable to expect that entrepreneurs reflect the dominant value of their culture. Thus, while they share some universal traits, others might be more culture-specific. Among the entrepreneurs in rural areas of Manipur, they rely on family ties in developing their business. Many of the entrepreneurs own and operate their entrepreneurial activities through joint families. They also consider the moral behaviour of the people while recruiting their employee. It may be due to the reason that most of the young people become more prone to bad habits like drinking, smoking, etc. And most importantly, many of the entrepreneurs complain about the young people of easily getting cheated by the insurgents and may use them for their anti-social activities. Such young minds have no firm ideas so they are sometimes easily carried away and insurgents use them to get information about their owners' business. These sometimes bring burden to extortion of money demands by insurgents to the emerging entrepreneurs in Manipur.

Entrepreneur established and re-organized its fundamental set of relationship with its rural and social environments of Manipur. It is a strategy characterized by widespread and more-or-less simultaneous change in the decision making pattern by any entrepreneur for developing their entrepreneurial activities. The need for entrepreneurial behaviour arises with the creation of a new entrepreneurial venture. They innovatively establish their enterprises which will allow it to survive and prosper in its existing socio-economic environment of Manipur. Once established, entrepreneurs are inducing the potential or actual rebel between their entrepreneurial activities and rural social environment. Perception of potential competent entrepreneurs may lead the organization to act practically in adapting smoothly their entrepreneurial activities to such change. The perception of entrepreneurs in their entrepreneurial activities is also being affected due to the changing environment to its own benefit. As mentioned by Mr. Y. S. Singh who is engaged in furniture works, that in his initial days of starting his entrepreneurial activities, he always thought of how to maintain workers for the survival of his unit. Once he established his unit, he again thought of different ventures like producing different types of furniture products like almirah, cot, sofa, dining set, etc. which are different from the products of other furniture houses. He has specially trained employees who are engaged in polishing and painting the furniture products. This enhanced the genuine look of his products. He also used many modern tools like electric wood driller, electric wood polisher, electric saw, etc. All his efforts make his furniture unit to compete with other furniture works in the area.

Technology Development and Entrepreneurship

New technology is very important in developing the entrepreneurial activities in the region. Manipur is always away from the technological developments. The rise in the technological innovation came only a few decades before. Most of the entrepreneurial units especially like the saw mills, furniture house, brick field farm, etc. were functioning by the manual labour. They relied mainly on their human power. This needed more workers but produced less products. At the same time, it also consumes more time for procuring their works. Nowadays, with the coming of new technology, the working behaviour also transformed into a more knowledge based work rather than a labour based one. The common idea among the new technologies in the workplace is that they substitute machinery for human labour in transforming inputs into outputs. This also led to increase in the investment for most of the entrepreneurial units really rely on modern technology.

For instance, the introduction of electricity in the rural area of Manipur allowed introducing electric-saw-mill that could produce more, faster and cheaper than what was previously possible when the saw mill were powered by the individual labour. Even in the printing press, a decade ago, they had to work day and night for print some pages of books or Journals. Nowadays, the introduction of offset-printing machine has changed the working pattern of the printing press in the rural life at Kakching. People are aware of such machines and they have less tension for arranging orders for printings like invitations, posters, journals, books, etc. So, the computerization of equipment and machinery in the last quarter-decades has been the prime move in reshaping the workplace.

However, the changes in technology in rural areas also have cut the shelf life of most employees' skill. A traditional working employee could learn one job and be reasonably sure that his or her skills would be adequate to do that job for most of his or her life for earning their livelihood. That certainly is no longer true with the intervention of new technologies in entrepreneurship development. New technologies driven by computer and flexible manufacturing systems among entrepreneurial unit are changing the requirements and demands of jobs and the skills employees need to do them. Repetitive tasks—like those traditionally performed in printing press (business) and by low skilled employees – will continue to be automated. A good number of jobs will be upgraded. For instance, a most professional worker who had been working long before the intervention of computer in Printing press should be upgraded to become more of an advanced skilled worker or assistant. Those workers who are not equipped to take on these expanded roles should be displaced.

Case study:Importance of Technological Knowledge in Entrepreneurship Development

Mr. Inaocha Singh (29 years) is a young dynamic person from Kakching. He often goes to Imphal to visit to one of his brother's friend, by name Khumukcham Joykumar Singh, at Konung Mamang Bazar, Imphal. Mr. Joykumar Singh was working as a computer assistant in the Private Institute at Imphal. Mr. Joykumar Singh introduced Mr. Inaocha Singh to his owner and allowed him to visit his private office frequently during their school vacation. Later, Mr. Inaocha Singh started his career by joining the basic course of hardware there. As Mr. Inaocha Singh became familiar with the people in the office, he was recruited as a helper and also started learning more practical knowledge of computers there. He became very interested in knowing more about computers. He talked to his parents about it and wanted to go for computer course while doing his higher secondary education. His mother is very soft hearted and always in a position to help her sons and daughter to fulfil their wishes.

In the following year, on the advice of Mr. Joykumar Singh, he appeared for an entrance test for the Diploma Course at Community Polytechnic, Takyel. His luck favoured him to get the selection. He learnt diploma course in Computer Education from Community Polytechnic, Takyel, Imphal. He also got his technical training from a private institute in Imphal from Sir Ibomcha Singh. Sir Ibomcha Singh gave him the technical knowledge and told him about the upcoming future of Computer Technology during his stay in Imphal. Sir Ibomcha Singh also explained about the disadvantages of growing unemployment situation of Manipur to him. Mr. Inaocha was impressed by their motivation to open a Computer Centre at Kakching which will be very new to the rural people of the region. He also imagined the demand of the emerging technological service at Kakching. So, he started his plan of opening small computer service centre at his home at Kakching. With the increase in demand for such services, he started earning Rs. 100 per day. By knowing the advantages of his work, his uncle gave him the opportunity to open a Centre at Kakching Bazar. Now, he owns a computer centre at Kakching Bazar. He gives service for printing, DTP works, photo editing, etc. as per the requirements of customers.

Work Culture on Entrepreneurship Development

Entrepreneurial behaviour in team-work represents a common perception held by the members of the entrepreneurial units. This feature was made explicit when we defined culture as a system of shared meaning in their society. It is expected that individuals with different backgrounds or at different levels in the entrepreneurial unit should tend to work together for the development of their entrepreneurial activities.

Acknowledgment that organizational culture among the workers in an entrepreneurial unit has common properties does not mean, however, that there cannot be subculture within any given culture. Most large entrepreneurial units have a dominant culture and numerous sets of subcultures. A dominant culture expresses the core values that are shared by a majority of the organisation's members. Subculture tends to develop in large organizations to reflect common problems, situations, or experiences that member face while working in their entrepreneurial unit. These subcultures are likely to be linked with their designations and geographical separation among the workers within the unit. The purchasing or selling members, for example, can have subculture that is uniquely shared by members of that entrepreneurial unit.

Case studies: Entrepreneur's relationship with workers and customers

Mr.Yambem Satya Singh is an ambitious man. His father was a cultivator and his mother was a housewife. But his uncles were engaged in some business activities. Their uncles had run a tractor service for agricultural activities. His father thrives on agriculture, but he wanted to do something different and be on his own. He feels that real greatness consists of being the master of himself.

He was very much influenced by his uncles who were engaged in business activities at Kakching Market. He had started a chicken hatchery under the name "Volga Hatcher" in the 1980s. It was running good for some short period with one hatchery machine. Again he invested more and bought again one more hatchery. But the problem started for him as the eggs were supplied from Calcutta which sometimes got spoiled on the way and also not reproduce chicken from it. So there was heavy loss to him. He was frustrated and had debt from different financial sources where he had to pay high rate of interest. Later he took the advice from his uncles who run their business successfully. With the advice of his uncles, he sold out one acre of agricultural land and paid off all the debts. But he never stopped thinking of starting his business again. He started a ladies shoes factory at Kakching market with a few of the local ladies who were already experienced in shoes making. In the meanwhile, he started making furniture with the banner "Yambem Furniture" with some of the local carpenters. He allowed everyone to make whatever the customer demands. This time luck favoured him as his furniture products like chairs, tables, sofa set, almirah, clothes hangers, dining table with new designs were sought after by the locality. He lived in Kakching Chumnang Leikai where people were traditionally involved in wooden furniture based business and fuelwood business. So, he too saw a scope of a healthy competition in this area of business. He could visualize the opportunity of exploring his creative talent in this field. His wooden furniture was creative and very competitive not only at Kakching Market but in the Imphal Markets too. He sold his products at different places of Manipur and received good response. He really worked hard to give his customers what they wanted and never compromised on quality.

The major problem Mr. Satya Singh faced initially while setting up his business was the arrangement of capital for starting his unit and the raw materials supplied to him because the wooden plank which they were using should be dried properly and preserved for the years so that it could meet the demands. This also enhanced the quality of products. He had to depend on banks and other financial institutions for financial assistance. He managed to overcome his fund constraints by being persistent. The problem of power supply was also another major hurdle in expanding his entrepreneurial activity.

Y. Satya Singh's high ambition and desire for accomplishment has not stopped him at just this business. His wooden furniture unit is doing well and is tossing more profits. But his drive for more growth and success has enthused him to diversify into other areas of business. He started his own saw mill, from the profit of the existing wooden furniture business. He is utilizing his financial resource in the most optimum manner for the growth of his enterprises. Mr. Satya Singh, a simple man, who started from Volga Hatchery to Yambem Furniture, is a proud owner of his well established business today.

However, he keeps observing the customer behaviour and needs and tries to deliver the goods in the most effective way. Success has not stopped Mr. Satya Singh from putting his hard labour and keen interest.

He has always associated himself with the social activities around especially in education and developmental works. He loves writing poem, short stories, etc. He is a man of different character.

Work Culture

Work culture is transmitted to employees in a number of forms, the most potent being story telling, rituals, material symbols, and language.

Story telling

Stories such as *Emoinu Ahongbi, Phunga Lairu, Henjuna, etc.,* circulate through many generations. They typically contain a narrative of events about the organisation's founders, rule breaking, ways-to-success, reductions in the workforce, relocation of employees, reactions to the past mistakes, and organizational adjustment. These stories anchor the present in the past and provide explanations and legitimacy for current practices. The workers are motivated with the phrases put forward by the entrepreneurs which have moral significance to solidarity among them. It helps in breaking the personal gap in their work space for organizing a friendly atmosphere among the workers. Some examples of the picture which they kept in the working place are like the pictures of 'Emoinu Ema Leirembi', 'Ema Laxmi', etc. representing the cultural values to them. They also kept the picture with the words written in Meeteilon like '*Nangonda Nungairouidouba Thabaktu Meidasu Touruganu*' (meaning – Never do thing which you feel not good to yourself), '*Angam tannabada ngambatana thouna phabara? Phattarea khanglabashingbu thadokpa ngamba – hendabara mashinabu thouna phaba?*" (the central idea of the words is the essence and value of perseverance, good manner and sacrifice in society) etc. This also has strong moral obligation towards truthfulness and symbolizes the spirit of avoiding toward other's cowardness or weakness. In addition to this, they have put the audio recordings of many Hindu and Meetei spiritual folk songs and play in their working place. It is mentioned that such practice indirectly brings the moral obligation towards their duties and the spirit of oneness.

Rituals

Rituals are repetitive sequences of activities that express and reinforce the key values of the organization—what goals are most important, which people are important and which are dispensable, etc. Performing ritual ceremonies during the yearly festivals like *Vishwakarma Puja* (Festival for the God of Tools and Implements), *Emoinu day* (festival for Goddess of Wealth among the Meeteis), *Cheirouba* (New Year of Meeteis), etc. enhance the working spirit among the individuals in their working place. This symbolically represents the spirit of work and moral obligation towards being a good human being as a part of society. Most of the entrepreneurs mentioned that observing such *pujas* and rituals give them a psychological relief from the potential threat like enmity among the people. Rituals enhance the spirits of oneness as well as the feeling of defending themselves from the evil spirit and jealousy. The *puja* is performed by the local priest on the auspicious day at the starting of their entrepreneurial units. Such *pujas* and ritual reflect the value of self-respect among the worker and the entrepreneurs.

Moreover, they organize charity function for the betterment of their society in the name of Manipur Statehood Day, Meetei New Year Day, etc. One of the best known ceremonies is the annual award meeting on the foundation day where the local students who have secured very high marks/grades in the Class X examination conducted by the Board of School Examination are felicitated. They also give awards or prizes to the upcoming sportsmen who have participated at various competitions.

In addition to this, sales men or workers are awarded based on their success in achieving sales quotas at every June of a year. This "show" acts as a motivator by publicly recognizing outstanding performance. Such ritual aspects reinforce personal determination and optimism, which enable them to overcome personal hardships, to find his/her own entrepreneurial unit, and achieve material success. It conveys to entrepreneurs that reaching their target is important and that through hard work and encouragement they too can achieve success.

Marketing Strategies

The role of market is very crucial in developing any kind of entrepreneurial activities in the rural life of Manipur. Entrepreneurs are always depending on their local market for the small production from their entrepreneurial units. The growth and stability of their entrepreneurial activities depend on the demand for their products from the locality— in and around the surrounding villages. Kakching is the main marketing centre for the surrounding villagers from Wabagai, Keirak, Tentha, Tekcham, Wangjing, Irengband, etc. From the surrounding villages, they also supply raw material for different entrepreneurial activities at Kakching. At the same time, these villages are also the customer for the finished products from such entrepreneurial units.

However, they also need good strategies of marketing for their products and changes of marketing networks with the Imphal businessmen. The change in marketing network takes place through a conscious effort to solidify an entrepreneur's ideas into a marketing plan with a clear marketing strategy. The plan must be prior in place to start up, but it is subjected to change as competition occurs and the entrepreneurial activities grow. If the marketing information is accomplished with care, this helps in making good marketing decision. Here, it discusses the marketing responsibilities and marketing strategies specific to new venture in the rural areas of Manipur. For instance, Mr. Rameshwor Singh, who is engaged with piggery unit at Mahadev Ching, Kakching, plans his business by seeing the marketing demand of pork (meat of pig) in the neighbouring villages and also from other districts like Ukhrul, Senapati, etc. He also considers the demand of piglets and matured pigs especially from Nagaland State and Mizoram State both for rearing and consumption. He has established regular contact with his friends from Ukhrul district and Senapati district to supply pigs from his piggery. Now, he earns a decent income of Rs. 70,000 per year from his piggery.

At Kakching, the most fundamental marketing consists of multitude activities that include decisions about the products or services, promotions, and methods of distribution of their products. The entrepreneurs should work different activities for their business. The ultimate goal is to facilitate exchange between an enterprise and its customers. Marketing is the process of conceiving that exchange, and then accomplishing the tasks necessary to deliver the goods or services in a manner that satisfies customers for their business. It focuses the enterprise on a target market to fill a gap or create a niche for their business activities. For example, Mr. Manglem Meetei, the proprietor of Kamdevo Silk Work, explained that running an entrepreneurial activity is a very strenuous work. He has to look for the products which are in demand by the customers and also affordable by the common people. Sometimes, he wants to produce the finest products which will fetch higher price than the common products like *Muga Phi, Muga Phanek, Muga Akapi, Eri Phi,* etc. But he is not able to do the same as there are only few people who will buy such expensive products. So, he promotes to produce as per the demand of the customers.

Among the entrepreneurial units, expected results are expressed in sales forecasts and operating budgets, but more importantly, they constitute the entrepreneur's strategic marketing objectives of their product in local markets. An allocation of resources reflects what an entrepreneurial unit has to use and the tactics employed to achieve results. Responsibilities are those activities required to implement a marketing plan. Control issues concern methods of feedback necessary to track performance. Feedback from the customers and the retailers provide planning information for future decisions in developing their entrepreneurial activities. Thus, the marketing plan solidifies the marketing strategy for customer's needs, sales forecasts, and marketing objectives. Consequently, the marketing plan synthesizes market research and the entrepreneur's strategy into a blueprint for action of how the entrepreneurial unit will grow or expand more in future. The plan is implemented through a marketing programme, which addresses the marketing activities.

Case study: Need of sincerity and hard work in entrepreneurship development

Mrs. Tamu Devi is a 48 years old married lady entrepreneur of Kakching Sumak Leikai. From her childhood, she wanted to do something of her own. When she was 17 years old, she saw one of her aunt making *tikei* (traditional *puja* material for producing incense). She had an idea that the imported *agarbatti* is comparatively costlier, then why not making a cheap and easily available *agarbatti* made from the locally available raw materials. Some of the raw materials were easily available in the market and the investment required was also very minimal. This brought her the idea of earning a livelihood by making *agarbatti* at home. At that time, she earned a profit of Rs. 800 per month. She was doing her domestic work at home and sometimes engaged in agricultural works during the agricultural seasons.

She invested Rs. 6,000 in her unit and employed two of her family members and started the unit. Gradually, the unit grew in size and the neighbouring unemployed ladies were also employed in her unit. In the initial years, she had problem of marketing. The local dealers used to come to her home and collect the *agarbatti*. Most often she distributes the *agarbatti* by herself by riding her scooter (Two wheeler). But with the increase in demand and advancement of time, more and more people came to her place to learn the making of *agarbatti*. She gave training to many young boys and girls. She keeps changing her selling strategy like offering special discount on bulk purchase or to regular customers. She also started saving money for her workers.

She is aware of the present entrepreneurship development programme organized by the government. She enhances her business to compete the emerging marketing fight with the outside state imported *agarbattis* (branded *Agarbatti* or *Dhup*). She has strong confidence to survive and grow to more heights. She likes to attribute her success to her strong will-power and faith on God. She believes that sincerity and strong will-power are the two significant aspects for an entrepreneur to develop their entrepreneurial activities.

From her childhood, she used to write poems, short stories. Some of her short stories had already published. She is not only an entrepreneur but also a social worker. She wants the young generation to have good education and serve the country. Most importantly, she wants to bring unity and solidarity among the different ethnic groups of the state. She also narrated her heart felt thanks to Late P.M., Indira Gandhi for her visit at such remote place like Kakching in Manipur.

Distribution of the products and services for entrepreneurship development

The entrepreneurs always look for new products and also try to provide good service to their customers. So, they identify their target customers well and their methods of distributions should be easily assessable to the local customers. In fact, the effective distribution strategies must be consciously selected ways to position their venture through market channels that match expectations of consumers with characteristics of products and services. So, different entrepreneurial units follow different networks of distribution of their products. This becomes the ultimate responsibility of the entrepreneurs for entrepreneurship development to compensate the existing socio-economic environment of the region.

Network of distribution of their products

Production based entrepreneurial activities need a proper channel for its production. The adoption of appropriate channel for distribution of products enhance in marketing. It can be categorized as below:

(1) *Producer – Customer:* This type of distribution of their entrepreneurial products is very common among the villagers. It is because of the reason that they have less production ratio compared with the urban dweller and the demands of their products are also less. So, the entrepreneurs themselves supply their products to the local people by travelling either by bi-cycle or with two wheelers. For instance, Mrs. Chaoba Devi who is engaged with pickles and spices business goes daily in the morning and evening in their neighbouring locality for supplying of her products. She gives the facility of getting her products at her customers' door step.

(2) *Producer – Retailer – Customer:* This type of distribution channel of their products is common especially for piggery, poultry, dry fish fermentation, bamboo shoot fermentation, etc. It is due to the reason that the entrepreneurs cannot give direct service for selling out their products as most of their entrepreneurial activities need more labours. At the same time, it is also more risky to keep their products for long time. It may spoil within a short period. At the same time, anyone from the locality can easily harm their activities by putting some poisonous materials like in poultry farm, piggery farm, etc. In order to avoid such inconveniences, these entrepreneurs supply out to their local retailers.

(3) *Producer – Wholesales - Retailer – Customer:* This type of distribution is very less among the entrepreneurial activities in the rural areas like Kakching. It is required only for some bigger units like brick farms, furniture units,

etc. Besides this, they also provide direct selling to their customers.

It can be mentioned here that some of the entrepreneurs have the facility to sell their products in bulk by giving discount to their wholesalers. But, most of the entrepreneurs carry out direct distribution of their products to their customers, for example, some entrepreneurs use hawkers or rickshaw pullers for selling their products.

Promotion of their entrepreneurial activities

The role of promotion is to facilitate exchanges between entrepreneurial activities and their customers. In the region, commercial enterprises are concerned with attracting customers; professional services are concerned with informing clients about their services. And non-for-profit entrepreneurial units must let their constituents know what they do. Different type of enterprises will have distinct promotional mixes utilizing a variety of promotional methods. The following are some of the effective promotional methods in the rural life in Manipur :

Advertising

Advertising is a form of impersonal broadcasting through commercial mass media. The pervasive type of promotional advertising is the one form that punctuates our daily lives. Advertising gives consciousness among the local people and certainly get their attentions through daily newspapers, radio, local cable networks, pasting picture in the public places, etc.

Publicity

In the rural area of Manipur, publicity is the most effective way of promoting marketing of their products. Publicity is the result of public service announcements or news generated through media, loudspeaker or mike.

Entrepreneurs have many publicity opportunities. For example, sponsorship of community events and non-profit fund raising events usually carry an incentive for businesses. Sponsoring a charity running event is also very common during the *Holi* festivals (locally termed "Yaoshang" festival).

Personal selling

Personal selling is the most common promotional mechanism which is used by the entrepreneurs. It is the personal effort of an entrepreneur to convince a consumer about their products that a purchase has fair exchange value for both parties. Personal selling can also be far more expensive than other methods of promotion, but it is most effective in the rural areas where people want to know their product in details.

Participating in trade fair

Modern way of promoting the product especially the new product is through participating in trade fairs organized by the government and Non-Governmental Organisations. Trade fair is organized in collaboration with Department of Commerce and Industries every year at Khuman Lampak in Imphal. Many visitors from different areas of Manipur visit during the fair. They offer discounts on their sales. The Department of Commerce and Industries distribute prizes for encouragement in their fields. Later the selected entrepreneurs are sent to the Regional trade fair at Guwahati and those selected from Northeastern Region participate Trade Fair held in Delhi for National Level.

Besides these, some voluntary organizations also organize various state level fair for specific categories like bamboo and cane products, water reeds products, indigenous food fair, etc. for the promotion of various traditional products from Manipur.

5

Functioning of Entrepreneurship Development Programmes

Considering the crucial situation of unemployment among the educated youth, complicated further by insurgency in Manipur, the State Government has started the implementation of some programmes with financial assistance from the Central Government for giving employment opportunities to the people of Manipur. Basically, the function of the entrepreneurship development programme is to help a person in strengthening his entrepreneurial motive for self-employment. It also aims at helping the youth in acquiring the skills and capabilities necessary for playing their entrepreneurial role effectively.

Several factors go into the making of an entrepreneur. Individuals who initiate, establish, maintain and expand new enterprises constitute the entrepreneurial group. The socio-political and economic conditions, the availability of industrial technology and know-how, the culture of business and trading among the people, the existence of markets for products and services and the incentives and facilities available for starting an industry or business, all have a bearing on the growth of entrepreneurship in the region.

Traditional Credit Scenario in Manipur

The traditional credit system known as *Marup* is an interesting aspect of socio-economic organization among the *Meeteis* of the Manipur. It is a typical co-operative and credit institution. It originated as one of the most important institutions for mutual help and cooperation in a locality at the time of death, marriage, birth and other personal economic problems. It functions as an institution for socio-economic security in every stage of one's life. It also runs as a traditional moneylending system for the development of entrepreneurial activities in the state. However, the *Meetei* people commonly consider that it helps in bringing social solidarity and strengthens unity among the people. Over time, it has expanded its function much wider than the social sphere and covers most of the economic spheres of the individuals, it caters to.

An interesting and unique operation mechanism of this institution is that each member of the organization contributes some fixed amount on a regular basis like daily, weekly, bi-weekly, monthly or even yearly or on other occasions like marriage, death, etc. within the members' families, and the money collected each time is provided to different members in rotation, as he or she wishes to finance a ceremony, buy needed items, investment in their business, etc. Once a member has received the amount, he or she is not eligible for subsequent distribution, but he or she has to continue regular contribution with a small interest until all the members receive the same amount. The nature of distribution may be on the basis of rotation. On emergency requirement of an individual, the members of the organization allow him/her to get it out of turn with a special request. There are various types of such *Marup* in Manipur like *Keithel* (Market) *Marup, Yumsha* (House building) *Marup, Luhongba* (Marriage) *Marup, Nahutpa* (Ear piercing) *Marup,* etc. It is a traditional system of mutual help among the people. This system generally operates either within family circles, one locality and workplace or among a group of friends.

Roles of Traditional savings and credit systems at Kakching

The roots of traditional saving and credit systems among Manipuris are typically diverse and overlapping. Generally, they are loans among family, relatives, and friends. Loans are often made reciprocally (as per needs of the individuals) and they often do not carry interest charges and are part of broader informal insurance relationships. Such systems can be divided into two types like the *Marup* and the *Tender* system. The *Marup* is a traditional credit system which has been practicing among the Manipuris from generation after generation. This practice has organized among the people for generating economic security during the needy hours. It helps not only for financial support but also helps them to organize themselves for establishing good relationship among the friends and families. The *Marup* is mostly made up of people in the same neighbourhood, with the others based on a shared workplace. Their membership ranges from five to over thirty members depending on the nature of the *Marup*, and the total collected money ranges from some thousands to even some lakhs. The large *Marup* in Manipur provides enough capital for members to make investments like the purchase of rickshaws, utensils for local festivals, decoration material in festivals or marriages, etc.

In the case of *Tender,* it has a clear beginning and end; the accounting is straightforward. The storage of funds is not required since money goes straight from one person to another through the collection by the group leader. *Tender*s come in a number of variations. Each *Tender* has implications for how it stays together, and who is attracted to join. The main variants involve the way groups determine who gets the collected money. The orders of receipt are not predetermined, and may be chosen randomly at the beginning of each cycle. Among the members of *Tender,* there is no strong relationship. So, there is more in economic relationship rather than social relationship among the members of the group. However, both systems have function in a similar manner. Some of the basic components are discussed as followed:

(1) A group of individuals, it can be a minimum of 10 members and to the maximum 35-40 members.

(2) Among the members, a leader is selected voluntarily who can read, write and also do arithmetic calculation.

(3) It is compulsory for all members to contribute a fixed

amount on a particular day to the head. The frequency of contribution may be decided by the head of the group with consultation with the members.

(4) The total amount which is collected from the members will be given to the member who is in immediate need of money or there will be a lottery system to decide who will receive the money.

Cycle of Marup or Tender

Now let us consider an individual who joins *Tender* with twenty neighbours, each of whom is willing and able to contribute Rs. 150 each month. His/her order of receiving the pot is a number between 1 and 20. Before ranks are determined, he/she can priori end up with any rank with equal probability 1/20, but on an average she will be the tenth recipient. After receiving, from the next month he/she should also pay Rs. 170 (i.e Rs. 150 + Rs. 20 as interest) till the cycle completes for the remaining members. This helps in speeding up the expected date of purchasing or investing in their entrepreneurial activities. So, it is better than saving on one's own. In fact, it is better for everyone except the last one person to get the pot, and they are no worse off than they would have been saving up on their own.

The most commonly cited reason that some entrepreneurs at Kakching joined a *Marup* or *Tender* was to save, particularly given their difficulties in saving at their home or business. Most of the people favour *Marup* or *Tender* since it helps them get money out of their home or business.

As far as saving goes, *Tender* has an important advantage that is missing from other informal mechanisms. The beauty is that *Tender* does not require a physical place to store money since it is on the same day that funds are collected and distributed again. The basic nature and pre-commitment associated with *Tender* participation also serves as a device to foster discipline and encourage saving in ways that may work. Participating in a *Marup/*

Tender thus provides a secure, structured way to save money that would otherwise be missing.

It can be observed from the empirical data collected from the field for analysis that many of the members from different *Marups* of Kakching mentioned that they are financially or socially supported through their strong relationship brought by it.

Methods of informal lending and security

Traditional loans are referred to as 'non-institutional' loans, in contrast with bank loans. But in fact all the following methods of arranging credit and security are not really informal but follow traditional forms. The following methods are in vogue in different parts of the state with variations and sometimes with different names.

Loushan (piba or thaba)

Among the Manipuris, it is the most common mortgage form of debt security for those having some land. In return for a cash loan, the borrower hands over a piece of land to the lender to be used by him for a stipulated period of time, in lieu of any payment of principal or interest. The term literally means that the moneylender uses the land for the set time and "gives it back" to the owner once he/she returns the same amount. In principle, the borrower can redeem his land by paying back the proportionate balance. But in fact lenders try to use the land as long as originally agreed upon. This method of security is popular among rural people because they give no other cash repayment and they have every prospect of recovering their land. Frequently, the lender will even have the owner sharecrop it for the duration of the loan.

Bandop

This is a loan of cash against some security which is, literally, "closed" to the owner, and the lender has the use of it for the duration of the loan. It may be land, gold, silver, ornaments, brass utensils, bicycles, motor vehicles, etc. The borrower has to pay the agreed principle and interest in cash to redeem his property, and therefore in the case of land it is less favourable to the borrower than the above method.

Phoudambi

Some people are mainly subsistence producers and their first concern about savings is crop inputs, for which they require some thousands for the agricultural season. About two-third of them are able to meet their costs from savings, while some borrow locally or get an advance from the owner of some land they sharecrop on the side. *Phoudambi* refers to a cash loan which is to be repaid in kind, usually at harvest. *Phoudambi* literally means "Paddy given as interest". It is common throughout Manipur. The rate is pre-determined and the produce is valued at something less than its normal market price. The most common form of *Phoudambi* is repayment of an agricultural loan in the form of part of the paddy harvest. They usually lend out money during the month of July/ August, i.e during the rainy season when people are becoming penniless and they collect it back preferably in the month of December/January after their harvesting.

Traditionally, in rural and backward areas of Manipur, the banks have usually not provided financial services to needy people with little or no cash income. It is so crucial for a poor man to get a bank account of his own. There is always some corruptive atmosphere in the region, which will take time to wind off from the region. There is also the reluctance of government employees to give their helping hand to needy people who are less aware of the modern financial norms and conditions. Moreover, most poor people have few assets that can be accepted by a bank as collateral (security). So, there is the need of some financial institutions like micro finance, which can offer back-up in certain situations. Such situations need the banks to have reconsideration on the prevailing environment in the region. It is because of this reason that government experts focus their main attention only on developing commercial banking sectors dealing in high-value transactions, and often neglect the delivery of services to households of limited means, even when these households comprise the large majority of their population. That is why the only means for the common people is often to rely on relatives or the local moneylender, whose interest rate can be very high to them. Moneylenders often threaten and accuse the borrowers who could not pay back the money in time. Even if there are certain misfortunes, the common man often falls into the hands of local lenders since their services are convenient and fast, and they can be very flexible when borrowers run into problem. Sometimes, the poor people are prepared to pay high interest rates for services like flexibility in repayment schedule. When they borrow money for a starting small business, they often borrow for other purposes like daily family maintenances etc.

Role of Financial Institutions for Entrepreneurship Development

At Kakching, financial institutions are playing a key role in providing finance and counselling to the entrepreneurs to start new ventures as well as to modernize, diversify and even rehabilitate sick enterprises. In this context, it is required to study the scope and operation of various development corporations and financial institutions which have been rendering financial assistance, directly or indirectly, to entrepreneurs and their various ventures.

In the rural areas of Kakching, the majority of the people depend on agriculture and they do not have surplus money. But the development of entrepreneurial activities needs more capital requirements. The need for capital is continuous. It is also necessary to generate capital for their growth in entrepreneurial activities. The growth and progress of their economy creates its surpluses with which further development is achieved, often at an accelerated rate. Financial assistance to entrepreneurs is granted by commercial banks, State Financial Corporations, DIC (District Industries Centre), etc. Credit facilities granted by commercial banks and

State Financial Corporations are covered under the Credit Guarantee Scheme for Small Scale Industries, which offers protection to credit institutions against possible losses on their lending to these sectors.

Financial Institutions in the study area

Public sector banks like United Bank of India (UBI), State Bank of India (SBI), Manipur State Co-operative Bank (MSCB), Rural Development Bank (RDB) have their branches at Kakching. Also there are non-government financial agencies and co-operatives that provide financial support for entrepreneurship development. Some of the women's self help groups, *Shagei Marup* (Clan Thrift Group), *Ningol-Piba Marup* (Families and relative thrift group), Local *Tender* group (Non-formal association among particular thrift group), etc. also provide money for local entrepreneurship.

The financial institutions make provision for long, medium and short term credit facilities for development activities and to accelerate the rate of growth and economic development. At present, credit facilities are made available in the area by various branches of Manipur State Co-operative Bank and Manipur Rural Bank. One branch each of United Bank of India (UBI) and Manipur State Co-operative Bank (MSCB) function at both the sub-divisional Headquarters, i.e. at Thoubal and Kakching. There are six branches of Manipur Rural Bank (MRB) located at Kakching, Waikhong, Sugnu, Yairipok, Lilong and Pallel. The study area enjoys credit facility for development activities through various co-operative societies as well. These banks provide short-term crop loans to the Scheduled Castes and Tribes of the area. Long-term loans are made available for farm mechanization, purchase of automobiles and starting new businesses and industries.

However, the near collapse of institutional financing in the state is a matter of grave concern as they play an important role in promoting economic activities. As mentioned by a bank manager of Manipur State Co-operative Bank at Kakching, the bank officials are threatened by the insurgent groups to give money. These insurgent groups target the bank officials and take them to their custody for not meeting their demands for money in time. They also impose personal threat to the bank officials to give loan through fake names and fake certificates. Sometimes, there are also cases that the surrendered militants also pressurise to give loan in the name of their group or group members. Warnings like keeping live bullets on officer's table, throwing hand grenades on the Bank manger's house, kidnapping the officials from the office, demanding five per cent of their salary to the insurgents, etc. are a common talk. For instance, the attack of Manager of United Bank of India, Kakching, in 2002 that led to killing of two police constables who were on duty at the bank. There is a need for more banks to be opened in the hill districts and the rural areas and enabling conditions created for stepping up lending activities. The credit disbursement from commercial banks in the state is low. So, the rural people in Manipur depended heavily on moneylenders and indigenous bankers. Commercial banks have now evolved new schemes to meet the varied credit needs of the small-scale sector after a careful study of its problems. In fact, the growth of this sector during the last decade is mainly due to the assistance it has received from commercial banks. These banks offer a wide range of package services/assistance to small industries. The scale and scope of their assistance has increased considerably.

On the other hand, in the paper work, Commercial banks have a wide-ranging financial assistance to small-scale units from equity to bill finance:

1. *Equity Support*: Under this scheme, the technically-qualified entrepreneurs get equity capital to start business. Interest-free loans ranging from Rs. 5,000 to Rs. 50,000 are sanctioned to strengthen their equity base. These loans are repayable in 7 years.
2. *Term Loans*: Banks grant loans for the construction of factory buildings and the purchase and installation of machinery and equipment. Loans are also sanctioned for purposes of expansion, modernization and renovation.

3. *Working Capital*: Small-scale industries are given financial assistance against pledge or hypothecation of stocks of raw materials, semi-finished goods. They are also given overdraft and bill finance facilities.
4. *Export Finance*: Small-scale units engaged in the export of their products are given full finance, from production to realization under pre-shipment credit facilities.
5. *Special Hypothecation*: This is sanctioned to small-scale units to supplement their working capital requirements.
6. *Clear Advance*: Banks also sanction clear advances to small scale industries to enable them to tide over unforeseen financial difficulties.

Micro-Finance Intervention and Entrepreneurship Development at Kakching

Some micro-finance organizations like WIGS (Women's Income Generation Centre), WCTP (Women Credit and Thrift Project), UNNACO (United Aroma Commercial limited), etc. started giving loans to the small farmers, manufactures and producers to start or expand their micro enterprises. This brings a new dimension to those people who desperately need help and safeguard for their livelihood. However, the role and service of moneylenders also continues to be valued in the region. Nowadays, micro-finance is also slowly being diverted to investment in horticulture, animal husbandry, farming, etc. It not only helps the people in producing more products, but also helps in providing marketing facilities and banking linkage to rural entrepreneurs. This leads to the habit of thrift among uneducated people.

In the development process of small or household enterprises in the rural areas of Kakching, micro-finance has evolved as a need programme to cater to the so far neglected target group people like women, poor, rural, deprived, destitutes, etc. It is mainly concerned for the empowerment of the poor and the alleviation of poverty by encouraging self-employment through entrepreneurship development. It also includes access to credit for poor people as a major aspect of many poverty elimination programmes. Such programmes become one of the promising ways to use scarce development funds to achieve the objectives of poverty alleviation. Furthermore, certain micro-finance programmes have prominence in the development of locally available entrepreneurial activities. The basic importance of micro-finance may be simple for example, if poor people are provided access to financial services including credit, the backward and rural people of the region may be able to become self-sufficient by expanding their own micro-entrepreneurial units like furniture work, motor servicing, piggery, poultry, etc. that will allow them to break out of poverty and indebtedness. It will ultimately benefit the people so that they will increase their income generation level. Furthermore, the poor are able to access financial services which previously were exclusively available to the upper and middle income population. Finally, the access to credit and the opportunity to begin or to expand such micro enterprises or small entrepreneurial unit may be empowering to the poor.

The basic problem of micro-finance in the rural areas is that poor people need money for different purposes such as for building houses that may involve saving and protecting diverse building materials for years until enough are available to proceed with construction, expenditure for school-going children, daily expenditure, etc. Children's schooling may be funded by buying chicken and raising them for sale as needed for expenses, uniforms, etc. So, the rural people sometimes not able to repay back the whole amount in time but they utilize the benefits of micro-finance in the study area.

Change in saving pattern among the rural people at Kakching

In the rural areas, informal methods of saving are very unsafe since there is no adequate security measure for the recovery of their lending money. For example, Mr. Godhadhor Singh has a saving of Rs. 50,000 from his daily work as well as from their agricultural products. They have planned for lending money to their neighbours so that they can earn extra income to their family. He asked his wife to look for some people who can give regular interest of Rs. 5 per cent per month for their capital. They started lending money to different people in their locality. Later, Mrs. Yaima Devi came to their house and requested to lend her some money and promising that she will give 6 per cent interest for their capital. They were impressed by Mrs. Yaima's words. Mrs Yaima Devi gave them regular interest without fail for some time. After six months, Mrs. Yaima left her home without informing them. Mr. Godhadhor Singh lost their money with no hope of getting back from Mrs. Yaima. In most of the cases, people with no option of saving other than informal saving, lose some money. It is found that micro- finance and micro-credit brings a paradigm shift to the rural people. The poor villagers are able to get out of poverty by borrowing, building micro-enterprises and increasing their income. The new paradigm places more attention on the efforts of poor people to reduce their vulnerabilities by saving more of what they earn and building up their assets. When they need financial help, they may approach the micro-credit institutions and get it as it is useful to borrow for consumption as well as for micro-enterprises. It becomes a safe, flexible place to save money and withdraw it when needed. It is also very essential for managing household and family risks. There is some advantages of micro-finance like the immense diversity of institutions serving poor people in developing rural Manipur. It achieved a great deal, especially in the backward areas and with entrepreneurial families. Another major achievement of it is the micro-credit awareness movement among the people against traditional moneylenders, who typically charge high interest rates per month and often keep the poor in their trap of poverty and exploitation.

Role of EDP (Entrepreneurship Development Programme) at Kakching

Though EDP has been recognized as an effective Human Resource

Development tool, the rural people at Kakching have various expectations from a single programme, like removing unemployment, enhancing awareness among the people, promoting small scale industries, developing industrially underdeveloped regions, providing financial assistance through EDP, etc. But it is needless to say that no one programme can achieve all these ambitious objectives. So, it is required to have different programmes for different problems suffered by the people in the state. EDP is one among the programmes implemented by the Government for the development of various small scale enterprises (either traditional or modern enterprises). It aims at encouraging the unemployed youth to become self-supporting (self-employed) by initiating new ventures for earning.

In rural areas at Kakching, EDP is primarily meant for developing or helping those first-generation entrepreneurs, who on their own cannot become successful owners of enterprises. EDP covers three major variables: locations, target group and entrepreneurial activities in the local environment. Any of these can become the focus or starting point for initiating and implementing an EDP. The type of the target group promoted among the rural people, the nature of the traditional and the non-traditional entrepreneurial activities promoted and higher probability of success in new ventures can decide the quality and impact of an EDP in the region.

The agencies conducting EDP and the trainers alone cannot develop entrepreneurs. They can only help people to set up their enterprises since many other support agencies like banks, micro-finance institutes, DICs, etc. are also involved to create better co-ordination and effective linkages with these support agencies. The trainer alone cannot control or influence external factors like providing loans, supplying modern technology, credit linkage with banks, providing raw materials, marketing facilities, etc. which are necessary for starting up an EDP. It is required to work out collectively for the development of entrepreneurship in the region.

In addition to this, it is required to give better awareness to the people about the process and strategy of EDP. This helps to get

EDPs their due importance and recognition among the young generation of the region for self-employment or sustaining their livelihood. The programme organized for the development of entrepreneurship focused on the locally available resources as well as the adaptability of the entrepreneurial types.

Role of Consultancy Organisation and Training Institutes

The various motivation campaigns or programmes taken up by the Government agencies tried to fill the information gaps which existed and are relevant for rural entrepreneurs. The entrepreneurs required a lot of information for setting up business. In that context, the contributors of these programmes were essentially in the area of disseminating knowledge on financial, technical and managerial aspects. To that extent, these programmes were not basically programmes towards entrepreneurship development, but were in the nature of supportive programmes for the existing and new entrepreneurs. For instance, Institute of Co-operative Management, Imphal, offers a wide range of training programmes in the area of Computer and IT, credit and banking, marketing, processing, consumer, handloom, handicrafts, general management, accounts audit, cooperative law, allied laws, etc.

In the context of the emergence of financial and training institutions in the state, it was visualized that creation of all external facilities is not a sufficient condition for the promotion of entrepreneurship development in the region. Equally important are the qualities of the individuals who respond to the external opportunities (i.e. availability of funds, financial incentives, etc.). Also, socio-cultural and organizational factors help people to perceive opportunities and learn to respond to them.

There is always the prevalence of competition, constantly changing marketing conditions, trying for the production of quality goods at a minimum cost, etc. among the enterprises. These all depend solely on the availability of technical know-how and available skilled workers, from time to time. Modernisation of technology and upgradation of technical skills, etc. for higher productivity also depends on technical know-how, which is essential for the healthy growth of entrepreneurial activities. But the technological know-how, however, depends on entrepreneurial research, particularly in the household enterprise sector, and not only ensures stability in marketing and profits, but is also essential for the very survival of the entrepreneurial units in the rural areas.

The Government of Manipur encourages the growth and development of rural entrepreneurship because of its contribution to the rural economy and to self-employment among the young generation of the state. The government agencies provide valuable assistance and advice to young household entrepreneurs or rural entrepreneurs since they cannot afford the financial cost of the unit as well as for providing their own staff of qualified specialists. In order to make this service as complete and comprehensive as possible, the government agencies organize training, awareness camps and financial assistance at the different districts of Manipur. For example, Yengkhom Inaocha Leima, age 37 years, belongs to a rural background where agriculture (farming) was the main occupation of their family. She got married and is a mother of three daughters. Her husband, Mr. M. Nungleiba Meetie, is an employee who is always ready to help in her aspiration of becoming an entrepreneur. She is a young and enthusiastic lady. She is a quick learner who always seeks for achieving her heights. After becoming a housewife, she devoted herself in their family welfare. Although, Mrs. Inaocha Leima could have easily got a decent job for herself, she is more of the creative type. With the strong desire to be on her own and be able to explore her creative talent, she wanted to start something on her own. She always kept her eyes open and thinking to open the first readymade show room at Kakching under the Manikchand Store banner. She started a survey of the private and public schools in and around Kakching for supplying school dress. With the help of her husband, she took loan from Manipur State Co-operative Bank. With the financial assistance from bank, she supported her venture to become a successful entrepreneur. In their show room, new models of shoes, bags, jackets, T-shirts, coats, trousers, etc. are also on display. She also kept school bags in the shop, with the contacts from Ken Bags Industries. She gave employment to two of her relatives with a monthly salary of 1500/- per month. This lady having strong will-power, rightly pointed out that "to be successful in business, one should be task oriented, hard working, broad minded, flexible and open to challenges".

On the other hand, WIGC (Women's Income Generation Centre), YVU (Youth Volunteers' Union), etc. are giving vocational training-cum-employment generation programme to a large number of women and girls. The most common and popular crafts training presently provided are *Kouna* (water reed) craft and Handloom. The *kouna* craft goes at times with cane and other allied materials.

Modernisation of Entrepreneurial units

Modernisation of programmes for entrepreneurial untis involved an integrated approach, for it was felt that it would not be possible to tackle and solve individual problems connected with modernization of their enterprises because of the prevailing imbalances in the production set-up and supply of raw materials for various entrepreneurial unit. The following are the main features of the modernization of entrepreneurial units:

1. Modernisation of management marketing skills, techniques, including the modernisation of attitudes and skills of the personnel at all levels.
2. Upgrading in quality of products in terms of standardization of designs e.g. mechanization of brick farm products in Bhubon Brick Field.
3. Modernisation of equipment and machinery like start using of computer at Pioneer's Printing Press, Kakching.
4. Modernisation and upgrading of technology in the sense of identification and use of low cost technology which is, at the same time, consistent with economy, efficiency, quality and which is affordable by the rural entrepreneurs

like using of modern electric saw, electric drillers, etc. in the furniture houses.

The agencies in Manipur conduct motivational contact programmes through seminars, workshops, media, etc.

Training Programmes for Entrepreneurship Development at Kakching

Most of the entrepreneurs who are engaged in different entrepreneurial activities lack the training in their respective fields. They started their entrepreneurial activities through personal experience or by imitating their neighbours. So, the majority of the individuals need training regarding the induction into the rationale and objectives of their jobs, etc. They need to train themselves in their specific skills and routines. This is shown in Fig. 5.1.

Fig. 5.1: Objectives of Training Programme among the Rural Entrepreneurs in Manipur

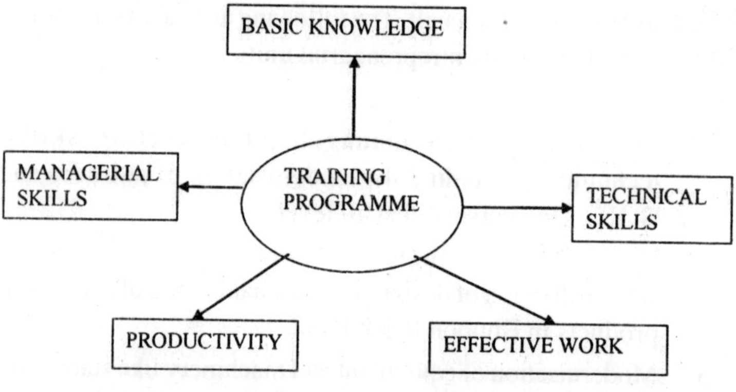

Source : Artisan Training-cum-Production Centre, Manipur.

Experienced and professional workers who were engaged in entrepreneurial activities (like carpentry, handloom, motor servicing, etc.) got training programmes to enable them to obtain more effective and advanced technical knowledge of their work. Certain workers may need training for specific purposes, the development of a new service, taking on a new role in the organization, preparing for retirement, etc.

However, rural entrepreneurs in Manipur suffer from various handicaps compared to the entrepreneurs in other states. One of the most important among these is the non-availability of technical and managerial personnel of the required calibre. The entrepreneurs from other states (like Bihar, Assam, West Bengal, etc.) can employ qualified staff who are specialized in different areas of production and management. Further, they can afford to retain capital investment from time to time for their entrepreneurial units. Besides, entrepreneurs at Kakching do not have the equipment and resources to train their own workers.

Role of EDP in Changing Entrepreneurial Behaviour

The objectives and planning of EDP in changing entrepreneurial behaviour need to be achieved through training. At Kakching, the contents and nature of the programme are largely depending on the stage of growth of entrepreneurs. Entrepreneurs in the rural areas at Kakching engaged in small business are usually owner-managers for self-sustaining their entrepreneurial units. In the beginning stage, most of the entrepreneurial units are more concerned with how the activities will be start properly and they play the role of workers rather than that of a manager. Maximum efforts were contributed for smooth running of their enterprises.

But as soon as the business or activity achieves constancy in terms of production/service, entrepreneurs start planning its growth and improvement. Then, his or her role as a worker gradually diminishes and proportionately the manager's role increases. As there is more progress of the industry/entrepreneurial activity, the manager's role will also increase. Thus, the role of a small entrepreneur is a dynamic one and follows a continuum between the worker's and the manager's role. For instance, Mr. Bhudhi Singh started his piggery unit at Kakching Irum Mapal, in the year 2003. He worked for the construction of the pig shed with some of his workers. He had a difficult time while searching for buying piglets from different places. At the same time, lack of money for investment was very difficult. He mentioned that wherever the workers face some problem, his physical presence was needed as the workers always wait for his decision. He worked along with the workers who are working in his construction of pig sheds. As his piggery unit expands from 15 pigs to 34 pigs, he engaged two workers from his locality. He allocated one person for arranging and feeding his pigs and the other person for cleaning and supplying water daily in the piggery unit. But the most difficult time in piggery is during the breeding of pigs as it needs more labour and proper selection of the timing for different pigs. For his unit, he has to be the manager as well as the best worker.

In order to maintain competence both as a worker at the beginning of the entrepreneurial activities and ultimately taking more managerial when their unit attains smooth production. Usually as part of the entrepreneurship development programme, they receive the motivational training that includes the preliminary knowledge of production, marketing and financial management. As enterprise grows on, they require another training intervention with formal management inputs to bear the increasing management responsibility.

Training Programme: Course Duration and Schedule

The training was set-up according to the training needs of participants, who are potential/aspirant entrepreneurs. The training programme lasts for one or two weeks (approximately). This training is aimed at increasing the participant's level of achievement, confidence, developing the right attitude and behaviour towards new venture. This also enables the participants to know the environment in which they operate their small business or entrepreneurial activities. The training programme covers such aspects as government incentives, entrepreneurial oppourtunities, etc. During the training session, the participants have the option to attend either in morning session or the evening session as per their convenience. But such options are only available to those programmes organized by the VOs/NGOs. Upon the completion of the course, each participant is awarded a certificate by the institute at the closing ceremony.

Case study: Training Programme in Embroidery and Wool Knitting

Miss N. Sumita Devi runs her own embroidery unit at Kakching. She belongs to an agricultural family, but her father is an employee at Manipur Electricity Department. This enterprising lady, since her young age, was always very ambitious and had an entrepreneurial bent of mind. She desired to be her own and kept her motivated to start her own business some day. She was always a very creative woman. So, to exploit her creativity she went to Imphal and gained a diploma in embroidery and wool knitting. This technical education gave her an edge in her business of embroidery, wool knitting, etc. She also joined the EDP conducted by Government of Manipur at Kakching Municipality. This further enhanced her confidence and gave her a professional outlook. This brought her into new entrepreneurial ventures. Slowly, she experienced a tremendous change in her personality. She realized that she had to become more sociable and enthusiastic to become an entrepreneur who can give jobs rather than seeking jobs.

Through attending training sessions and awareness camps, she became aware of the universal problem faced by women entrepreneurs regarding the role conflict between a job and domestic chores. Since women entrepreneurs in rural areas achieved exceptional success but very often found the problem in running both simultaneously.

She started an embroidery under the banner "Laxmi Embroidery and Wool Knitting Centre" when she was twenty years old. She was very interested in this art from her childhood. The neighbours used to praise her work and started ordering her. The family income was not so low. Her brothers also helped in her financial needs.

After completing her Intermediate examination, she did not go for further studies. She wanted to get into the business of embroidery. The elder members of the family gave support by supplying machines for her unit. She started the unit with just one machine and earned about Rs. 500 per month.

In 1985, she heard from one of her friends about embroidery and wool knitting training at Imphal. She appeared for the interview and was selected. During the training programme she could develop relationship with the DIC officials. She gained more knowledge about entrepreneurship through the training programme. After attending the training, she gained confidence to do something on her own.

After two years, she was able to upgrade the unit by adding three more machines with the financial support of her brothers. At present, she is earning about Rs. 3500-5000 per month. She started a training programme on embroidery and at present there are ten students undergoing the training. She takes Rs. 50 per month per student as tuition fee. For marketing her products, she has no problem because the rates that she charges are similar to the rates prevalent in the market. As she says, "I am trying to keep my level best and latest design for embroidery. Therefore, nobody bargains with me. My services are in great demand". Now, she has registered her unit. She plans to apply for a loan to expand the business. She wants to add the tailoring unit also. By doing so she will be able not only to increase her income but also help some unemployed youth by giving them employment in her unit.

Role of AITC (Artisan Training-cum-Production Centre), Thoubal

Artisan Training-cum-Production Centre was established during the Fifth Five-year Plan under the Directorate of Industries, Manipur. The syllabus of the training centres was prepared at the level of I.T.C. (Industrial Training Centre, Manipur). After observation and evaluation at various levels, it was considered essential to amend the syllabus to suit the local artisans. Accordingly, various committees were constituted and suggestions were invited from the Instructors/ Superintendents and the same have been compiled and consolidated and the committee considered to have two different courses viz.:

(1) Elementary Course of one year.
(2) Advanced Course of one year.

The Government of Manipur has approved the new syllabus of two different courses, i.e. Elementary and Advanced Course *vide* their letter No. 61/16/91-IND dated July 1991. The main objective of the syllabus is to cater to the needs, of each and every individual who is interested to take up a suitable training course of his or her choice. The syllabus is prepared on the basis of average persons according to their ability in two categories (i) Elementary Course and (ii) Advanced Course with one year duration each except for Wool Knitting & Embroidery which will be of six months, duration each. The training courses are considered suitable for self-employment. The contents of all courses in different trades are focused on the scientific aspect, with theoretical as well as practical classes. The Elementary courses in Carpentary, Blacksmithy, Weaving, Bamboo & Cane, Tailoring & Cutting have been pursued with special interest.

In view of the present needs of qualified/skilled artisans in various trades the State Industrial Training Centre (I.T.C.) advisory committee has decided to modify the existing syllabus of different trades like weaving, cutting and tailoring, carpentry, blacksmithy, foundry, bamboo and cane, carpet weaving, wool knitting, embroidery, etc. The main aim of the training course is to impart training to the interested youth as per the new syllabus with modern tools, equipment and techniques. After satisfactory completion of this course, the trainee could be provided with a set of tools and equipment for self-employment. The Advanced Course Training is essentially meant for artisans who are already trained in a specific trade from a recognized institute, who are matriculates or passed an examination of equivalent standard and are desirous to improve their professional skill.

The State Director in-charge of the training programme has sanctioned trade-wise intake capacity for the different training courses as shown in Table 5.1 against each trade for each academic session.

Table 5.1: Courses offered and intake of seats at AITC, Thoubal

Sl. No.	*Name of the Trade*	*Intake capacity*	*Duration of training course*	*Title of Certificate*
1.	Wool knitting	12	6 months	Short term course
2.	Embroidery	12	6 months	Short term course
3.	Cutting and tailoring	12	12 months	Elementary course
4.	Carpentry	12	12 months	Elementary course
5.	Blacksmithy	12	12 months	Elementary course
6.	Foundry	12	12 months	Elementary course
7.	Bamboo and Cane	12	12 months	Elementary course
8.	Carpet Weaving	12	12 months	Elementary course
9.	Hand Weaving	12	12 months	Elementary course
10.	Advance Hand Weaving	12	12 months	Advance Training course
11.	Advance Carpentry	12	12 months	Advance Training course
12.	Advance Cutting and Tailoring	12	12 months	Advance Training course
13.	Advance Blacksmithy	12	12 months	Advance Training course
14.	Advance Foundry	12	12 months	Advance Training course
15.	Advance Bamboo and Cane	12	12 months	Advance Training course

Source: AITC, Thoubal, Manipur.

In training centres like Porompat and Thoubal, the number of sanctioned seats have increased in order to meet the present demands of more skilled artisans in the thickly populated valley districts in Manipur.

Table 5.2 : Report of students in AITC from the period 2000-06

Sl. No.	*Name of the course*	*2000-01*		*2001-03*		*2003-04*		*2004-05*		*2005-06*		*2006-07*	
		A	B	A	B	A	B	A	B	A	B	A	B
1.	Carpentry (adv)	5	NA	X	X	X	X	4	4	6	4	X	X
	Elementary	11	NA	6	5	X	X	11	7	2	2	7	4
2.	Blacksmithy (adv)	2	1	X	X	X	X			X	X	X	X
	Elementry	4	0	3	2	X	X			6	3	5	4
3.	Cane-bamboo (adv)	3	3	X	X	X	X	X	X	X	X	X	X
	Elementry	6	2	6	4	X	X	9	6	10	6	8	3
4.	Weaving (Adv)	6	3	X	X	X	X	4	2	X	X	X	X
	Elementry	12	8	8	0	X	X	17	9	19	16	22	9
5.	Tailoring & Cutting (adv)	7	4	X	X	X	X	9	4	6	6		
	Elementry	411	33	71	1	X	X	28	8	24	2	21	2
6.	Foundry (Adv)	1	1			X	X						
	Elementry	4	2			X	X					4	4
7.	Carpet weaving (Elementry)	6	4	121	1	X	X			5	5	10	6

Source: AITC, Thoubal, Manipur state (from the period 2000-06).
Note: Adv. = advance course; A= no. of students enrolled in that particular year, B = no. of students passed out, NA = Data not available, X= students not enrolled.

ITI (Industrial Training Institute)

The Directorate of Craftsmen Training, Manipur was set up in 1980. The Director General of Employment and Training, Government of India is responsible for laying down the policies and training standards. The responsibility for the day-to-day administration and implementation of training programmes in the ITI rests with the State Government. There are 11 (eleven) Industrial Training Institutes in the State. These institutions have been playing an important role in producing skilled manpower for the industrial development of the state. The Department implements two schemes, namely:

(1) Craftsmen Training Scheme and
(2) Apprenticeship Training Scheme.

The main objectives of ITI are:

1. Making an increase in industrial production for the betterment of the socio-economic condition of the people.
2. Solving the unemployment problems among the educated youth by promoting self-employment.
3. Giving upliftment of training standard by replacing outdated tools/machinery with new ones.
4. Giving training especially to Ex-ITI trainees to make them more skilled.

Under this scheme young persons in the age group of 14-40 years are trained through institutional system of training in 11 (eleven) Industrial Training Institutes with the capacity of 1340 seats in Engineering and Non-engineering trades. The period of training for most of the Engineering trades is 2 (two) years while that of Non-engineering trade is 1(one) year. The minimum educational qualification for admission to these trades varies from Class X/HSLCE to XII classes (Science or Commerce) or its equivalent. The training in the industrial training institutes is given with facilities like free workshop, free raw materials, free games, free recreation, free study tour, free hostel accommodation, etc. Stipends of Rs. 120 (Non-Hosteller) and Rs. 150 per month are awarded to all the trainees.

Problems of Entrepreneurship Development

Infrastructural lags

Being a weak infrastructural base, Manipur is one of the most backward states in the country. As per the index of the Relative Development of Infrastructure report prepared by different

Table 5.3 : Details of the existing ITI

Sl. No.	Year of Est.	Name of ITI and Place	Trade Unit	No. of Seats
1.	1959	ITI, Imphal West District	19	352
2.	1993	Women ITI, Takyel, Imphal West District	4	80
3.	1972	ITI, Saikot, Churchandpur District	6	92
4.	1972	ITI, Ukhrul District	3	48
5.	1974	ITI, Senapati, Senapati District	4	60
6.	1974	ITI, Tamenglong, Tamenglong distict	2	32
6.1.	2003	ITI, Tamenglong, Tamenglong District	8	128
7.	1980	ITI, Jiribam, Jiribam Sub-division	2	32
8.	2003	ITI, Imphal East, Phaknung	8	132
9.	2003	ITI, Ningthoukhong, Bishsenpur	8	128
10.	2003	ITI, Kakching, Thoubal	8	128
11.	2003	ITI, Chandel	8	128
		Total	**80**	**1340**

Source: ITI Imphal, Manipur.

agencies, Manipur occupies a low place in the list. The level of development in infrastructure such as roads, power, irrigation, etc lags behind other states of the country.

It is noticed that the density of road per 100 sq. km. of area in 2001-02 for the state was only 51.2 kms. as against 74.73 kms for all India. In 2002-03, the per capita energy consumption for Manipur was 72.9 kwh. as against 373 kwh. for All India. The area served by a post office in Manipur in 2002-03 was 32.13 sq. km while that of All India was 21.12 sq.km. The per capita income for Manipur for 2002-03 was only Rs. 12,230 (Q) as against Rs. 18,912 (Q) for All India. The Net State Domestic Products in 2002-03 was Rs. 3047 crore (at current price) as against that of Rs. 10,964 crore for All India and that of Meghalaya, which has similar area and population with that of Manipur, was Rs. 3,842 crores.

Unemployment

According to the Government report, unemployment is the biggest challenge in the region. The state has a very high rate of unemployment, particularly among the educated youth. The number of persons on the live register in Employment Exchanges which was of the order of 2.28 lakhs as on 30.06.1993 increased to 6.30 lakhs as on 30.12.2007, showing an increasing trend. The maximum level of unemployment is in the age group of 30-40 years and that too among the highly qualified/professionally qualified youth.

The problems of educated unemployed remain acute with ugly manifestations. As a result of this, the state has been experiencing many problems on the socio-economic development programmes due to unrest among youths for quite some time. In the present situation, there is little scope for generation of employment opportunities in the Government sector. There is also a dearth of organized units, be they in the field of industries or other activities, for generation of employment opportunities. There has thus been greater stress on generation of self-employment schemes.

In the region, employment programmes are being taken up under 3 broad groups viz. creation of general employment opportunities, supplemental programmes for specific target groups/ areas for employment generation and special schemes for the educated unemployed. The first one is contemplated to be tackled with growth of the agricultural sector as a result of expansion of irrigation facilities, increase in cropping intensity, expansion of new agricultural practices, development of horticulture, fisheries, forestry, etc. For specific target groups, the important schemes are SGSY (Swarnajayanti Gram Swarojgar Yojana), SGRY (Sampoorna Gramin Rojgar Yojana), and IAY (Indira Awas Yojana). To tackle the menace of unemployment in the country, the Central Government has already enacted the National Rural Employment Guarantee Act (NREGA) which is approved only for Tamenglong district and has started implementation for April, 2006. Job Cards have been issued to all the 17,880 households which demanded employment. In terms of individuals, 45,172 persons have been provided jobs out of 60,636 applications registered. However, two more districts viz. Churachandpur and Chandel have also been covered under the programme from 2007-08 and all the 9 districts in the state will now be covered under the programme from 2008-09.

Lack of sufficient financial resources and exploitation by private moneylenders

The formal processes in accessing banks in the study area are discouraging for the people who need financial help. Such a time-consuming process makes people lose interest in taking loans from the public sector banks and other financial institutions. Meanwhile, they need to put one government employee's signature as a guarantor of the proposed loan. This is because, if the borrower fails to pay back the amount, the financial institution will directly take a certain amount from the guarantor's salary every month till it recovers the total amount. Such problems make everyone reluctant to be a guarantor. Often, people depend on local private moneylenders. The moneylenders charge heavy interest and often harass the people while recovering the loan. Nowadays, it needs to give *patta* or gold of the same value as security.

Skilled labour migration from rural areas

Recently, many shop and market complexes get products from big towns such as Imphal. Also, the products from Myanmar and China are available in Kakching in plenty at much lower prices. The local entrepreneurs find it very difficult to compete with them to attract customers for their products.

The youth and skilled people have started to migrate to other places in search of settled jobs and daily incomes, leaving behind their small business activities. The youth, who are trained for entrepreneurship development, find jobs easily outside their village from sources of instant income. Therefore, this local spirit of entrepreneurship is damaged.

Extortion by militants

Monetary demand and physical harassment of the local business-men by militants in Manipur is becoming a common phenomenon. Due to the increasing extortion by militants of different groups, the local entrepreneurs face difficulties in running their entrepreneurial activities. Entrepreneurs become helpless in the hands of militants as militants frequently enforce them to close down their entrepreneurial activities for not providing their monetary demands. Sometimes, the militants ask the local entrepreneurs to come with huge amount of money to the remote forest for negotiation. Such inconveniences make the local entrepreneurs to feel regret that they are not working for themselves but for the militants. They work day and night to earn their livelihood but the money goes easily to the hands of militants. To stop the extortion spree in Manipur, the activities of police commandos have been enhanced. After identifying the individuals collecting money for different UG groups, police commandos have mounted strict vigil on the movement of these individuals.

These measures have been taken up with the belief that rampant extortion activities can be checked only when strong punitive actions are initiated against those persons (sympathizers) collecting money for UG (Underground) groups. The state government's initiative to set up SPOs (Special Protection Officer) came after rebels gunned down three youth, including two girls, at Heirok on March 24 and a 55 year old man at Lilong Chajing of Imphal East district. The angry villagers had requested the government to provide them with arms to combat militants. The cabinet had also decided to recruit 200 SPOs at Lilong and 300 SPOs at Heirok. The government provides .303 rifles and a monthly remuneration of Rs. 3,000 each for their duty of protecting themselves. The SPO's working pattern would be supervised by respective superintendents of police of Heirok and Lilong Chajing. But the proscribed United National Liberation Front (UNLF) and Kanglei Yawol Kanna Lup (KYKL) had threatened "capital punishment" for five villagers of Heirok who had played the pivotal role for appointing the SPOs and had procured arms from the government. The outfits had ordered Heirok locals not to venture out from their village for defying their earlier warning not to join the SPO force.

There are many incidents which affect the public life of Manipur. For instance, the bomb attack at the State Assembly in

2007, the slaying of migrant workers in 2008 and killing of innocent people are some of the actions that have severely threatened the law and order situation in the State. Even though many UG cadres were apprehended from official quarters of MLAs and Ministers at Babupara in August 2007, no further action could be initiated till date due to strong pressure from political circles. All these situations bring an unbearable environment for the development of entrepreneurial activities in Manipur.

Manipur Government Planning for Developing Different Entrepreneurial Activities (Special Employment Generation Programme)

In order to uplift the unemployed rural youth in Manipur, the State Government has started the implementation of the "Special Employment Generation Programme" (SEGP) with financial assistance from the Central Government for giving employment opportunities to educated unemployed and uneducated unemployed youths during the Annual Plan 2004-05. It was informed that this is a three year programme with a provision of Rs. 30 crores for 2004-05, Rs. 70 crores for 2005-06, and Rs. 50 crores for 2006-07. The scheme is a loan scheme given at low rates of interest through the Manipur State Co-operative Bank (MSCB) for generation of employment for the youth of Manipur. The schemes implemented are based on agriculture, horticulture, fishery, veterinary, sericulture, health, transport, trading/business, etc. for the unemployed youth in the state.

Providing self-employment and employment opportunities to the youths of Manipur, both educated and uneducated, falling in the age group of 20 to 45 years is the main focus of the programme. However, the selected person should not have availed financial assistance under any other Government scheme and as such a 'No Due/No Benefit certificate' from DIC (District Industries Centre), KVIB (Khadi and Village Industries Board), MANIDCO (Manipur Industries Development Cooperation), etc. would be required to be eligible under this programme. Preferences are given to women, disabled, educated youth, married persons and those above the age of 35 years.

Considering the rural social environment, this scheme has a wide range of economic activities (like poultry, piggery, duckery, dry fish fermentation, mushroom cultivation, pineapple cultivation, ginger cultivation, cane and bamboo work, tailoring, carpentry, four wheeler repairing, T.V. and radio servicing, readymade garment, etc.) so that the beneficiaries may have a wide variety to choose a suitable scheme. This is aimed at ensuring that each beneficiary is assisted with a scheme and scale of finance which is best suited to him/her.

For smooth implementation and transparency of the scheme, the maximum ceiling of loan admissible under the Scheme will be Rs. 5 lakhs per loanee. However, this condition does not follow in respect of purchase of truck, the upper limit of the scheme is Rs. 8 lakhs per loan. In spite of all, it is all aimed at better coverage of more unemployed persons; preference to schemes of lower cost are also given by the bank.

For identification, selection and sanction of loan, the Deputy Commissioners call for applications in the prescribed loan application form of the bank concerned from interested unemployed persons as per the sectoral allocations, district-wise and month-wise targets. The screening of all loan applications received within the stipulated period are done by the District Level Committee for the Special Employment Generation Programme. The eligibility and fulfilment of the parameters for loan are decided as per the guidelines and the check-list and recommend. Those loan applications fulfilling the various parameters of the guidelines are forwarded to the MSCB (Manipur State Co-operative Bank) and other assigned participating banks in batches. The MSCB (Manipur State Co-operative Bank) and other assigned participating banks scrutinize the technical aspects and other parameters required to be fulfilled as per banking norms of the loan applications recommended by the District Level Committee of each district and forward those loan applications which fulfil all requirements for sanction of loan to the Planning Department. Subsequently, the applications forwarded by the banks to the Planning Department are placed before the State Level Committee for SEGP constituted by the Government for this purpose. In the process, the Committee also ensures that the sectoral allocations and district targets are maintained and shall thereafter makes its recommendations. The Planning department obtains the approval of the Government on the recommendations of the State Level Committee and conveys it to the banks for sanction of loans based on technical soundness, viability, documentation, etc. The name of the trades and the number of beneficiaries are given in Table 5.4.

Table 5.4 : Number of SEGP beneficiaries and name of the trade or schemes

Sl. No.	*Name of the Trade/Scheme*	*Amount in lakh*	*No. of beneficiaries*
1.	Readymade clothes	2.00	1
2.	Iron and Steel Industries	1.50	1
3.	Beauty Parlour	0.51	1
4.	Dry fish fermentation	2.00	2
5.	Fishery	1.82	1
6.	Duckery	0.86	1
7.	Meat shop	1.25	1
8.	Piggery	1.75	2
9.	Poultry	1.51	2
10.	Grocery	1.00	3
	Total		**15**

In the SEGP (Self Employment Generation Programme), there are twenty six trades or schemes. In the study area, it is found that 49 people got the benefit of Self Employment Generation Programme for different trades like readymade business, iron and steel industries, beauty parlour, dry fish fermentation, fishery, duckery, meat shop, piggery, poultry and grocery. The beneficiaries initiated their new venture with the financial support given. For example, Mr. Tairenjao Meetei is happy to get financial support of Rs. 1.82 lakhs for initiating fishery unit of his own. He never thought of getting such financial help from the government. He applied for it casually when one of his friends informed him about the information of SEGP given in the local newspaper. He struggled a lot for getting the form for applying SEGP among the big crowd from the Directorate of Commissioner's Office at Thoubal. He spent two days to get the form and also spent one and a half week to get all the documents from different departments for applying it. Sometimes, his wife misunderstood him as she did not know the problem of communicating the government official for issuing a small document also. But it is like "Dream comes true" for him. Later he got the loan from the government and his plan for initiating new venture in fishery came true because of the financial help given to him by the government. He mentioned that most rural people like him are suffering from non-availability of financial assistance as the number of people who need such financial assistance are also high.

Feedback on Entrepreneurship Development Programme in Manipur

The entrepreneurship development programme aims at giving self-employment which takes care not only of the progress in economic life of the rural people but also of meeting the social needs of the rural people. It has become the catalyst for the removal of poverty and seasonal unemployment.

As is well-known, the wage employment programme of NREGS at the district/block levels, with the selection of works being decided by the Zilla Parishads or local Counsellor in consultation with the other elected representatives like local MLAs, etc. are operating throughout the rural and tribal areas of Manipur while special priority is given to areas suffering from seasonal unemployment. However, it has a long way to go for the needy rural youth at Kakching and the surrounding villages as there are hundreds of needy youth who do not avail the benefits of the schemes. So, the effectiveness of such schemes depends critically on the extent to which the Government officials at Thoubal District, as concerned officers, can assume a pivotal role in implementing the various components of the programme.

For the development of entrepreneurship among the rural people, it is well-known by now that the SEGP, managed by the state government, is an important scheme for financing the rural potential entrepreneurs (i.e. youth for starting various entrepreneurial activities in Manipur).

On the other hand, Entrepreneurship Development Organisations/institutions are in a hurry to complete the programmes and do not bother much about what happens to the trainees. It is also mentioned by one of the informant that he got surprised to listen the comments given by the officer during a training session in Imphal. Sometimes, everyone blame each other for the issue and the official sometimes scolded the trainee that they come to the training centre only for availing the loan but not for developing their skills for setting up their own enterprises so they are less interested about anything like the course and the training programme, etc. Their main aim is to finish their programme as soon as possible. At the same time, doubts were also raised regarding the capabilities of the trainers. It was felt that EDPs are being used as a means to generate surplus income for the ED organizations by shortening the training programmes with the link of government official. This also minimizes their expenditures in organizing the training programme. The image of these organizations/institutions and the trainer-motivators working therein is not very different even in the eyes of bankers or officials of DICs who are engaged in the entrepreneurship development in the region. The support of officials at the local level questioned the attitude of even the head of the ED organizations. If it is a venture creation activity, there should be a long-term training programme that can motivate participants properly instead of one day/one week training programme for entrepreneurship development. In addition to these, they should also have evaluation programme. So, they are predominantly commercial in orientation. For ED organizations/institutions, what matters is saving money by cutting cost from training expenditure, without much concern for the quality of EDPs.

On the other hand, they also face the difficulty of lack of adequate skills and information on viable projects, technology, project cost, market, etc. The entrepreneurs find themselves very vulnerable and lost their interest for creation of new entrepreneurial activities and so the growth for entrepreneurship is stagnant somewhere. However, the ED organizations/institutions complained that even the best conducted EDP in Manipur is sometimes not able to produce the desired results because of the fact that the prevailing psychological environment and the hostile attitude of the support system, especially bank and the industrial development corporation is not adjusted with the socio-cultural environment of the rural life of Manipur. It is mentioned that though there are many good schemes on paper, in practice they are beyond the reach of the trainee, if they do not have a sound economic background. For instance, Mr. M. Chandrakumar Singh, 29 years old, has a daughter. He got diploma in Medical Laboratory Technician. His parents were worried that he may not get job as a permanent government employee in Manipur State. He visited the government offices for applying for loans, seeking information about the new schemes which he can apply for initiating for his venture. But the government officials were reluctant to give the information to him. Sometimes, he was very disappointed by such responses. But, he always dreamed of starting a clinic of his own for his earnings. His father is an unemployed educated person but very skillful and helpful. They have agricultural land that produce paddy with good yield every year for their consumption. They also produce potato, garlic, onion and mustard oilseeds from their field. There is no financial problem in their family.

He was too independent by nature to do any work. He always had a strong desire to do something independently. He was fortunate that his elder cousin brother was a doctor and her cousin sister was nurse. And it was his elder brother who showed Chandrakumar the tremendous scope of a diagnostic laboratory at Kakching. Chandrakumar took the proposition seriously. He arranged the capital investment from his family members and purchased some equipments on credit. Then he started his own laboratory attached with the Beda Pharmacy. There he started his network with the doctors and Babina Clinic at Imphal. During the initial stage of his establishment, Dr. Birchandra Singh extended his moral support to him. He is always service conscious. He has one more laboratory technician in his laboratory. In this short span of time, he has already established a good reputation in the area. A successful entrepreneur, M. Chandrakumar attributes his success to his father and guide to his entrepreneurial journey.

6

Socio-cultural Changes in Entrepreneurship Development

Entrepreneurship development brings changes among the rural lives at Kakching. Entrepreneurship is an important ingredient for economic development and the dynamic entrepreneurs are considered to be the agent of change in the society. In the rural and backward areas of Manipur, growth and development of industries, therefore, depends on the development of entrepreneurs with respect to the existing socio-economic and cultural environment. Due to many reasons like low achievement motivation, passivity to the environment, lack of command over resources, and lack of financial support, there is slow progress in development of entrepreneurs in the backward areas specially in the North-eastern states of India. However, a good number of various types of indigenous entrepreneurs of first generation have come up in the region especially due to the various supports from family and friends etc. Most of the first generation entrepreneurs have good educational background, better commitment and higher achievement motivation.

However, socio-cultural and technological change in rural and tribal areas of Manipur is very slow unlike the changes which are taking place in the complex urban areas. To understand the changes which are taking place in the rural and tribal areas, it requires a study of correlating diverse fields such as economy, social, cultural etc. Entrepreneurship is one of the emerging ways of earning in all the rural and urban section of India.

In developed states, economic structure is very dynamic and extremely competitive due to the rapid establishment of new firms. Some dynamic entrepreneurs manage and lead their entrepreneurial activities not only to remain in the business but to expand it for the further growth in their enterprises. With the clear vision, they look for growth for their business. They seek professional advice and also get help from external resources having professional teams. Challenging their competitors is in their entrepreneurial spirit. They rather compete their business competitors instead of avoiding them by taking or sharing risks in a way that leads to success.

In order to improve the social life among the rural people, improving economic life is very important. Economic life and social life are also very closely interlinked. In other words, entrepreneurship development is based on bringing in human capital and investment by themselves or other financial agencies. It is based on stimulating local entrepreneurial talent and subsequent growth of indigenous companies. These in turn create jobs and improve economic life to a region and community. Thus, a rural entrepreneur is someone who is prepared to stay in the rural area and contribute to the creation of local wealth and generate employment in the rural areas. For this reason, the rural entrepreneurs generally have a strong relationship with the involvement of family members and also have a relatively strong impact on the development of rural communities than urban areas.

Changing Sources of Entrepreneurship

The understanding of sources of entrepreneurship and the promotion of entrepreneurship is as important as the understanding of the concept of entrepreneurship. On the other hand, if it is considered, entrepreneurial characteristics are very necessary, and then active promotional policies and training programme can contribute to entrepreneurship development in the rural and backward regions of Manipur. Moreover, entrepreneurial skills and motivation to entrepreneurship development can be acquired through training. Some of the characters like risk taking, self-esteem, creativity and innovative behaviour can also be either enhanced through attending training and personal experience.

Entrepreneurship and entrepreneurial skills are culturally and socio-economically more conducive to some community than others. The factors that contribute to enhance entrepreneurship development are an inheritance of entrepreneurial tradition, family position, social status, educational background and the level of education, etc. Whether educational background influences potential entrepreneurs or not is a matter of debate. This popular idea of an entrepreneur is that of a totally self-made man, lacking in formal qualifications. This is of course is not in conflict with findings that entrepreneurs who are better educated are more successful than the less educated ones.

Entrepreneurial activities in rural areas are not thriving but the conclusion that entrepreneurship is not something inherently alien to rural and backward areas of Manipur. While this feeling could have some legacy/tradition due to the slower pace of changes occurring in rural areas compared to urban areas of Manipur like Imphal city. Such entrepreneurial activities help in attaining a sustainable and healthy rural economy and environment in order to ensure a high quality of life for individuals, families and communities.

Entrepreneurship Development Scenario in Rural Areas

In rural areas at Kakching, diversification of entrepreneurial activities such as blacksmithing, carpentry, weaving, piggery, poultry, grocery, bi-cycle repairing workshop, etc. takes place. Such diversification of entrepreneurial activities other than those solely related to agricultural activity, enhances the development of rural entrepreneurial activities, for example, the use of locally available human resources other than using the agricultural land. The entrepreneurial combinations of these resources are training relating to wood crafting, water reed mate making; bamboo and cane crafting, and other technical training, retailing and wholesaling of their products, servicing like motor repairing works, van repairing centre, electronic repairing (like T.V., radio, mobile, etc.). So, dynamic rural entrepreneurs can also be found. They are expanding their activities and markets and they find new markets for their products and services beyond the local boundaries.

However, behind each of the success stories of rural or household entrepreneurship, there is usually some sort of institutional support like training programme, financial institutions, etc. Besides, an individual or group entrepreneurial initiative or motivations that enable environment supports these initiatives are of utmost importance. The identification of potential entrepreneurs and generation of such a conducive environment for entrepreneurship also needs socio-economic and political stability in the region. The inputs into an entrepreneurial process, technical and capital supports, buildings, communications and transportation infrastructure, distribution channels and skilled labour are easier to find in urban areas. In urban areas, entrepreneurs usually have the option for seeking professional advice. In addition to these, they can also avail more market opportunities which are lacking among the rural entrepreneurs and so it narrows down the scope of their enterprises. Therefore, it requires not only the development of local entrepreneurial capabilities but also a coherent regional/ local strategy.

Economic Development and Entrepreneurship Development

At Kakching, the problem of economic development represents itself as an organizational one. The Kakching market also has the possibilities for significant expansion of the entrepreneurial activities. But, it lacks the mobility of its capital; and narrow network to exploit the existing resources. The economies of the entrepreneurial activities operate through personal organization with respect to its particular production and distribution of the products. Most of the entrepreneurs are at marginal level of living. They are unable to actively search and create new sources of profit. However, there is a significant progress in patterns of economic activity among the entrepreneurs who are engaged in different entrepreneurial activities like poultry, piggery, furniture work, bamboo shoot fermentation, fuelwood and charcoal business, tractor for tilling the field and rice mill for husking paddy etc.

Regarding the flow of goods and services in the study area, people look for low capital investment. Specially, the entrepreneurs who are engaged in piggery, furniture work, bamboo shoot fermentation, fuelwood and charcoal business expand their social network for supplying their raw materials in developing their entrepreneurial activities. For instance, for the bamboo shoot fermentation business, the raw materials are supplied from the remote hilly areas like Lamkang village, Khonggam village, Purum village, etc. They need to establish strong feeling of confidence and trust with the people of these villages for the regular supply of the raw materials. Since, the hilly backward areas of Manipur are affected by the insurgency; it is sometimes very difficult to mobilize among the people for such kind of entrepreneurial activities. The people of such remote areas always develop suspicion to the outsiders as an informer to the government intelligence or social motivator of the insurgents. In addition to this, some of the services like repairing of T.V., radio, tape recorders, etc. are also carried out by the entrepreneurs with the help of the neighbouring towns or from the Imphal city. Some other services like school van, jeep, tractor, telephone booth need capital investment for their expansion. There is a good cooperation among the entrepreneurs and the customers. Most of the entrepreneurs engage with such entrepreneurial activities are educated unemployed persons.

Considering all the changes, the entrepreneurs still continue with simple technology in the production of food, weaving, and construction of houses etc. The economy was predominantly based on settle agriculture. There is a widespread permanent cultivation; the lands are individually owned, and there are also facilities for minor irrigation. Weaving and spinning are widely practiced. But, most of the bamboo and wooden basket, crafts etc. are produced by the hilly people. Barter system was an important form of exchange in the hills as well as in the plains, but now currency is circulated. So, there are changes in the exchange system of Manipur.

To sum up, the rural people at Kakching are passing through a phase of economic change with the emergence of new entrepreneurial activities. The phases of economic change with the emergence of entrepreneurship are discussed as subsistence economy as part-time earning work after harvesting the crops, household business and independent business activities. The first phase of economic changes existed among the people of Kakching when their forefathers depended mostly on the agricultural activities. After their harvesting, they started spending their time in small earnings like selling fuelwood and charcoal, bamboo shoot fermentation, dry fish fermentation, etc. at their home. But, their economic life confined to the agricultural activities and the attachment towards the land was very high. Later, they developed their entrepreneurial activities encouraged by their contacts, for supplying fuelwood, charcoal, etc. regularly. Such encouragement of entrepreneurial activities generated earning for self-dependent. For instance, Mr. P. Ibotombi Singh informed that economic life of his grandfather was totally depending on the annual agricultural products from their agricultural field. Vegetable products from their kitchen garden are the only economic supplement besides their agricultural products. After harvesting of crops specially in the month of September, his father started fuelwood business at his home with the help of his close friend Mr. Koshil Maring from Komlathabi village. Sometimes, Kosil Maring also supplied charcoal along with the fuelwoods. But the business was not a regular one as it run only after their harvesting only. Once the rain started, they have devoted their time for agricultural activities. Later, when Mr. Ibotombi's father was not there at home, Ibotombi looked after the stored fuelwood. He grew his interest to develop his new venture as it gives extra income. After his father passed away, he was the only person who took care for the household business. He motivated his friends from the surrounding hilly villages to give regular supply of fuelwood, charcoal. Nowadays, he is getting supply from different villages like Karunthel, Komlathabi, Machi, Phunal, etc. There is a continuous impact of the new modern economies which is evident from the fact of the emergence of earning venture. There is a new trend on the nature and extent of the economic transformation in the present rural life of Kakching. The modern economic activities are changing the traditional rural economy. These changes may be the result of new link of rural market with the bigger city markets or urban market. This change in market linkage has introduced many innovations in the rural areas. The rural and tribal people are buying their modern luxurious articles. For example, the tribal and the rural people started using T.V., CD players for watching movies, dining tables, electric cookers, etc. As mentioned by an informant that he has bought a T.V. which he had been thinking to buy long before. He also mentioned that working in his piggery unit is very tedious work. It needs more labour. Once he enters his farm, he finds a row of works to be carried out. So, after coming back from his work, he feels to get leisure with his daughters by watching the T.V. at his home.

At the same time, the rural and tribal people also find wider market for their goods. This has encouraged tribal and rural economic activity. For instance, Mrs. Bino Devi, who is engaged in dry fish fermentation, has her name for the quality of dry fish products. Locally, dry fish is known as *Ngari*. Dry fish have different varieties which differs in their quality and the taste and the types of fish they prepare. Some of the varieties like *Utong Ngari, Phabou Ngari, Yelou Ngari, Ngakha Ngari, Thumyakpi Ngari,* are commonly available fish in the market at the study area. The moods of preparation of most of the dry fish varieties are same but it varies in the period of preservation for the dry fish. The longer the period of fermentation, the higher the price for the dry fish. In most of the cases, they keep to the maximum of six months to one year. In some varieties, they prepare it by properly washing and drying in the sun for few days, as shown in Table 6.1.

Table 6.1 : Types of Dry fish *(Ngari)* and their mode of fermentation

Sl. No.	*Types of Ngari*	*Rate per Kg (Rs.)*	*Mode of fermentation*	*Period of . fermentation*
1.	*Utong Ngari*	240-280	Washed and dried	6-12 months
2.	*Phabou Ngari*	80 -120	Washed and dried	2-3 weeks
3.	*Yelou Ngari*	130-150	Washed and dried	1-2 months
4.	*Ngakha Ngari*	70-110	Washed, dried and pounded	3-5 weeks
5.	*Thumyakpi Ngari*	70-90	Washed and dried	1-2 months

Source: Primary data from the field-work.

On the other hand, the agricultural rural people are selling potatoes, vegetables, etc. of new varieties at the market. And the artisan tribes in the neighbouring viliage are producing bamboo crafts, fruits, etc. for earning money by selling to the entrepreneurs engaged in such business. Now-a-days, the commercial banks have just started giving loans to poor people in the rural areas. This has shaken the moneylender's business and their exploitation to the rural poor.

Farm Technology and Social Transformation

It was assumed that the people of Kakching live under a great pressure and are always in search of livelihood. Their population is concentrated around the market. There was a time when the people were all dependent on the nature. They worked hard putting in enormous effort for the betterment of their life.

Among the people of Kakching, agriculture was entirely of subsistence nature. Due to the development of entrepreneurial activities, changes occurred slowly. They became aware of some of the technical knowledge of modern agricultural technologies and different ways of earning through several activities like poultry, piggery, weaving, carpentry, motor cycle workshops and services, handloom enterprises, embroidery and knitting works, grocery shops, photo and xerox service centre, brick-field, etc. They also started using fertilizers and pesticides to enhance agricultural production. Nowadays, they are gradually experiencing transformation towards its end on account of adoption of agricultural innovations. This ultimately leads to a change in the working habits and lifestyle of the people in the region. Similarly, consumption of inputs like chemical fertilizers, insecticides, pesticides etc. have started. The use of tractors has also started among the farmers. Consequently, there is surplus in foodgrains production. It indicates relationship between adoption of new technologies and socio-cultural transformation. Adoptions of new technologies are also related to the existing social environment. It is known that the use of the tractor for agricultural activities is displacing the family labour. Consequently, occupational diversification has taken place in the study village. The traditional agricultural practices are undergoing phenomenal transformation like lessening of manual agricultural labour due to the utilization of modern agricultural implements, implementation of herbicides, etc. And the urban culture is emerging in the rural areas of Manipur like attending training programmes given by the local voluntary organizations like Advance Voluntary Organisation, Sena Athletic Clubs, Juvenile Club, Ideal Youth Club, etc. Through these local voluntary organizations, the government official provides fertilizer, pesticide, etc. during the agricultural season. However, the nature of adoption of agricultural technology is mainly confined to the use of tractors, sugarcane crushing machines, water pump, and sprayers for insecticide and pesticides for performing agricultural operations. Most importantly, there is also the mechanization in some of the entrepreneurial activities like carpentry work, brick-field work, ironsmith, goldsmith, etc. This brings changes in their production as well as the working habit among the workers who are engaged in different kinds of entrepreneurial activities in the area.

Rural Entrepreneurship and Technological Advancement

Entrepreneurship development needs technological development in order to advance their entrepreneurial activities. It is very necessary for the technologically backward and indigenous technology capabilities to master new technologies. It is, therefore, not surprising that during the past few decades a major effort has been made by the entrepreneurs for the technological transformation and mechanization of their traditional system in the process of their entrepreneurship development. However, the technological transformation in entrepreneurial activities, use of mechanical power in rural areas at Kakching is sometimes beyond the scope as they need huge investment of capital.

Technological progress enhances economic and social transformation of the entrepreneurship development. It contributes to the growth of entrepreneurs' per capita output, to shift output and employment out of traditional working processes, and to capital and skill formation. Most importantly, mechanization of working implements can be mentioned as one of the most advancement in the process of entrepreneurship development in the rural areas of Manipur. Before, it was localized to some of certain mainstream states of India only. It is because of the personal interest of the entrepreneurs as well as the interference of the Manipur State Government while developing entrepreneurship in the region. It does not bring any appreciable benefits among the entrepreneurs in the rural areas of Kakching.

The rural entrepreneurs also face the challenge of revitalizing their indigenous technologies and indigenous technologies must become development-oriented with a thrust towards technologies that satisfies basic needs. This will give self-satisfaction that leads towards self-reliance based on social participation among the entrepreneurs in the rural areas. This will also minimize the burden of commercialization of technologies in the remote areas of Manipur. The problem in commercialization in rural technologies is that the major percentage of the population living below the poverty line does not have the purchasing capacity to meet its demands. On the other hand, the state government agencies and the financial institutions in Manipur try to transform rural technologies of the entrepreneurs who are engaged in different entrepreneurial activities. Such agencies gave a scope of getting the emerging technological know-how among the entrepreneurs. Even in the small state like Manipur, there is technological gap between urban entrepreneurs and rural entrepreneurs.

Occupational Mobility and Social Change

Tribal and rural communities in Manipur are undergoing changes under the impact of industrialization, modernization, urbanization, cultural contact, modern education, development programme and other forces. As informed by the Oja Naran Singh and Oja N. Ibotombi Singh, the people of Kakching have their own traditional or indigenous religion, i.e. Sanamahi Cult. They perform traditional rituals for different purposes like worship to the Emoinu Lairembi, Nongpok Ningthou, Panthoibi, etc. Due to the influence of Hindu religion, they also have adopted the various ritual practices like Laxmi puja, Durga puja, etc. Both the religious practices are performed by many of the people in the study area. Though there is also relatively slow adaptive nature of the rural people in Manipur, the different forces of changes are operating for the development of entrepreneurial activities. This leads to change in occupational and ritual pattern and the value system among the people of Manipur. For instance, Mr. Sanatomba Singh worships both the *Laxmi* (the Hindu Goddess) and the *Emoinu* (the Meetei Goddess) at his cycle workshop. He plays *bhajan* on his tape recorder at every morning and also burns incense stick. He mentions that this prayer gives him mental satisfaction and enhance his spirit and devotion to his work. So, it also jointly creates a conducive environment to the development of entrepreneurs among the young generation of rural Manipur. Such changes in traditional occupation and economic life are interlinked in all aspects of society. Therefore, a change in traditional occupational structure due to entrepreneurship development becomes a vital force to bring about changes in the society.

Agricultural labour to Non-agricultural labour

Rural populations who traditionally come from the agriculturist type have adopted a new economic life of casual worker or labourer and whatever wages they get is their income. They work in agricultural or non-agricultural work on a casual basis. They may get employment on daily basis. During the agricultural season, the agricultural work is mostly available in the locality itself within a radius of a few kilometres. But such labour work has limited period that covers only two months during the sowing season and two months during the harvesting season. The non-agricultural work potentialities are situated in the local as well as at distant places in different districts.

The non-agricultural labourers are mostly engaged in different small industrial works. It is believed that the non-agricultural labour type is the result of increase in the pressure on land due to population growth and opening of different small entrepreneurial activities in the rural areas. As a result of these factors, people from the neighbouring villages like Pallel, Khongjom, Irengband, etc. come to work as labourers at Kakching. They sometimes come in group to the working place, which include male and females, specially in the brick farms. With the opening of such industrial activities, they have found alternative employment in the entrepreneurial activities. Most of the villagers working in these units are unskilled labourers. The villagers are found to be taking the work either as subsidiary occupation or as main occupation. The occupational changes are also very obvious among the artisans. So there is gradual disappearance of village crafts, due to the existence of such activities. Along with the occupational changes there is a considerable increase in income and expenditure patterns of the families working in these units. The change in the material culture has been considerable. The young women have changed their mode of dress and also changes in their food habits, lifestyles, etc. On the other hand, the traditional recreational practice have started degenerating as the workers become mentally and physically fatigued due to these new type of jobs. They are becoming more money oriented to meet their immediate needs.

The Changing Market Exchange

From the entrepreneurial activities, different new products have to be developed. The products, goods and services, have to be sold for sustaining their entrepreneurial activities. Crucial for this are prices and quality of their products. In this development process of entrepreneurial activities, quality is given priority among most of the entrepreneurs. And the enterprise has to develop from marketing in the locality as well as the surrounding villages. The basis has to be quality development of their product and services. In order to emphasis this aspect of development and to make clear that development does not automatically and only mean increased production. But, the study of marketing of their products and exchange of services among the entrepreneurs was associated with life activities of the people in and around the study village. The rural people in Manipur, irrespective of Meetei, Hindu-Meetei, tribals, etc, worship many deities and deified ancestors in a number of ceremonies. Every state of cultivation or other economic pursuits are started after performing a rite.

However, changing marketing strategy and exchange system among the entrepreneurs were studied against their background of living in order to know their habits concerning to sale, purchase and consumption of the rural people. The role of middlemen in the rural areas, while supplying the products or raw materials in Imphal city especially to the Non-Manipuri entrepreneurs or businessmen, is also a new phenomenon of market exchange.

By its nature, the rural backward economy affords restricted scope for exchange transaction. The basic needs of the people are comparatively less and also limited in variety. The rural people produce most of their foodgrains, vegetables, firewood, fruit, fish, etc. Most of them consume locally produced vegetable from their own kitchen gardens. The kitchen garden itself is the result of personal labour. Likewise, people who are engaged in small entrepreneurial activities like fish-farming, piggery, poultry, duckery, dry-fish fermentation, bamboo-shoot fermentation, etc are also depending on the personal labour. In some cases, they use paid labourers for such purposes.

During the 1920s, the self-sufficient character of the rural economy at Kakching was more prevalent. It also restricts the scope of exchange transaction in their daily life. These have also reduced the volume of buying and selling goods. In those periods, whenever, they need anything, they took their grains in bullock-cart or in small boats to take it to the Imphal (urban areas) for the exchange. The limited use of money as medium of exchange activities leads to barter economy. Moreover, Kakching people were habitated in clusters on inaccessible hill slopes at Wairi Thingel near Pallel of Chandel District and later at Keraching, where transport involves heavy cost. They adopted stable cultivation and used improved method of agriculture like using HYV crops, irrigation by water pump, etc. This change has necessitated more exchange transaction.

The rural people at Kakching want more iron implements, HYV seeds, mechanized tractors for tilling field, fertilizers, etc. Besides these, they require more cash for payment of purchase of certain other goods. This has shaken the very foundation of self-contained Kakching economy. The Kakching people are starting different entrepreneurial activities besides continuing their traditional agricultural activities. The Kakching Keithel (market) grew well and the people in and around the village like Maring, Khoibu, Anal, Mantak, etc. are now seen depending on the Kakching Market.

The growing contact with the outside village and the neighbouring town has created a new outlook and generated new wants for starting different entrepreneurial activities which are successfully running there. There is now a growing demand for material like metal utensils, dresses, furniture, fertilizers, house building material, iron implements, household consumption goods, etc. As a result, the buying habits and activities among the people have increased in recent time. For instance, Mr. Thoiba Singh has good time of selling his furniture products specially during March-April (Phairen-Lamta) months. It is because these months are considered as an auspicious month for marriage, building houses, etc. So, people from different villages come and order for their furniture products.

When the harvest of potatos and mustard oilseeds are done, the middlemen from the locality gather the products and send it to Imphal city at low rates especially to the non-Manipuri businessmen who can invest more amount during harvesting. Non-Manipuri businessmen sell it again at double the price during the off-season. The middle men are also exploiting the rural people prominently in the local market. The local middle men catch them before reaching the market and try to negotiate in lower price of their goods. Sometimes, these middle men take advantage of the villager's inability in calculating the amount of their goods. Such middlemen group fix the price without the consent of the villagers who produce their goods for selling in the market. The tribal and rural people who toil the years round for the production of their foodgrains, bamboo-crafts, etc. do not get the benefit of selling them due to their inability to access the current fair price. Besides, the local moneylenders also lend money to the village people as they know the timing of the needy hours of the villagers who come to the market for buying their agricultural needs. They offer small loans to them for their agricultural activities and collect with interest year after year. During the agricultural season, mostly the women visit the market and men keep themselves engaged in the agricultural field.

In fact, the Kakching *Keithel* (market) is at a distance of only 44 km from Imphal town. It is also the central place approaching to a large number of villages in the Kakching sub-division under Thoubal District of Manipur. At Kakching Keithel, men and women of all age groups come freely. Traders from Imphal bring readymade dress and clothes which are either from Guwahati or Moreh. People from Kakching also started business activities like stationery shops, grocery shops, cinema halls, cycle workshops, etc. The local businessmen know the necessities and demand of the rural people. Sometimes, when there is road blockade, public strike, or during festivals, etc., they charge higher price for the commodities which are badly required by the local people. Moreover, rainy season is the most crucial season for villagers when the rural entrepreneurs are totally depending on the local market. During these months, the rural people are very busy in agricultural work and also they cannot go often to the Imphal market for the fair price of their needs.

Role of market in social relationship

Kakching as the centre have each fixed separate weekly market places locally known as *Hao-Keithel*. In the rural areas, weekly markets play an important role in the life of the people. The tribal people too come with their produce. One can easily see in the early morning about the importance of the market as various activities are taking place in the morning. Regular bazaar jeeps ply from a central place to different neighbouring villages. This rural market brings together people from different ethnic groups for not only economic but also secular and religious activities in the region. Tribesmen and villagers from the region meet there to transact their business activities. The mode of economic transaction is barter for native goods, i.e. produced in the region, like foodgrains, local hand-woven clothes, baskets, etc. and cash for the non-native goods produced in the urban region or outside the region, viz., salt, readymade clothes, cosmetics, soaps, etc.

On the other hand, the impact of rural markets on their traditional life too has shown an attitude of accepting innovation. The market is the most powerful channel of communication among the rural areas. Economy has percolated through the market. And also the market has obtained a place in the social organization of the rural people. This proves, for the best place of meeting. Any announcement of community interest may be broadcast here and it will get relayed all-over the area immediately.

Entrepreneurship Development and Social Organization

The Meetei are organized into seven clans, locally termed as *Salai*. Each is bounded by the recognition of mythical ancestors and close blood relationship called *Yek,* i.e. Sub-clan. So the Salai are exogamous units which provide a regulation of marriage between different clan. These clans are *Mangang* or *Ningthouja, Luwang, Khuman, Angom, Moirnang, Sarang Leishangthem* and *Khaba-Nganba. Ningthouja* clan has the largest population which is followed by *Khuman* and *Moirang* clan. There is another social group locally called *Bamon* (the Hindu Brahmin). They do not belong to the native origination. They are Hindu priests who served the people during rituals, festivals, marriages, etc.

Each clan comprises a number of kin-groups locally called *Yumnak.* And they have very close relationship within the members of each such *Yumnak.* It is a collection of patrilineally related household, be they living together at the same place or not. They also recognize a closer relationship called *Sagei* within the *Yumnak.* Both *Yumnak* and *Sagei* recognize originating ancestors. But the ancestor of the latter is more immediate and less depth. Again, a *Yumnak* has a name where a *Sagei* does not have separate name and only refers to the name of the *Yumnak* to which he belongs. A

Sagei has ritual, social, economic and political functions. But a *Yumnak* has only social function of exogamy

In addition, the local group at Kakching is a distinct social unit as per their household location (not according to their blood relationship). It comprises a number of families, living in a common *Leikai* (locality) functions for their common welfare. Again, these local groups grew to be a bigger unit than the family itself. The people of the local group are helping hands for one another. Among the people at Kakching serves as an economic, social and religious unit and on all occasions the whole family members are bound by a common link. There is a great degree of economic and social co-operation within the people at Kakching.

Both the Hindu and Meetei of the study area characterize similar feature of social system. They are patrilineal and patrilocal group. With respect to their economic, political and ritual life, they exhibit almost similar characteristics. The only difference is to be found in their ritual practices. Among the rural people of Kakching, the head of the household took major decisions related to economy, political and religious matters. This way, the formation of family organization among the people follows. At the same time, an individual, when sons grow into adulthood, and get married they may continue to live in the same group. They continue to do the same things as their father. They may be living in the same house but in separate rooms or in newly constructed house close to the original one, i.e. they are dependent on the father in all respects even though they have separate residence. This is one phase of changing the family organization among the entrepreneurs. By establishing a separate independent residence, the married son makes their own living and eat their food prepared separately from their parents but do other things jointly with their parents. With respect to residence or food they are independent; in other respects (land or business) they are still dependent on the parent.

In the next phase, the married sons go independently by father's agricultural land, i.e. they cultivate the part of the land and live independently. But the religious services are still in the hand of their father and many of their major household decisions are taken by their father. In the final stage, father's property (land and other) are divided formally among the brothers. This may happen during or after their father's lifetime. All brothers possess their own residence in the same locality, have independent food, ownership of land and carry religious activities in their own way. In certain cases, the married sons go into directly separated/divided their kitchen after their marriage, but the ritual service may or may not be in the hands of their father. So, extended family is playing a major role among the entrepreneurs at Kakching.

Beyond the family groups, the entrepreneurs are organized in terms of clan and lineage. They organize themselves during their ritual offering for their clan. They offer collectively to their ancestral festivals too. It is mentioned that entrepreneurs from Moirang clan namely Mr. Koireng Meetei, Mr. Lukhoi Singh, Mr. Kokngang Meetei, Mr. Chandrakumar Singh have organized the yearly ritual *puja,* i.e. Apokpa Khurumba. They contributed Rs. 5000 each and handed over to the temple keeper for financing the ritual *puja.* Such close interactions among the entrepreneurs of the same clans give a platform to share and extend their sense of brotherhood. The most powerful function of a clan is that it regulates trust among themselves for their entrepreneurial activities. And the most powerful function of a clan is that it regulates marriage system. A clan is always exogamous, i.e. all the marriages must be contracted outside the clan. Members of a clan look back to a common past, claim particular area as a place of their origin. Social control beyond the domestic household is exercised by the clan and lineage. Ritualistic activities are organized around clan and lineage.

Kindred relationship among the entrepreneurs

Kinship is a dominant feature of rural life of Kakching. Because of residential distance and dispersal of members, it is not possible to maintain a closer lineage affiliation as before. When relatives are living at a closer distance within or outside Kakching, they are invited to participate in their household rituals or festivals. The relatives may even be called upon to settle the internal conflicts between families. With due course of time, neighbour are now taking over customary role of kinsmen. In fact, at the time of emergency helps, neighbours are the persons who extended aid to the seeking family. This circle of friendship has expanded due to their expansion in their entrepreneurial or economic activities. They have also organized voluntary organizations like Keithel Social Welfare Association, Eco-park Association, etc. Such organizations enhance the spirit of solidarity and oneness among the entrepreneurs in rural areas at Kakching.

Entrepreneurship Development and Family Structure

The institution of family has always been considered as an important institution among the rural lives of Manipur. There are different features like composition and structure, major forms and intercultural variations, social functions, relationship to other social structure and the manner of its response to changes in the larger society. Family is considered to be a dependent factor, an institution which responds and adjusts to change in other parts of society with the change of time.

The relationship between entrepreneurship and family and other factors like education, religion etc. have a role in enhancing individual's participation in the occupational and hierarchical system of a society. Among the people of Kakching, the head of the family is the authority. They are patriarchal in nature. The inheritance of property (i.e. from father to their sons) by all sons equally was the system. The brothers in the family have equal share and the younger sons are encouraged to stay with their old parents and so they become equally competitive for earning their livelihood after their marriage. It encourages enterprise and individual initiative. Apart from these, the family is considered as an important factor for influencing individuals and social attitudes to remove the obstacles in the development of entrepreneurship.

The process of changes in the family also responds to forces of modernization. The study at Kakching reveals that family system in the rural area is not only undergoing changes due to the pressure of economic forces but also because of social mobility and urbanization. Among the entrepreneurial families, the nature of authority has also undergone changes in favour of younger generation who have the light of education and the good network of market information etc. The parents come to know the wisdom of the young generations in decision making roles in the family. It is also observed that the family culture and the value of sharing and sacrifice have strengthened the cooperative value of the entrepreneurial systems. The cooperative working has some advantage in the entrepreneurial activities as one cannot always look for the specific activities. If there is no cooperation among the family members, it leads to the dysfunction in the enterprises.

Family and entrepreneurship development have sometimes been treated as naturally separate institutions. But the present study reveals that they are inextricably intertwined and one is affecting the other. Changes in family composition and in the roles and relations of family members have produced a new environment among the entrepreneurs in the rural areas of Manipur that they are growing sometimes smaller and losing many of their previous role relationships within the family. Such transformations in the institution of family have implications for the emergence of new business opportunities. And it also helps in resource mobilization process by expanding the entrepreneurial horizon among the rural people.

This change in family composition leads to the change in the roles of women and children, sometimes extending strong bonds with their extended families that have the same kind of entrepreneurial activities. It emphasizes on how the characteristics of entrepreneur's family system, i.e. transitions, resources, norm, attitudes and values etc. can influence the process involved in venture creation, i.e. opportunity recognition, the decision making, resource mobilization, and the implementation of founding strategies etc.

In the rural areas, the entrepreneurs are not the sole decision-makers, but rather, are concerned in their network of social relations. Thus, individuals do not decide to start a business alone, instead they consult their family and relatives. As per their belief, they look for the "Good Fortune Day", i.e. the inauguration day, to their local priest. According to the decision given by the local priest, they organize small rituals on the inauguration day. Every relative of the family is invited for ritual to give blessing to the newly inaugurated enterprises. They offer sweets to the *Ema Emoinu* (the local Deity of Wealth), *Keithel Lairembi* (Deity of Market) for their blessings to bring them good luck. Thus, the family members also take initiatives while developing their entrepreneurial activities. They often visit them and discuss the progress of their work.

Among the rural entrepreneurs, the kinship relationship and communities' ties enhances the process of developing groundwork for new ventures. More importantly, family represents a very crucial element in creation of potential entrepreneurs in rural life of Manipur. So, family plays an important role in the mobilization of financial resources and venture creation and deserves greater consideration in the entrepreneurship development.

The study provides the importance of family members as a supply of human resource. So, among the entrepreneurs in the study area, it is found that although family members may not represent a direct source of funding or financial support but they are often play important sources for establishing indirect source by using their social network of financial support. Hence, the family ties sometimes part of the resource mobilization process in entrepreneurship development among the rural people of Manipur. In some cases, parent often develop solution to the problem associated with their enterprises.

One might expect the growing number of employed women especially in sericulture work, embroidery, tailoring and wool knitting, brick farms etc. and their increasing contribution to household income, to lead to more sharing of task with their husband. So, women who work full-time in their enterprise have to do less housework. Thus, the number of hours per week or days that women spend doing household work decreases as they start spending their time in their entrepreneurial work. Such situation brings rotation of work schedules in the family. The presence of young children among the entrepreneurial families increases the likelihood of a split-shift arrangement among spouse for baby day care. They allocate their works within their family members. Such allocation of work lessens their workloads and also helps in sharing the burden of their work. For instance, Mr. Rameshwor has shared his work with his wife (Memcha Devi) in their piggery unit. She goes daily when her husband comes back for lunch and look after the piggery unit. She also helps in communicating with the supplier of rice husk which is the main feeding for pigs. These changes in women's role have certainly spurred the growth of several entrepreneurial activities, and have created opportunities for organization within them to develop new products and services. In addition, due to the increase in work pressure to the entrepreneurs, there is also a need of help from their extended kinship which cuts across household boundaries.

Entrepreneurship Development and Changing Marriage Preferences

About a decade ago, people of the rural areas considered those people as of socially less values who were engaged with some entrepreneurial activities because they do not have government jobs. They have social stigma that they are unable to get government job and they are running such pity business. So, the villagers are not willing to give their daughters to those men who are engaged in such entrepreneurial activities. Instead, they want to give their daughters to those persons who got job in the army, constables, peon, clerk, teacher, etc. who have permanent government jobs. And also, rural people considered business as a last option for earning their livelihood as they cannot predict their profit.

In due course of time, development of entrepreneurship has given positive impact that they can sustain their life through proper utilization of the available market facilities. People came to know that the local entrepreneurs can also lead a good life. For instance, some entrepreneurs like Mr. Y. Satya Singh of Yambem Furniture, Mr. Sanatomba Singh of Cycle Workshop, Mrs. M. Muktamani

Devi of Mukta Shoes, etc. got reputation at their locality. Such dynamic entrepreneurs are the eye opener among the rural people at Kakching. They start giving training to the young people to have a better life of their own. The social stigma to the local entrepreneurs of being an unemployed person is slowly eradicating. Parents are now allowing their daughters to accept marriage proposal from the local men entrepreneurs. So, the two parties (relatives of bride party and bridegroom party) negotiated easily even if they eloped against the will of their parents.

Social Networks

Among the Manipuris, there was always diversity in social relationship with different communities. They have strong community feeling and this feeling sometimes brings trust among the people in the region. Moreover, the feeling of religious purity and pollution among the Hindu-Meeteis were also very strong. Few decades ago, the tribal and rural backward people were never allowed to enter the houses of Meeteis or Hindus of Imphal City. The Hindu or Meeteis considered tribal people as dirty and polluted people. Tribal people were not allowed to marry a Hindu or a Meeteis from the plain areas. This is due to the reason that the hilly people were economically backward as compared to the plain people. And also the food habits of the hill people are very different as they are more habituated with the non-vegetable foods. These make a hierarchy among the people of Manipur in the name of tribal and non-tribal. Among the people, it was perceived that the tribal are those who are staying in the hills following a different religion other than Hinduism or Meeteism. However, the hierarchy among the tribal and non-tribal is vanishing. For instance, Mr. Ibotombi Singh, who is engaged in firewood and charcoal business, has good relationship with the hilly people from Chandel, Komlathabi, etc. He visits many villages as he has to travel for the supply of firewood from the hilly villages. He mentions that most of the tribal villages helped him when he was in trouble during the rainy season especially due to the unavailability of shelter in the remote hilly areas. Hilly friends cook food and also give shelter in their house. He also helps the hilly people during their visit for medical treatment at hospitals, admission of their children to the valley schools, etc. Due to the increased social interactions, tribal and non-tribal intermarriages are taking place. They are becoming more free in involving in any social gathering. They start inviting each other in any ceremonies of the family. Tribal people also invite their friends from the neighbouring town to participate during the Christmas and the Hindu or Meeteis are also inviting their tribal friends to participate in special festivals, i.e. Holi, *Ningol Chakkouba, Cheiraoba* festivals etc. So, these days, people of different ethnic groups co-operate each other.

Religion and Entrepreneurship

Among the people of Kakching, it is difficult to separate festivals from religion. During the festivals, different systems of supernatural belief and practices are performed. For example, during the *Laiharaoba* (forest god festival), Mr. Surjit Singh offered a traditional flag locally known as *Satrang*. It is especially offered to god for prosperity and good health. They also believe that such offering to god avoids evil eyes to them. In addition to these, he also offered candle light to the forest god in the hope that the candle light burns out all their ill-fate in their future life. There are similarities in the mode of religious practices/offerings among the Hindu-Meetei or Meetei cult followers. But they perform different rituals or *pujas* for the various gods and goddesses. Meetei people believed *Shidaba Mapu* as the supreme deity of them. He is the creator of the Universe and Sun is considered the visible symbol of strength and moon as the symbol for peaceful life. They offer water and flowers in the morning to the Sun for His divine blessings of strength and in the evening, they offer incense smoke to the Moon to give a peaceful life. Meetei believed that after death, the soul of a deceased person enter into their community or family of the ancestor's spirit. This happens on a particular day (*Apokpa Khurumba*) when they offer feast to their ancestor. And also, the ancestor spirits are usually remembered when one is seriously ill, misfortune in their activities. Offerings are made to them by their relatives during every feast or festivals. In addition to this, there are some deities who assume to control the prosperity in life viz. *Emoinu, Phouoibi, Keithel Lairembi*, etc. They are all female deities and are believed to bring success in wealth creation, business, marketing, etc. *Keithel Lairembi* is associated as the Goddess of Market who gives good fortune to the people who does business at market. So, most of the entrepreneurs offer some sweets locally called *Kabok* to *Keithel Lairembi* for her blessings to make good fortune for the day in their entrepreneurial activities. They also conduct *pujas* and offer *Kabok* to *Sanamahi Lainingthou* at the evening after returning from their entrepreneurial units. Later, the offerings are distributed to their family members. Such offering to *Sanamahi Lainingthou* are not allowed to bring out of their house as it is considered only for the household members.

Household God, i.e. *Sanamahi Lainingthou* constitutes household spirit to which sacrifice or offerings one made on behalf of each individual household. Among the Meetei, household spirits are worshipped by the head of the family in a particular place of the house, known as *Sanamahi Kachin*, a place at the south-west corner of the house. They offer *puja* to *Sanamahi Lainingthou* for the well-being and long life. They also offer prayers to the *Jatra Jumbi* (Main post of the house) for the mysterious power to defend themselves from other persons who will do harm to them. Besides this, many people adopted Hindu religious festivals like Holi festival, Diwali festival, etc. During the festivals, the Hindu-Meetei offer vegetables and sweets to the Hindu Temples in their locality. In addition to this, they also play *Laishon* (prayers) in their Tape recorders in every morning and evening at their working place for their spiritual satisfactions.

Adoption of Traditional Ritual Practice in Entrepreneurial Activities

In rural areas of Manipur, the people have their traditional mindset believing on 'begetting good fortune for good deeds'. They work hard and also have the emotional attachment towards whatsoever they do in their daily lives. Every morning, most of the businessmen perform *puja* and clean their *Lai Khurumpham* or *Laimang* (a place kept reserved in front of the Traditional God and Goddess) which they keep in their houses. They offer flowers or water while praying for prosperity and good health. Symbolically, water represents peace of mind and the origin of all life, whereas flowers represent the ingredients of life like prosperity, luck, etc. In certain cases, people who have nothing can offer water only which is also considered as most auspicious and meaningful. In certain cases, some of the people offer *Tinthou* (a type of wild grass which is considered to be a medicinal plant) or *Langthrei* (a type of herbs which is considered to have a medicinal value as well as religious value). In every special rituals performance or practice among the Meeteis, *Tingthou* and *Langthrei* are the most important ingredients. If these two are not available at different seasons, Meetei people keep some branches or roots of it, as a symbolic representation of the two. The Meetei people consider *Langthrei* as an auspicious flower which is to be offered to Meetei Gods and Goddesses. However, indigenous Meetei people consider *Tulsi* (a plant which is considered very auspicious by the Hindus) as religiously less important than *Langthrei*, even sometimes ignored to bring to some of the holy places of Meeteis. It is due to the religious egocentrism among the Hindus and Meeteis. But most of the people who follow both the religion have considered these plants as auspicious. They put some leaves of it to water and use it for the ritual purification. Nowadays, many people follow both the religions and sometimes very difficult to find out who belongs to which kind of religion (Like Hindu or Meeteism). Moreover, both Hindus and Meeteis differ only in their beliefs. For people who belong to Christianity, food habits, dressing pattern, etc. are quite different from those of Meeteis and Hindus. Christians claim that the Manipuri Hindus or Meeteis are more rigid in their religious practices and they never allow other religious groups to take part in their ceremonies.

For ritual occasions of the Manipuris at rural areas, the cooperation of several functionaries like *Maiba/Maibi*, *Panji* (astrologers), *Arangpham* (Arrangers), etc. are necessary. Formerly, within the community, the head of the particular family officiated as priest, locally known as "*Piba*". His service is hereditary. They also perform *puja* for the inauguration of any entrepreneurial activities or stone laying (founding) ceremony (locally termed as *Jatra Hunba* in Manipuri). They also perform ritual purification if any robbery or bad accident had happened inside their business unit. Such ritual practices highlight the importance of religious value among the people/entrepreneurs at rural areas of Kakching. They have strong belief of Hindu philosophy on *Dharma* and *Karma*, etc. It is mentioned that they strongly follow the principle like "Good works favour good fortune". In the annual village god festivals, the entrepreneurs offer goods, money, fruits so as to fulfil their mental and spiritual desires. These strengthen the community solidarity against the divisive tendency between the individuals either in business or political realms or religious life.

At the same time, the rural people expect that every man to be self-sufficient. And he has to look after his family. The ritual manifestations of this nurturing of the acquisitive or earning tendency is expressed in the community norm that the expenses for marriage of their sons and daughter, the death ceremony of a male person and his wife should be met as far as possible by the earnings of the dead person that he/she has left behind. Every old person tries to keep something in the form of agricultural land and gold ornaments or cash which will cover expenditure for his last rites. The community life encourages individual enterprise in a struggle to get rich.

The community life also tends to value many community affairs in monetary terms. High prestige is attached to wealth and strong moral life. In the Hindu temple festivals or Forest God Festivals, one attains prestige by contributing most. It is publicly announced during the festivals. It also encourages others to donate for the welfare of the society. The wealthy contribute money to become *Phamnaiba* (Guest of the Day). Sometimes, this is specially given to the Local MLA or Ministers or High official when they visit the village during the festivals. During the Holi festival, they collect donation from the entrepreneurs for the construction of village road or Community Hall, Temple, etc.

Role of Religious Functionaries

Among the Meeteis or Hindu-Meeteis, the head of the family or lineage is called *Piba*. He is responsible for the propitiation of the spirits or deities of the family or lineage respectively. At the village level, *Maiba* or *Maibi* (Medicine men or women) along with the oldest man from the village are responsible for propitiating village deities and spirits.

Village God is served by *Laishangba* assisted in his work by *Maiba* (traditional priest) and *Maibi* (traditional priestess) and few other elder people called *Phamnaiba*. *Laishangba* is hereditary who serves the village God. The *Maiba* and *Maibi* have the power to predict future with their oracle power locally known as *Laipao*. At the time of prediction in the village God festivals by *Maibi*, the temple courtyard and the veranda is crowded by the villagers. Men sit outside, while women sit inside the courtyard and veranda. The *Maibi*'s head is covered with a thin veil. She sits in front of the deity and rings the brass bell in her left hand, chanting all the while in the archaic Meetei language. Her body shakes in frenzied motion; her voice choked with occasional loss of breath. Some men will take notes of *Maibi*'s oracle. The *Maibi* predicted the events of the coming years of communities, families, and individuals without pointing specifically to anyone. After about fifteen minutes, a *Maiba* sprinkles some water with *Tairen* leaves over the *Maibi* and her shaking began to lessen in its intensity. The *Maiba* who stands behind *the Maibi*, places his hands over, and presses the navel of the *Maibi*. He murmurs some *mantra* to the *Maibi* and the shaking of the body stops.

The *Maibi*'s oracle is important to the entrepreneurs to any expedition, and in period of crisis, they consult a *Maibi* to seek advice, addressing her as *Ima* (mother). A *Maibi* is responsible for performing propitiatory rites for the inauguration of entrepreneurial activities. They perform *puja* and chanting *mantra* to avoid evil eyes in their activities. It is believed that the successful performance of such *pujas* often led to speedy rise in their entrepreneurial activities.

Festivals and Entrepreneurship Development

The festivals among the people of Kakching link with the people's social and economic life. Any event like *Lai-haraoba* (Forest God festival), *Heikru Heitongba* or *Heyang tanaba* (Traditional boat race), etc. during the lifecycle process takes an important celebration leading to villagers' participation. During the festivals, entrepreneurs also participate and pray for the betterment of their business activities. They often donate money for the celebration of village God. On the other hand, some ritual like *Apokpa Khurumba, Sagai Laiharaoba*, etc. are also organized among the families on a particular day fixed by the people or by the *Maiba/Maibis*. Certain rituals are associated with agricultural operations, prosperity of village, to avoid natural calamities, and their general well-being.

Lai Haraoba festival is celebrated in spring season (April or May). This is the period when a number of plants and trees sprout flowers and fruits. The *Laishangba* of the village informs the villagers about a particular day fixed for "*Lai Unathetpa*", i.e. symbolic representation of "avoidance of outsiders" entering into the village. He also informs the villagers about the timing for ritual offering to god. On the following day for the celebration of "*Lai Haraoba*", the celebration of "*Lai Haraoba*" begins. Actually, people believe that rituals must be performed in order to please their deities which in turn influence their course of life. Some festivals are importantly held traditional by the people. But some festivals are Hindu festivals like *Holi, Durga Puja, Saraswati Puja, Dol Jatra*, etc. In fact, *Lai Haraoba* festival is for the remembrance of their past culture. And it also highlights the traditional social relationship between the hills tribes and the valley dwellers. During the festival, they perform dance and act like how the people of valley and hills practice agriculture. It is also followed by dance which shows the symbolic exchange of fruits, rice, goods, and vegetables, iron implements between the valley and hill dwellers. It also shows the system of exchange between the communities. They still celebrate this festival with traditional value, social gathering, fun and merrymaking.

Individual Behaviour and Entrepreneurship Development

More and more individual behaviour today faces a changing environment that requires everyone to adapt. The changing nature of work habit made every entrepreneur to adjust to a multicultural environment.

Competition is changing everywhere. It is necessary for established entrepreneurs to defend themselves against both local competitors who develop new products and services and small entrepreneurial firms with innovative offerings. Successful entrepreneurs are considered to be the one that can change in response to the competition. They are very fast on their feet, capable of developing new products rapidly and getting them to market quickly. They rely on short production runs, short product cycles, and an ongoing stream of new products. In other words, they are flexible. They require an equally flexible and responsive workforce that can adapt to rapidly and even radically changing conditions. For instance, Mr. Naorem Joykumar Singh, the proprietor of "Linda Furniture Work", always looks for the trained and skilled workers. He wants to produce quality and new design of products which are in demand by the customers. He frequently visits Imphal along with his workers to see the new designed produced in Imphal. He motivates his workers to listen carefully about the comments and feedbacks given by his customers. And also, he openly discusses with his workers about the possible upgrading of their new machines for their units.

Some of the rural entrepreneurs are reluctant to approach banks because of the limited availability of guarantee, making it difficult for them to formulate and develop a viable business plan. They face a different behaviour while interacting with the bank officials. So, they often resort to raising most of the capital from their personal savings from family or friends, or sometimes both. Because of the risk of limited earnings in the start-up phase, many rural entrepreneurs find it difficult to access significant start-up capital. It is possible for them to start a business if their family has the start-up capital readily available.

The inconvenience of the rural and backward people for travelling and transportation from the rural areas, business among the rural and urban entrepreneurs limits the opportunities to acquire specific training. They also face severe competition when embarking on gaining access to the market place. In the urban areas, they are more able to organize themselves, more freely in the society and interact with their peer groups. Within the wider area of society such as administration and government agencies, rural people suffer more than urban people in maintaining and approaching the government officials. Rural people are often encouraged to stay longer when they are attending official meeting, resulting unnecessary delays in receiving responses to their queries.

86 (62.77 %) respondents concurred that one of their most daunting challenges was dealing with uneducated-labour force. Some of them could be rude, unsupportive and unwilling to accept the authority of the entrepreneur. The female entrepreneurs face such problem more. Another major gender-related challenge for women entrepreneurs was that of providing their credibility to both their suppliers and customers. The respondents agreed that the acceptance of their authority was a major problem they need to overcome against patriarchy. It was exacerbated if the female entrepreneurs worked in a non-traditional sector. They often had to deal with a situation where neither supplier nor customers took them seriously and seemed to believe that these women entrepreneurs will not be able to achieve their target. More seriously, some suppliers and customers believed that the rural entrepreneur would not be able to pay them on time to meet the required production. Therefore, rural entrepreneur had to work much harder to convince customers, suppliers and even their

employees that they were capable of running an effective and efficient enterprise. For example, Mrs Joymary Devi has been working for the past seven years in her embroidery and wool knitting unit. She took order of stitching clothes like Phanek, bed covers, pillow covers, sofa cover, mosquito net, enaphi, kamsha, etc. She put her best effort to give the quality product for satisfying her customers. She also motivates her workers to complete their works before the dateline of their order. In spite of her efforts, some customers complained of her for not maintaining the quality and timing of her products. In such cases, she promises them to pay back the money if she fails to give her product on time with the quality which she promised to give to them. In order to avoid such inconveniences, she started a small show room of her products so that customers can have of their own choice.

Changing lifestyle and food habits

The daily routine of rural people at Kakching starts when they get up around 4.30 a.m. in the morning. Morning bath is a common habit for the people who are engaged in small business activities as they are considered polluted if they do not take bath after their sleep at night. They think that if they go to their workplace without bathing, it will bring bad luck for the day. After their bath, they usually offer prayer to their household god and also to the goddess of wealth either "*Emoinu Ema*" for Meetei or "goddess *Laxmi*" for Hindu-Meetei. At the same time, they also offer water and *tulsi* leaves to the Sun god for giving strength, blessing for long life and good fortune of the day.

Due to the development of entrepreneurial activities, their life-style and food habits are also changing slowly. Generally, the rural people prepare their meals twice in a day, i.e. lunch and dinner. Very few people who are well-off take breakfast everyday. Most of them take lunch instead of breakfast in the morning. The people of Kakching prepare lunch at the morning and take it in between 7.30 a.m. to 9.30 a.m. However, as the working habits change, their food habit also changes in order to adapt with their changing lifestyle. Most of the entrepreneurs start taking breakfast as they have to reach their workplace early in the morning. They cannot wait for their morning lunch. Instead, they take some breakfast and tea at home and leave for their work. Ultimately, their lunch timing changes between 11.30 a.m. to 12.30 p.m (which is considered very late among the rural people at Kakching) as per their convenience in the work schedule of the day.

Moreover, there is also the alteration in the division of labour among the family members. In general, men look after the activities like agricultural work, business activities, attending social activities, etc. and women take care of the household activities like cooking, sending children to the school, buying vegetables from market, collecting vegetables from cottage garden (*Engkhol,* i.e. Cottage garden in Manipuri). But, some of the women whose husbands are engaging in entrepreneurial activities start taking active role to assist their husbands in their entrepreneurial units. Women are encouraged to take major role in their entrepreneurial activities while their husbands are away from their entrepreneurial unit. For instance, Mr. Yaima Singh is very happy to get help from his wife while he is away from his medical shop. As she is well educated lady, she can handle all accountant work and manage to assist the workers in selling the medicines. He mentioned that it is a great help to him as he need not necessary to worry about the monetary account while she is in their medical shop.

Changing traditional agriculture to modern agricultural farming

Commercial farming started at Loushi Pat in the 1990s by some of the pioneers who have cleared the wetland at Loushi Pat which was under the Kakching-Irengband-Tekcham areas. The wetland is surrounded by Kakching from the south, Irengband and Mairenbam from the east, Tekcham from the North. The wetland were totally untouched by the surrounding people due to its problem of floods and difficult transport facilities. By the end of 1980s, a movement came out by some of the villagers to construct a Kattcha

Road with the hope to connect Kakching Wairi to Tekcham village. Due to the lack of availability of labour and government assistance, the construction of road stopped at the middle of the Loushi Pat. Kakching Wairi Laukol Lowyai Lambi Development Committee (a voluntary Organisation) played main role in the construction of the road. The local people voluntarily came out and extended their help in the construction of road. With the coming of this new road there is a drastic change among the local cultivators/farmers in terms of their transportation, irrigation facilities, cropping pattern, etc. In short, it transformed the traditional agricultural pattern into commercial farming. People started cultivating mustard oil seed, potatoes, cabbage, chilly, onion, garlic etc. especially at the Loushi Pat area which were once abandoned by the people.

Mr. M. Tairenjao Meetei and Mr. M. Ibohal Singh were the pioneers among the agro-entrepreneurs who started modern agricultural practices for providing employment to the local wage labour. They face many problems to motivate the rural people for initiating such new venture. The villagers are very suspicious of their products regarding the taste of potatoes, mustard seeds etc. The villagers sometimes complained that the crops which they cultivate at Loushi Pat were less tasty and less nutritious. But these pioneers never stop their activities and never regretted. Mr. Tairenjao and Mr. Ibohal Singh offer descent wages to all his labour who come daily to their farm for plantation of potato, mustard oil-seeds, cabbage, pumpkin, papaya etc. The local labours are also engaged in different available works like watering of plants and vegetable, digging of pits, etc. Both the pioneers had also sacrificed their labour and money for the construction of the Loushi Lowyai Lambi (Road). They are now becoming the living legend of the Loushi Loukol agricultural transformation. Mr. M. Tairenjao Meetei organizes his activities and also encourages other neighbouring people to start cultivation of vegetable and other crops after the harvesting of rice. Nowadays, he organizes for marketing the yield by collecting from the rural people and sends them collectively to the Imphal city. He is now planning to expand his fishery farm as a part of his entrepreneurial activity. Besides these positive results, he faced many problems. There is also the risk of flood before the cultivation of potato, mustard oilseeds etc., if the monsoon season starts early in the region. This is due to the reason of poor drainage facility which cannot divert the water accumulated in the field. The rural people are now concerned about the possible solution of this problem with the help of government assistance. In addition to this, there is also always the risk of getting reasonable price for their products. They also suffer from the higher inputs cost with the rise in prices of fertilizers, labour wages, increased vulnerability to pest etc. Sometimes, instead of access to lucrative markets, they end up losing their domestic market to imported goods from Guwahati and Moreh Market. People started using tractors for tilling the fields. They are also using modern agricultural pesticides, fertilizer etc. for getting high yield. Such introduction of larger number of crops in their traditional cropping pattern gives more employment to agricultural labour round the year. On the other hand, crop diversification can be viewed as a strategy for profit maximization or risk minimization. This also encourages adoption of more new technologies in agricultural activities.

7

Summary and Conclusion

Entrepreneurship has become an important area of study and it is also considered to be a new way for creating wealth, generating employment and providing new and better goods and services. So, initiating entrepreneurship is an important aspect of changing the rural world. The values, customs and traditions that gave continuity to rural life have been undergoing change. But, such changes depend on the socio-economic and cultural factors of the rural society. With changes like globalization, deregulation, open competition and technological change which are taking place, rural society is becoming an entrepreneurial society. Ultimately, developing the spirit of entrepreneurship among the young is very important for enhancing the scope of self-employment among the rural and backward people.

Many studies highlight entrepreneurship as a quality which can be acquired by an individual and is a function of various factors like psychological, socio-cultural, economic etc. Studies conducted by Schumpeter (1961), McClelland (1961), Pareek =(1967), Nandi, (1973), Rao,*et al.* (1975), Akhauri (1977, 1978), Cantillian (1955), Lucy Mair (1984), Adam Smith (1984), Geertz (1967), Firth (1967), Barth (1960), Singer (1967), Epstein (1964), Nafziger (1975), and others suggest that these factors play a key role in the development of entrepreneurship.

Development of entrepreneurship lays foundation for new ventures, and for better life in the rural and backward areas. This results in the modernization of an underdeveloped economy. It will also provide new opportunities for earning and generate socio-economic growth in the rural and backward regions. The present study has stressed the importance of entrepreneurship for socio-economic development in rural areas, particularly the people of Kakching in Manipur. Many educated youth from Kakching take up entrepreneurial activities for generating income; at the same time, it helps them to elevate their social status in the society. Even though the job of an entrepreneur is difficult due to unavailability or inadequate availability of resources and insurgency problems; there are some improvements in the development of entrepreneurial activities in the study area.

The present study explores the dynamics of entrepreneurship development among the rural people of Kakching in Manipur. An attempt has been made through the study to map out the development and changes of entrepreneurial activities among the rural people of Kakching. It stresses on the contribution of family and kinship in developing entrepreneurial activities, significance of social networking, and cultural values in entrepreneurship development, feasibility and accessibility of the entrepreneurship developmental programmes, etc. in the study area. It also highlights the development of entrepreneurship propelled not only by economic needs or psychological inclination, but, also, by the cultural ideas like morality, values, religious spirit etc. of the rural life.

Historically, people of Kakching progressed slowly in the field of entrepreneurship development in the larger context of Manipur. The original professions of the people of Kakching were blacksmithy and cultivation from their forefather's period. Iron smelting was a popular activity of the people as iron ore of high quality was found in the eastern paddy fields of Kakching.

Literally, "*Youtsungba*" means "iron smelting" in Manipuri. It has a long history associated with the origin of the people of Kakching. The tradition of iron smelting among the people of Kakching can be traced from their myths, legends, oral traditions, religious festivals etc. The local God *Khamlangba* is associated with the discovery of iron. His search for iron in the ancient land of *Takhel* (presently called Tripura), his marriage to a *Takhel* lady, his arrival at Imphal and ultimate migration to *Kereaching* (a place near Kakching Khullen Turel Wangma) and founding of an iron smelters' colony at Kakching is meticulously written down in the ancient *Puyas* (the King Chronical of Manipur). It can be considered as the oldest of the entrepreneurial activities associated with the people of the region passing through generations after generations as part of indigenous knowledge. The technology of iron smelting which were in possession of the people of Kakching is a matter of great archaeological, historical and cultural interest. However, the history of different entrepreneurial activities in Manipur can be broadly divided into three developmental stages. Typically, it can be broadly divided and discussed as Pre-British Period, British Period and the present phase or the third phase. The first stage began with the dawn of Manipur history and lasted up to the Pre-British period, i.e. till 1891. This period can be regarded as the golden age of all the traditional entrepreneurial activities like handloom, crafts, and other household industrial activities in Manipur. The second period which can be termed as the British Period began with the defeat of Manipur in the Anglo-Manipur war in March 1891. In the initial days of British rule, Manipur handloom and handicrafts and other business activities continued to flourish. The third phase started with the extension of Indian Empire to the Manipur state and the open trade relationship with Myanmar. This led to the initiation of influx of Indian products like cotton, consumption goods, medicinal goods, fertilizer products, house building materials, etc. Such flow of raw materials/ goods in Manipur made the young generation to initiate new ventures for earning. So, it is considered as the turning point for the development of entrepreneurial activities among the youth in the area.

Nowadays, people of Kakching manage to develop a new way of life by initiating new ventures through entrepreneurship development. Utilizing the available resources, rural entrepreneurs modernized their traditional entrepreneurial activities, at the same time many of them are also involved in different entrepreneurial activities which are new to their rural environment. Although it is still in an incipient stage, these entrepreneurs are playing an important role in the growth of rural socio-economic life. By investing in their entrepreneurial activities, the entrepreneurs are not merely seizing the opportunities that could help them expand their business but also contributing significantly to promotion of development at Kakching.

Besides agriculture, different communities of Meetei at different places of Manipur were associated with various entrepreneurial activities. For instance, Meetei at Sekmai, Pheiyeng and Andro have their traditional alcohol preparation, Meetei at Thongjao have pottery, Meeteis at Moirang have fishery etc. as their traditional entrepreneurial activities. However, the Meetei of Kakching were mainly associated with the iron smelting. In addition to this, they are also engaged with handloom, wood crafting, carpentry, timber and fuelwood business, charcoal business, bamboo shoot fermentation, fishery, piggery, etc. from generation to generation.

Different mythological stories of the Meetei show that there is a strong relationship between the religious sentiments and the entrepreneurship development. It can be traced from various *pujas* and offerings performed by Meetei on different occasions in their lifetime. The entrepreneurs perform specific *pujas* and recitation with strong religious sentiments according to their own religion as well as Hindu belief system of Gods and Goddesses while inaugurating their newly established entrepreneurial units. They also perform daily offerings and *pujas* as per their convenience and belief of their Gods or Goddesses and offer charity in the name of their entrepreneurial unit so that the Almighty will forgive all their sins and give blessings for their growth and prosperity. Some of their traditional sentiments of Gods and Goddesses contribute to the solidarity among the entrepreneurs and their workers within their entrepreneurial activities. It also enhances the moral obligation and self-respect among the people of the region. The Meetei of Manipur worship different God and Goddesses viz. *Atiya Guru Sidaba, Pakhangba, Sanamahi, Leimaren, Phunga Lairu, Apokpa, Umanglai*, etc.

Irrespective of *Meetei* or Hindu *Meetei*, they all have belief in the Goddess *Phunga Lairu Emoinu.* They believe that ritual and *puja* offered to her will bring good fortune to their family and solidarity among themselves. While conducting rituals, the local *Maiba* or *Maibi* (religious functionary or physician) recites *mantras*. They perform rituals in different timings in consultation with the local elders and ritual performers. They perform ritual during *Engga* (May-June) for blessing of wealth, *Langban* (August-September) for blessing to beget children, *Poinu* (November-December) for blessing for their long life. These rituals morally help them in performing their duties. In addition to these, fire place of every household is considered to be a special place for the deity "*Emoinu Ahong-Achoubi*". Her divine power is considered to be very magnificent. Everyday there should be light on it and every dawn, there should be a offering of incense smoke to the deity. It is also considered to be a place where the bad spirit infected from outside can be driven out by getting the light/heat from this fire place. Nowadays, most of the Meetei entrepreneurs keep photo of *Emoinu* near their money box or at their working place so that it will bring luck and prosperity to their entrepreneurial activities.

Entrepreneurship is also considered as a broader phenomenon as an expression of entrepreneurial behaviour among people of Kakching, i.e. the establishment of a new business ventures or self-employed individuals. Starting a new business or deciding what way to take for earning, the rural people are always on alert at the possibility of changes that may improve their life. They are potential innovators or imitators of someone's success seeking a new and better way to do things.

The individuals' employment choice and their innovations are closely associated with the influence of the social capital of the existing rural life. The social networks are crucial factors in the decision making like whether to become an entrepreneur or not. So, entrepreneurship does not take place all of a sudden. It is always embedded in networking of social relationship either within the family or friends or peer groups, etc. Moreover, entrepreneurs have strong obligations and expectations among themselves that depend on their trustworthiness. They help each other in various aspects like financial assistance, exchanging information etc. in organizing their entrepreneurial activities. So, the influence of social capital in entrepreneurship development in rural and backward areas includes trust and social networks, culture, belief system etc. Entrepreneurs observe their workers, habits of drinking, playing cards, etc. In addition to these, they are very much afraid of workers who are not from Kakching because of the extortion demands of money from different insurgent groups of the region.

The traditional saving-credit system *Marup*, is another aspect among the Meetei of the Manipuri socio-economic organization. It is a typical co-operation and credit institution of mutual help in a locality at the time of death, marriage, birth and other economic problems. Besides, it also runs as a traditional moneylending system for the development of entrepreneurial activities among the rural people of Kakching. It also helps in bringing social solidarity and strengthens unity among the people. There are various types of such Marups like *Keithel* (Market) *Marup, Yumsha* (House building) *Marup, Luhongba* (Marriage) *Marup, Nahutpa* (Ear piercing) *Marup,* etc. It is a traditional system of mutual help among the people. This system generally operates either within family circles, one locality and workplace or among a group of friends. The root of traditional saving and credit systems among Manipuris are typically diverse and overlapping. Such traditional financing system facilitates or acts as giving loans among family, relatives, and friends. Loans are often made reciprocally (as per needs of the individuals) and they often do not carry interest charges and are part of broader informal insurance relationships. Some other methods of informal lending systems like Loushan, Bandop, Phoudambi, etc. are other forms of traditional lending system.

There is a wide range of different entrepreneurial activities in rural areas like Kakching. These include poultry, fishery, piggery, dry-fish fermentation, bamboo-shoot fermentation, charcoal and fuelwood business, cycle workshop, printing press, saw mills, rice mill, oil mill etc. The crucial factors contributing to this diversity are capital availability and the entrepreneurs' willingness to take risk etc. Such heterogeneity of the rural enterprises engaged by rural people reflects not only the dynamism of the indigenous economy but also the rural entrepreneurs' potential in developing different entrepreneurial activities. So, without confining their activities simply to entrepreneurial activities, they also explore ways and means of widening their areas of operation and boosting their social and economic position in rural life. To attain their goal, a number of rural entrepreneurs are diversifying and reinvesting their profits in various enterprises.

Majority of the entrepreneurs establish their unit at their young age. The late entry of entrepreneurs having a higher level of education may be on account of two different reasons. First, their entry into entrepreneurial activities might have been delayed on account of the time that they required to spend on education. Second, it might have been delayed due to their aspiration for higher opportunity which will give a stable life. In the rural areas at Kakching, education is always conceived as a means to improve one's socio-economic position in society. It also reveals the possibility that those who have a higher level of education choose entrepreneurial pursuits because they are unable to get government jobs. Moreover, the early entry into entrepreneurial activities is also affected by the capital investment required by the family of entrepreneur. It is found that the sons or daughters of the business owners or the employed personnels enter into entrepreneurial activities easily because of their strong economic support. Most of these entrepreneurs bank on their own family resources for their entrepreneurial pursuits. The main reason is said to be the willingness and ability of the parents to support the new ventures of their children. Very few young people in rural backward areas get the chance to enter government employment and so they do pester their parents for help, for self-employment. In any self-employment venture, family backing highly essential. Thus, the development of enterprises in the rural areas is also depends on the family income i.e. they are encouraged to venture out for their new hope when the families have surplus income. Naturally, the entrepreneurs who have the backing of their family members enter in large number when compared to others who have poor family financial support.

The rural people need information which is a vital input in self-employment. They can get such information initially only from other established entrepreneurs from the city or from other states. This becomes one of the basic problems of the rural youth from Kakching. Most of the entrepreneurs are hailing from agricultural background. This proves that the confidence given by the parents or friends play a vital role in inducing youth to enter into entrepreneurship. Exposure to the techniques of business is another factor which provides necessary mental courage to take up new venture. Education improves the quality of entrepreneurs and it enables them to acquire skills in personal management, financial management, market forecasting, etc. There is no doubt that education and training are two important inputs in entrepreneurship development. But education alone cannot mould a person for entrepreneurship. Though, it can be said that it is only one among the many factors, it is a very badly needed factor for efficient entrepreneurship.

Coming to the role of decision making by the entrepreneurs, they feel the strain of decision making. They take advice from their spouse, parents and friends for making a final decision in their crucial hours. All of them have risen to the occasion for playing their role in developing their enterprises and they are found to be very competent in their activities. Regarding the main requirement of entrepreneurs for developing their entrepreneurial activities in the changing environment, better access to support agencies, education, management capacity etc. are other important factors and the most difficult thing to provide for themselves. Further, collective action to deal with new products and process standards, marketing facilities are also an important factor for entrepreneurship development.

However, in rural areas of Manipur, the entrepreneurship development is certainly going up, though they face a number of challenges. Therefore, such development has implications for the entire economy and people's livelihoods. There are lots of changes in the nature of modern entrepreneurship involving tremendous amount of technological input and market orientation which require capital resources, and marketing extension. There is a need for improving product planning, provision of market information, securing market for entrepreneurs, and provision of alternative and market orientation in terms of improved marketing practices.

Due to entrepreneurship development, socio-cultural and technological changes are taking place. But such changes in the rural and tribal areas of Manipur are slow unlike the changes taking place in the complex urban areas. Even then, entrepreneurship is becoming an important ingredient for economic development and the dynamic entrepreneurs are considered to be the agent of change in the society. With the entrepreneurship development in the region, there is a progress of economic activities in the area by entrepreneurial activities. In addition to this, there are micro-electronic advancement and mechanization of working implements among various entrepreneurial activities.

There is also a change in traditional occupational structure due to entrepreneurship development and it brings various changes in the rural life at Kakching. The study also traces the occupational mobility of the first generation entrepreneurs related to their parent's and grand parent's generations. The data indicates a strong shift towards entrepreneurship from the primary and traditional occupation like agriculture. This movement is prominent in the occupational transition from entrepreneur's father's generation to entrepreneur's generation. However, the tendency to return back to primary occupations from entrepreneurship is not noticed in the intergenerational occupational mobility, and the significance of a primary occupation like agriculture was reduced progressively in the intergenerational occupational transition. The direct entry of sons into entrepreneurial activities is noticed. The entire process of occupational transition showed a remarkable degree of drop-outs from the ancestral farming occupation. Moreover, rural population who comes from the agriculturist or artisan type have adopted an economic life of casual worker or labourer and whatever wages that they get as their income. They work in agricultural or non-agricultural work on a casual basis. Nowadays, the non-agricultural labourers are mostly engaged in different small industrial works. It is believed that the increased non-agricultural labour type is the result of increased pressure on land due to population growth and opening of different small entrepreneurial activities in the rural areas. As a result of these factors, people from the neighbouring villages like Khongjom, Wangjing, Keirak, etc. come to work as labourers. They sometimes come in group to the working place, which include male and females, especially in the brick farms. With the opening of such industrial activities, they have found alternative employment in the entrepreneurial activities. Most of the villagers working in these units are unskilled labourers.

The contributions of Entrepreneurship Development Programmes (EDPs) in the study area for creating healthy ventures, diversifying the base of entrepreneurial activities, creating self-employment are comparatively lesser than the urban areas. At the same time, some organization such as YVU (Youth Volunteers Union), WIGC (Women's Income Generation Centre), etc. have been created over the years to help entrepreneurs in venture launching by providing consultancy, training and counselling support. However, such development is not uniform as the benefit goes mainly to some people who already have contact with such organization. There are many constituent/factors in the whole process of entrepreneurship development. There is also no proper collaboration between the training institutes and financial support system. Moreover, the potential entrepreneurs who undergo Entrepreneurship Development Programmes (EDPs) require self-motivation towards their venture so that they will be able to launch their venture and become their own master. The rural youth, sometimes, join the training programme for the sake of getting loan which is provided by the Government. In addition to this, there is bias in the selection of training centre to access the potential of the proposed location for conducting the programme, promotional campaign, etc. In order to widespread the message of EDP among the rural people, it requires proper identification and selection of potential entrepreneurs for the programme. So, the people in the rural area are not able to access the benefit of entrepreneurship development programmes. And it is also mentioned by the entrepreneurs that there is also the lack of adequate and timely promotional campaign which often results in poor local response to the programme. Further, as one entrepreneur sadly mentioned that the culture of recommendations from somebody (like local MLA, government officials, ministers, etc.) for applying training programmes, loans are important rather than submitting application form in time. So, applying for EDPs loans are more critical to the rural people. And filling up the application forms has become more of a ritual in most ED organizations and there is also very less coverage of issues by the local medias like newspapers, cable networks, radios, etc. The expectation of entrepreneurs are not fully met. In addition to this, the officials of the support system (Managers/Officials of DIC) and Bank Managers criticize each other regarding selection procedure of entrepreneurs. A few of the bank officials mentioned that the EDP organizers do not bother even to check the list of activities for the purpose of bank finance. As a consequence, banks find it difficult to finance the project proposed by the EDP trainees. Such situation brings a state of confusion. Everybody accuses the other.

To sum up, a number of young unemployed youth have come up with various entrepreneurial activities for creating their own livelihood. Such developments in entrepreneurial activities are slowly spreading to the rural areas too. They always strive for a chance of creating their own livelihood. The rural youth are looking for various entrepreneurial opportunities that have been emerging in and around Kakching. It is observed that rural youth are eager to earn and they do not want to depend on their parents after their long study. They want to do something and help their parents. They want to use their talent, knowledge, etc. in starting different entrepreneurial activities. This is reflected in the fact that many youth are engaged in entrepreneurial activities (as worker) for getting some income. However, it is difficult to start a modern entrepreneurial activity for new entrepreneur as such activities need more capital investments. Most of the rural entrepreneurs start small enterprises, but they always have their vision for achieving bigger one by investing their profits. At the same time, 15 (10.94 %)

entrepreneurs started different entrepreneurial activities so that they can widen their scope of earning. By doing so, they develop their entrepreneurial skills.

From the study, it is observed that entrepreneurs can emerge from any family background. Some new entrepreneurial activities like P.C.O. and Xerox services, photo studios, etc. which were not very common earlier, became very popular. This has opened up opportunities for entrepreneurial activities in the area.

Among the communities, the entrepreneurs have strong association with their moral values, ethos, and belief system, etc. in developing their entrepreneurial activities. They also have distinct and traditional way of enterprising and networking for organizing and maintaining themselves. Entrepreneurship development makes the younger generation to engage in productive activities. In the study area, there are various entrepreneurial activities engaged by rural entrepreneurs usually owned and operated by an individual entrepreneur with little access to institutional credit. Most of the entrepreneurs engaged in such activities were assisted by the family members or by hired labourers.

The much debated view that caste system and joint family are an impediment for entrepreneurship development and the spirit of entrepreneurship, and the negative influence of the Hindu philosophy of *Artha* and *Karma* on entrepreneurship is not supported by the finding of the present study. As the data presented in the preceding chapters demonstrate the rural entrepreneurs at Kakching exhibit entrepreneurial spirt, though they have strong moral obligations, cultural values and sentiments. Rather such factors enhance the smooth running of their activities. And it shows that there is no lack of entrepreneurial spirit among the people of the study area. Instead, strong moral obligations and cultural sentiments enhance trust and solidarity among the workers and entrepreneurs in networking their entrepreneurial activities.

Although they are at an incipient stage, young entrepreneurs are playing an important role in the growth of an indigenous capitalist. By investing in their entrepreneurial activities, they are expanding their business. The crucial factors contributing to this diversity of activities among the rural entrepreneurs are capital availability and entrepreneurs' willingness to take risks etc. for entrepreneurship development. However, they are the agent of change in the rural society. They explore ways and means of widening their areas of operation and boosting their social and economic positions. To attain their goals, they reinvested their profits in various enterprises. Some of them are fairly stable in their entrepreneurial activities in terms of functioning, maintaining, operation, scale of production, etc. of their units.

As the number of working adults increases, a tendency also develops in families leading to change in lifestyles and food habits, etc. There has been increasing interest among the people to remain fit. This has resulted women entrepreneurs setting up beauty parlour, etc. to meet the growing demand for beauty care services. Once the field of entrepreneurship assumed to be for men only, nowadays women have also entered into this field. More and more women are coming forward to take up entrepreneurial activities.

To improve the socio-economic condition of the people of Kakching, it needs for an all-round development in different aspects of society. Entrepreneurship development is one among the different aspects of it. Entrepreneurial activities can be encouraged in the district with more regular supply of power, increase of flow of raw materials, increase local demand of the products, and upgradation of traditional skills of the people.

Bibliography

Agrawal, H.N, 1989, Public Sector Commercial Banks and Entrepreneurship Development in India, in "Entrepreneurship Development in India" edited by Sami Uddin, Mittal Publication, Delhi, pp. 121-126.

Alex, Stewart, 1989, "Team Entrepreneurship", Sage Publication, New Delhi, London.

Arghiros, Daniel, 1997," The Rise of Indigenous Capitalists in Rural Thailand: Profile of Brickmakers in the Central Plains", in (ed) Rutten Mario, Carol Upadhya, 1997, *Small Business Entrepreneurship in Asia and Europe: Towards a Comparative Perspective*, New Delhi, Sage Publication.

Asghari, Mohiuddin, 1983, "Entrepreneurship Development Among Women: Retrospect and Prospect", *SEDME*, Vol. X, March 1983.

Ashokan, 2004, "Rural Entrepreneurs— Problem and Prospect of Village Industries sponsored by Kerala KVIB", *SEDME*. Vol. 31, No. 1.

B.C. Mitchell, 2004, "Motives of Entrepreneurs: A study of South Africa", *The Journal of Entrepreneurship*, Vol. 13, No. 2, 2004, July-Dec., Sage Publication, New Delhi.

Barnett, H.G., 1953, "Innovation: The Basic of Cultural Change", New York, McGraw Hill.

Barth, Frederik, 1959, "The Role of the Entrepreneurs in Social Change in Northern Norway", Bergen, Universitets Forloget.

Barua, Indira and Anita Devi, 2004, "Women's Market of Manipur: An Anthropo-Historical Perspective", *Journal of Human Ecology*, 15(2), pp. 129-133.

Berger, Brigitte (ed.). 1992, "The Culture of Entrepreneurship", Tata McGraw Hill Publication Ltd., New Delhi.

Berna, James G., 1960, "Industrial Entrepreneurship in Madras States", Bombay, Asian Publishing House.

Bourdieu, Pierre and Wacquant J.D. 1992, "An Invitation to Reflexive Sociology", The University of Chicago Press, Chicago.

Bourdieu, Pierre, 1977, "Outline of a Theory of Practice", translated by Richard Nice, Cambridge University Press, New York.

Bourdieu, Pierre, 1986, "Form of Capital", in Richardson, John G. (ed.), *Handbook of Theory and Research for the Sociology of Education*, New York, Greenwood Press, 241-58.

Bourdieu, Pierre, 1998, "Practical Reason: On the Theory of Action, Polity and Press", Blackwell Publishers Ltd., U.K.

Chandra, Mohan, 2002, "Entrepreneurs and Venture Capital in Technological Innovation, Invention Intelligency", July-August 2002.

Cochran, C. Thomas (1965), "The Entrepreneurship in Economic Change", *Explorations in Entrepreneurial History*, Vol. III, No. 1, pp. 25-37.

Cochran, C.Thomas (1968), "Entrepreneurship" in *International Encyclopedia of the Social Science*, Vol. 5, pp. 87-90.

Cle, Lesger, 1997, "The Visible Hand: Views on Entrepreneurs and Entrepreneurship in Holland (1580-1850)", in (ed.) Rutten Mario, Carol Upadhya, (ed.), 1997, *Small Business Entrepreneurship in Asia and Europe: Towards a Comparative Perspective*, Sage Publication, New Delhi.

Das, Rajat Kanti, 1985, "Manipur Tribal Scene (Studies in Society and Change)", Inter-India Publication, New Delhi.

Devi, Th. Prabha, Devi A. Shyammuhini, 2005, "Problem of Women Entrepreneurs: A Case Study of Imphal and Kamrup District", in (Seminar paper presented in the National Seminar conducted by Manipur University, Deptt. of Commerce, sponsored by ICSSR, New Delhi).

Ducker, Peter F., 1985, "Innovation and Entrepreneurship", Heinemann, London.

Epstein, Scarlet, 1964, "Social Structure and Entrepreneurship" in *International Journal of Comparative Sociology*, Vol. 5.

Firth, Raymond, 1934, "Primitive Polynesian Economy", London, Routledge and Kegan Paul.

Firth, Raymond, 1967, "Themes in Economic Anthropology", London: Avistock Publication. (A.S.A. Monograph 6)

Foster, G.M. 1962,"Traditional Societies and Technological Change", Allied Publishers, New Delhi.

Fox, Richard G., 1969, "From Zamindar to Ballot Box: Community Change in North India Market Town", Ithaca: Cornell University Press.

Geertz, C., 1967, "Peddlers and the Princes", University of Chicago Press, Chicago.

Ghosh, Bishwanath, 1998, "Entrepneurship Development in India", National Publishing House, New Delhi and Jaipur.

Ghosh, G.K. and Ghosh Shukla, 1977, "Women of Manipur", A.P.H. Publishing Corporation, New Delhi.

Hadimani, R.N., 1985, "Dynamic of Industrial Entrepreneurship", Ashish Publishing House, New Delhi.

Hazlehurst, Leighton W, 1996," Entrepreneurship and the Merchant Castes in a Punjabi City", Duke University Programmes in Comparative Studies on South Asia, Monograph 1.

Hazlehurst, Leighton W. (1968), "Caste and Merchant Communities: Structure and Change in Indian Society", cited in R.A. Sharma, *Entrepreneurial Change in Indian Industry*, Sterling Publishers, Delhi.

Hoselitz, B.F. (1964), "A Sociological Approach to Economic Development and Society", New York.

Huang, Ping, 1997, "New Private Entrepreneurs in China: Family Relations and Social Connections", in (ed.)Rutten Mario, Carol Upadhya, (ed.), 1997, *Small Business Entrepreneurship in Asia and Europe: Towards a Comparative Perspective*, Sage Publication, New Delhi.

James, J. and S.J. Berna, 1958, "Pattern of Entrepreneurship in South India", in *Economic Development and Cultural Change*, Vol. VII, pp. 343-361.

Jan, I.J., Stein K. 2004, "Sub-culture and Entrepreneurship : The Value of Social Capital in Tanzanian Business" , *The Journal of Entrepreneurship*, Vol. 31, No.1.

Jay, Inge Jessen and Stein Kristiansen, 2004, "Sub-cultures and Entrepreneurship: The Value of Social Capital in Tanzanian Business", *The Journal of Entrepreneurship*, Vol. 13, No.1, 2004.

Jayanta Kr. Gopal, 2004, "Rural Credit Scenario in North East India", *Kurukshetra*, Vol. 52, No.4, February 2004.

Jeremy Boissevain, 1997, "Small European Entrepreneurs, in (ed,) Rutten Mario, Carol Upadhya, (ed.)", 1997, *Small Business Entrepreneurship in Asia and Europe: Towards a Comparative Perspective*, Sage Publication, New Delhi.

Joshua, Thomas C. Gopalkrishna, Ranjan Singh R.K.; 2001, "Constraints of Development of Manipur", Regency Publication, New Delhi.

Kenneth, Loucks, 1991, "Training Entrepreneurs for Small Business Creation (Lesson from Experience)", Oxford & IBH Publishing Co. Pvt. Ltd., New Delhi, Calcutta, Bombay.

Khankhoje D.P. and V.S. Kaveri, 1992, "Development of Rural Industries, SSI and Tiny Units and the Role of Banks – A survey", *SEDME*, Vol. XIX (4), December 1992.

Kondaiah, C., 1990, Entrepreneur Development in Rural Areas, SEDME, Vol. XVII, March 1990.

Kupper, Adam and Kupper Jessica, 1985, "The Social Science Encyclopedia", Routledge Publication, London, Boston and Wesley.

Levine, H.B, 1985, "Entrepreneurship and Social Change: Implication from a New Zealand Case Study", *Human Ecology*, Vol. 44, No. 4, 1985, pp. 293-300.

MacIver, and Page, 1986, "Society: An Introductory Analysis", MacMillan India Ltd., Madras.

Mair, L., 1984, "Anthropology and Development", MacMillan Press, London.

Mali, D.D., 1988, "Development of Micro, Small and Medium Enterprises in India: Current Scenario and Challenges", SEDME, Vol. XXV (4), December 1988.

Mali D.D., 2000, "Entrepreneurship Development in North East: Experience and Strategy" (ed.), Indian Institute of Entrepreneurship, Guwahati.

Mali, D.D. and Dutta Gautam, 2000, "Promoting New Entrepreneurs", Indian Institute of Entrepreneurship, Guwahati.

Mali, D.D., 2001, "Micro Entreprise Development—Policies and Programmes", Indian Institute of Entrepreneurship, Gawahati.

Mali, D.D., 2002, "Entrepreneurship: A Four Stage Approach to Self-employment and Entrepreneurial Career", Indian Institute of Entrepreneurship, Guwahati.

Manjusri, Chaki-Sircar, 1984, "Feminism in a Traditional Society: Women of the Manipur Valley", Shakti Books: Vikas Publishing House Pvt. Ltd., New Delhi.

Maria, Miniti, 2007, "Entrepreneurship: The Engine of Growth", (ed), Vol. 1, Praeger Publication, Westport, Connecticut, London.

Mark, Lazerson, 1997, "Entrepreneurship in Italy", in (ed.) Rutten Mario, Carol Upadhya, (ed), 1997, *Small Business Entrepreneurship in Asia and Europe: Towards a Comparative Perspective*, Sage Publication, New Delhi.

Mathivaanam, Samuel C., 1991, "Voluntary Agencies and Social Change", Manas Publication, Delhi.

McClelland, David C. and Winter, D.G., 1969, "Motivating Economic Achievement", New York, Free Press.

McClelland, David C., 1961, "The Achieving Society", Princeton, Princeton University Press.

McCrory, J.T., 1956, "Small Industry in a North Indian Town: Case Studies in Latent Industrial Potential", Government of India, Ministry of Commerce and Industry, Delhi.

Mitchell, B.C. 2004, "Motives of Entrepreneurs: A Case Study of South Africa", *The Journal of Entrepreneurship*, Vol.13, No.2, 2004.

Muttayya, B.C, Lohanathan, 1990, "Psycho-social Factors Influencing Entrepreneurship in Rural Areas", *The Journal of Rural Development*, Vol. 9(1), pp. 237-281, Hyderabad.

N.Roshini Kumar,1996, "Industrial Development in Manipur: A fresh look in Development Experience in Manipur", in *Development of Manipur*, Vol- 1, edited by N. Mohendro Singh, Institute of Development Studies.

Nan Lin, 2001, "Social Capital: A theory of social structure and Action", Cambridge University Press, Cambridge, England.

Nandy, A., 1974, "Entrepreneurial Cultures and Entrepreneurial Men", *Economic and Political Weekly*, Vol. VIII, No. 47, Bombay, Nov., pp. 98-105.

Owen, R.L., 1976, "The Anthropological Study of Entrepreneurship" in *The Anthropological Approaches to the Study of Complex Societies*, edited. by Agrawal, B.C., Space Application Centre, Ahmedabad.

Pande G.S. 1998, "Entrepreneurship development among the disadvantaged and tribals" in *Economic Development of Tribals: Approach, Method and Strategy*, edited by Kishor C. Pandhy, Sarup and Sons, New Delhi.

Pandian M. Soudara, 2001, "Rural Entrepreneurship: Growth and Development", Kanishka Publisher, New Delhi.

Paranjape, 1987, "Entrepreneurial Background and Performance", *Economic and Political Weekly*, Vol. XXII, No. 10, March 7, pp. 409-411.

Pareek, Uday, 1996, "Organizational Behaviour Process", Rawat Publication, Jaipur.

Pareek, Uday and Manohar Nadkarni (1971), "Development of Entrepreneurship: A conceptual Model Developing Entrepreneurship", Learning Systems, New Delhi.

Parrat Saroj Nalini Arambam, 2005, "The Court Chronicle of the Kings of Manipur: The Cheitharon Kumpapa", Routledge Publication, London and New York.

Prassian, G.P., 2000, "Entrepreneurship Development in Hill Areas of Manipur: Problems and Prospects", in *The Rising Manipur*

(Including other North East States) edited by M. Horan, Manas Publication, New Delhi, pp. 212-225.

Rao, C. Hari Narayana, Uma Mohan Ch., 1998, "Grass-Root Entrepreneurship and Rural Industralization", *SEDME*, Vol. XV, (March), 1998.

Rao, Kallu P, Thomas Shaji, 1992, "Performance of the Manipur Rural Bank—An analytical study", *Journal of Rural Development*, Vol. 11(4), pp. 443-459.

Rastogi Shashi Ranjan, 1989, "Entrepreurship Development in India and the Role of Banks", in *Entrepreneurship Development in India* edited by Sami Uddin, Mittal Publication, Delhi, 1989. pp. 117-120.

Ray Datta B. 1992, "Anatomy of Regionalism in North-East India Hills : A preliminary Observation, in Tribal Studies of India Series T-149", *Tribal Transformation in India*, Vol. III, "Ethno-Politics and Identity Crisis" edited by Budhadeb Chaudhuri, Inter-India Publication, New Delhi, 1992, pp. 474-485.

Rutten, Mario, 2003, "The study of entrepreneurship in India: In need of a comparative perspective", in *The Oxford Indian Companion to the Sociology and Social Anthropology*, edited by Veena Das, Oxford University Press, London.

Rutten Mario, 1997, "Cooperative and Differentiation: Social History of Iron Founders in Central Java" in (ed.) Rutten Mario, Carol Upadhya, (ed.), 1997, *Small Business Entrepreneurship in Asia and Europe: Towards a Comparative Perspective*, New Delhi, Sage Publication.

Rutten Mario, Carol Upadhya, (ed.), 1997, "Small Business Entrepreneurship in Asia and Europe: Towards a Comparative Perspective", New Delhi, Sage Publication.

Rutten Mario, Carol Upadhya, 1997, "In search of a Comparative Framework: Small scale entrepreneurship in Asia and Europe", in (ed.) Rutten Mario, Carol Upadhya, (ed.), 1997, *Small Business Entrepreneurship in Asia and Europe: Towards a Comparative Perspective*, New Delhi, Sage Publication.

Rutten Mario, 1995, "Farms and Factories: Social Profile of Large

Farmers and Rural Industrialists in West India", Delhi, Oxford University Press.

Rutten Mario, 1994, "Asian Capitalists in the European Mirror", Amsterdam, Free University Press, *Comparative Asian Studies*, No. 14.

Sang-Bok Han, 1997, "Local Level Entrepreneurs in Rural Punggi, Korea: Economic Behaviour and Lifestyle", in (ed.) Rutten Mario, Carol Upadhya, (ed.), 1997, *Small Business Entrepreneurship in Asia and Europe: Towards a Comparative Perspective*, New Delhi, Sage Publication.

Saxena Manoj Kumar, Dr. B.K Kukregti, Dr. Sandhya Gihar, 2004, "Entrepreneurial Attitude of Tribal Youth and Role of Education in Enhancing Entrepreneurial Competencies among Tribes", *Vanayajati*, Vol. XLXII, April 2004, No. 2.

Schumpeter, J.A., 1934, "Change and the Entrepreneur", Cambridge, Harvard University Press.

Schumpeter, J.A., 1967, "The Theory of Economic Development", Oxford University Press, New York.

Sharma, P.K. and Nageshwar Rao, 1994, "Research Trends in Entrepreneurship and Small Business in India: Directions and Prospects", *SEDME*, Vol. XXI (4), December 1994.

Sharma Sameer, 2004, "Entrepreneurship Development in Networks of Weaver Cluster of Pochampalli", *Journal of Rural Development,* Vol. 23(3), pp. 335-353.

Singer, Milton, 1973 (ed.), "Entrepreneurship and Modernization of Occupational Culture in South Asia", Durham, Duke University Press.

Singer, Milton, 1972, "When a Great Tradition is Modernized", New York, Praeger.

Singer, Milton, 1966, "Religion and Social Change in India: The Max Weber Thesis Phase Three", *Economic Development and Cultural Change*, Vol.7, No.1, 1-12.

Singh H. Nabakishore, 1981, "The Problem of Unemployment in Manipur", *Economic Affairs*, Quarterly Journal of Economics, Vol. 26, Q. 2, April – June 1981.

Singh Sheobahal, 1985, "Entrepreneurship and Social Change", Rawat Publication, Jaipur.

Singh W. Nabakumar, Shajahan Sardar, 2003, "The Socio-economic Development of Koireng of Manipur", *The Oriental Anthropologist*, 2003: 3(1), pp.68-73.

Singh Yogendra, 1988, "Modernization of Indian Tradition (A Systematic Study of Social Change in India)", Rawat Publication, Jaipur.

Sinha Dipendra, 2003, "The rise of Entrepreneurship in India", in *The Knowledge Economy in India*, edited by Ritcher F.J & Parathasarathi Banerjee, 2003, Palgrave MacMillan, New York.

Sinha, M. K., 1990, "Role of Nationalised Banks in Rural Development" in (ed.) *Modern Management Series: Rural Programmes Management*, by M.K. Singh, A. Bhattacharya, 1990, Discovery Publishing House, New Delhi, 34-35.

Srinivas, M.N., 1966, "Social Change in Modern India", University of California Press, Berkeley.

Schumpeter, J.A., 1967, "The Theory of Economic Development", Oxford University Press, New York.

Smith, Adam, 1977, "Wealth of Nations", Harmondsworth, Penguin.

Sundar I. and R. Asokan, 2004, "Regional Variation in Performance of Self-Help Groups", *Social Welfare*, Vol. 50, No. 10, January 2004.

Thomas M. Begley, Wee Liang Tan (2001), "The Socio-cultural Environment of Entrepreneurship: A comparison between East-Asia and Anglo-Saxon Countries", *Journal of International Business Studies*, Vol. 32, No. 3, (3rd Qtr., 2001) pp. 537-553.

Timmons, J.A., 1987, "Characteristic and Role Demands of Entrepreneurship", *American Journal of Business*, 3(1987), pp. 5-17.

Timothy, G. Habbershon, 2007, "The Family as a Distinct Context for Entrepreneurship", in (ed.) *Entrepreneurship: The Engine of Growth*, Vol. 3, Praeger Publication, by Mark P. Rice and

Timothy G. Habbershon, 2007, Westport, Connecticut, London.

Tripathi, Dwijendra, 1984, "Business Communities of India: A Historical Perspective", Manohar Publication, New Delhi.

Trivedi, Madusudan, 1991, "Entrepreneurship among Tribals", Printwell Publication, Jaipur.

Varadarajan, R and Ramalingam, 2001, "A study of Entrepreneurial Value in Coimbatore City", *SEDME*, 28.3, September, 2001, pp. 83-90.

Veronica, Mole and Dave Elliott, 1987, "Enterprising Innovation –An Approach", Frances Pinter (Publisher), London.

Wayne, G. Broehl, 1978, "Village Entrepreneur : Change Agents in Indian's Rural Development", Harvard University Press, Cambridge, Massachusetts, London, England.

Walsh, J. P., 1995, "Managerial and Organisational Cognition: Notes from a Trip Down Memory Lane", *Organisation Science*, 6, No. 3 (1995): 280-321.

Weber, Max, 1976, "The Protestant Ethic and the Spirit of Capitalism", translated by Talcott Parson, London, George Allen & Unwin.

Yadav, C.P. 2000, "Encyclopedia of Entrepreneurship Development", Anmol Publications Pvt. Ltd., New Delhi.

Young, Frank (1971), "A Macro-sociological Interpretation of Entrepreneurship" in Peter Kibly (Ed.) *Entrepreneurship and Economic Development*, New York : The Free Press, pp. 1-40.

Government Reports and Other Published Materials

Fifth Economic Survey, 2005, Instructions to Enumerations/ Supervisors, Central Statistical Organisation, Ministry of Statistics and Programme Implementation, Government of India, January 2005.

Government of Manipur, 2008, Economic Survey Manipur (2007-08), Directorate of Economics & Statistics, Government of Manipur, Imphal.

Government of Manipur, 2005, Draft Annual Plan (2006-07)

Proposals, Vol. 1., Planning Department, Government of Manipur, Imphal.

Golden Jubilee (1956-06), 3rd July, 2006, The Manipur State Co-operative Bank Ltd., Assembly Road, Imphal.

Women's Income Generation Centre (WIGC), 2008, Annual Report for the Last Three Years, WIGC Publishers, Thoubal Wangmataba, (Manipur).

Youth Volunteers' Union (YVU), 2007, Annual Report (2006-07), YVU Publishers, Thoubal Manipur.

Locally Published Material on Manipur Culture

Arambam Nipamacha S. 1989, *Meiteigi Paourou Paotak Akhomba*, Khongngangthaba Press, Kurai Lamlong Keithel.

Elangbam Kala Meitei, 2006, *Phouoibi Khurumba,* Shree Gourachandra Press, Imphal.

Elangbam Kala Meitei, 2006, *Lainingthou Amashung Ema Leimaren Thounirol*, Shree Gourachandra Press, Imphal.

Moirangthem Irabot S. and Moirangthem Khomei S. 2006, *Karigidamak Shageigi Apokpa Khurumnai*, Moirangthem Apokpa Sheba Kamiti, Khangngabok.

Moirangthem Rajendro Singh, 2001, *Manipurda Lai Haraoba Amasung Kakching Haraoba*, Moirangsathibi Publication, Kakching Bazar.

Moirangthem Birmangol, 1999, Naorem Amuyaima Singh (1895-91): Pandit Achouba Shana Konung Shahityagi Apunba Khomjinba, Rural Peace and Progressive Society, Kakching, Kakching.

Mayanglambam Gourachandra, 1997, *Manipurda Yotshung Yotsha; Traditional Iron Smelting and Forging in Manipur*, People Museum, Kakching

Mayanglambam Gourachandra, 2002, *Maitreibakki Puwarida Kakching*, Museum, Kakching.

Leishram Birendrakumar Singh, 1999, *Manipuri Khunung Eshei Khomjinba*, Sahitya Akademi, New Delhi.

Index